READINGS
—— ON ——
CONVERSION
TO JUDAISM

RABBI AARON M. PETUCHOWSKI

READINGS
— ON —
CONVERSION
TO JUDAISM

edited by
Lawrence J. Epstein

JASON ARONSON INC.
Northvale, New Jersey
London

For credits, see pp. 193–194.

This book was set in 11 pt. Electra by Alpha Graphics in Pittsfield, New Hampshire, and printed by Book-mart Press in North Bergen, New Jersey.

Library of Congress Cataloging-in-Publication Data
Readings on conversion to Judaism / edited by Lawrence J. Epstein.
    p. cm.
   Includes index.
   ISBN 1-56821-417-0
   1. Proselytes and proselyting, Jewish. 2. Judaism—United States.
 3. Judaism—Israel. I. Epstein, Lawrence J. (Lawrence Jeffrey)
BM729.P7R43 1995
296.6—dc20   94-40779

Manufactured in the United States of America. Jason Aronson Inc. offers books and cassettes. For information and catalog write to Jason Aronson Inc., 230 Livingston Street, Northvale, New Jersey 07647.

This book is dedicated to Michael, Elana, Rachel, and Lisa
for their kindness, their eager help,
and the unending joy they bring.

Contents

Acknowledgments

It is with great pleasure that I acknowledge the help of the many people whose efforts and support made this volume possible.

Arthur Kurzweil is particularly insightful about Jewish life and the way the interests of his authors and his audience can meet through books. I am most grateful for his long-standing advice and help.

This is my third book about conversion to Judaism, and so my debt has now accumulated to an enormous number of people and institutions. In particular, for this volume I must thank Dru Greenwood, Rabbi Avis Miller, and Lena Romanoff for their original contributions to the volume. All three of these remarkable people have provided me with numerous insights into the conversionary experience.

The search for particular articles required the help of many who worked in a wide variety of libraries. In particular, I want to acknowledge the help of the librarians at Suffolk Community College. They have become accustomed to my frequent, esoteric requests for material and have refused to quit before finding that material someplace. Marge Olson, especially, deserves a special note of thanks.

My rabbi, Howard Hoffman, is extremely supportive and helpful in my work on conversion.

Many friends also helped with their discussions. I'd like to thank Dr. Edward Hoffman for his useful observations and probing questions.

As always, my writing would not be possible without the constant support of my wife, Sharon, and our children, Michael, Elana, Rachel, and Lisa. The book's dedication to the children is a small indication of how much they mean to me.

Introduction

It would have been very hard to predict twenty years ago that the subject of conversion to Judaism would emerge as a crucial issue in American Jewish life. In those years, perhaps mythically remembered, a Jewish man married a Jewish woman and had two Jewish children. People outside Judaism rarely inquired about becoming Jewish, much less followed through on such an inquiry.

Contemporary American Jewish life isn't mythic anymore. Since 1985, more than 50 percent of people who are Jewish who married have married an unconverted gentile. People on a spiritual search look at a variety of options, including Judaism. Some of them, indeed, examine Judaism, study it, find it attractive, and become Jewish.

There are close to 200,000 people in the United States who have converted to Judaism, about 90 percent in the context of a romantic relationship, such as a pending or current marriage to someone born Jewish. The remainder came to Judaism independent of such a romantic relationship, drawn because of Judaism's beliefs or practices, or because of the tenacity of the Jewish presence in history, or for some other reason. These Jews by choice rather than by birth have infused an enormous amount of spiritual energy into Jewish life.

Their presence, the reasons for their original attraction to Judaism, the nature of their conversions, and the effects they are having have prompted a lot of dialogue within Jewry. Some of this dialogue is heated. The importance of the issue, and the intensity of feelings aroused in the discussions about conversion, have produced many words. Some of those words, uttered in a moment of argument, are forgotten. However, other words, pondered over, considered, have been put down to record the quiet religious revolution taking place in front of us.

It is now time to collect some of these important words, to see the role of conversion, to sharpen the debate, to inform the Jewish community about this issue.

The book begins with a memoir by Lena Romanoff that emotionally imparts a profound understanding of conversion.

When I first began studying conversion, I had the assumption that conversion simply was not a normative Jewish activity. I don't remember exactly having been taught that specifically, but it had been in the Jewish air of my upbringing. I was therefore more than a little surprised when I first systematically studied conversion in Jewish thought and history. I discovered that there was a vast and overwhelmingly supportive discussion of conversion in the most sacred of Jewish sources. I learned that Jews, according to some historical accounts, very actively sought converts at key moments in their history. This was all news to me, because I had thought conversion was some new idea used in some way to combat intermarriage. The first part of this anthology includes some discussion of how seeking converts fits into Jewish theology and history.

There are many disputes about conversion, including significant disputes among the movements about such matters as the appropriate motivations for conversion, the requirements for a conversion, and who may legitimately conduct a conversion. There are books, including an anthology, on that subject, so I have focused instead on another key issue: should Jews actively seek converts? Several prominent Jewish thinkers address this and related issues in the second part of the book.

Because so much of the contemporary discussion about conversion takes place within a more general discussion of intermarriage and ways to communicate with the intermarried, I asked two key leaders, one in the Reform movement and one in the Conservative movement, to write original essays for this volume on this subject. Dru Greenwood and Rabbi Avis Miller cogently present the important issues.

Conversion does not just take place in the United States. It is also a significant issue in Israel. I have tried to provide the appropriate background by including material on this subject in the third part of the book.

Because the subject of conversion to Judaism is fraught with so much controversy, let me note some points here. The first problem is language. As I have noted elsewhere, there is no appropriate, Jewish way to discuss those who have embraced Judaism. They are simply Jewish. Their status should not be considered as somehow separate from other Jews by this discussion of their religious quest. Some people who have become Jewish do not like the word *convert*, thinking it sounds un-Jewish or having some other objection.

The other terms, such as Jew-by-choice, choosing Jew, proselyte, new Jew, and so on, are used at some places in the anthology. We don't have a clear, good language in English to discuss those who join the Jewish people. I hope those who do not like the word *convert* will forgive its usage; I employ it because it is linguistically the simplest term and the one most widely understood.

Also, I have tried to present various positions within the Jewish community even when I differ with the author's conclusions. In a discussion of conversion, open, scholarly debate is much needed. I hope this anthology contributes to such a discussion.

⊰ Prologue ⊱

Lena Romanoff

White Roses in December

Conversion to Judaism is frequently discussed as a theological, historical, or social issue. Talmudic references are given. Famous studies of intermarriage and conversion are cited. Issues are argued over. It is, however, crucial to start a discussion of conversion with its central importance: conversion always involves a story. People convert or not. People break each other's hearts or help those hearts soar.

We begin, then, with one story. Appropriately, the story is by Lena Romanoff, herself a convert, and someone who is incredibly insightful about conversion. This story, appearing for the first time, is a story of separation and reconciliation. The tangled emotions of love and loss, of lying as an act of generosity, of the unintended lessons of that generosity, are told here in a quiet yet dramatic form.

Lena Romanoff is the founder and director of the Jewish Converts & Interfaith Network. She is the author of *Your People, My People — Finding Acceptance and Fulfillment as a Jew By Choice* (Philadelphia: Jewish Publication Society, 1990). She serves as scholar in residence in synagogues throughout the United States and Canada, speaking about intermarriage, interdating, and conversion. She also counsels interfaith and conversionary couples and their families.

No one can know the joy or the pain that leads a person to conversion. I am reminded of this fact every December first when the cold winds move defiantly through my stately old oak trees and rustle the dry leaves. Every December first, since 1985, I have been receiving a dozen long-stemmed pearly white roses from a dead man. Let me explain.

Joseph Steinman owned a chain of florist shops in Philadelphia. On a glorious bright day in July, Mr. Steinman called me and made an appoint-

1

ment to discuss his son's intermarriage. However, he never did keep his appointment and my phone calls remained unanswered. Six months later, Mr. Steinman called me again. His speech was now halting, his voice feeble. He had not been able to keep his appointment because he had suffered a stroke. There was a sense of urgency in his voice when he begged me to meet him at the hospital. There I found a fragile and worn old man with sagging cheeks and skin like parchment. He seemed much older than his sixty-five years.

He folded himself into his bedside chair and told me that he wanted me to persuade his daughter-in-law, Edith, to convert to Judaism. He knew he was very sick and wanted to die knowing that his only son, Jeffrey, would give him Jewish grandchildren. I told him that I did not believe in coerced conversion and that probably my persuasive ability would be limited. Mr. Steinman's eyes pleaded with me and his words urged me to try.

His relationship with his son had been strained since he and his wife (now deceased) had refused to attend their son's wedding. He had not seen his son in three years and every one of their phone conversations started with premeditated pleasantry but inevitably became undermined by the deep chasm that existed between them. Mr. Steinman had not forgiven his son for marrying a gentile. Jeffrey had not forgiven his father for not attending the wedding.

Unfortunately, Mr. Steinman's medical workup revealed something of greater concern than a stroke: metastatic stomach cancer, a death sentence. Doctors spoke hopefully to him about his remaining months, but later they would privately talk to me about his few remaining weeks.

I hesitantly promised to be present when his son and daughter-in-law were due to visit the next day. My heart ached for Mr. Steinman and I resolved to talk to his son and daughter-in-law about his last wish.

The following day Mr. Steinman's face was streaked with the afternoon sun. He was in a cheerful mood. His eyes beginning to dance, he told me that he hoped I could perform his miracle. I had my doubts, but I had also grown weary of giving him explanations that he chose to disregard.

Together we waited. He pressed his fingers against my cheek, full of hope. His son finally arrived, alone. At the time I would rather have walked through fire. Mr. Steinman clutched my arm. There was palpable fear in the worried father's eyes.

Father and son exchanged formal greetings. They did not embrace but spoke courteously. Mr. Steinman introduced me and spoke of my work, counseling interfaith couples. Jeff's eyes narrowed; I could sense his discomfort. The room was quiet except for our breathing, the rustle of the bed sheets, and the beeps from the monitor.

Blessedly, the technicians whisked Mr. Steinman away to endure more futile treatments. Jeff and I were alone. The floral scents of the bouquets of roses, carnations and chrysanthemums intermingled with the stale odors of blood, alcohol and urine. I could not remain in that hospital room; I suggested that we go to the coffee shop. There we spoke for three hours. I learned that his wife, Edith, had refused to make the trip because she was convinced that her father-in-law so disliked her that her mere presence might upset him. Indeed, she had felt "unwanted, unwelcome and unloved" by Jeff's parents. Jeff conceded that he sometimes wished that Edith would consider conversion but he could never ask her because it was too sensitive an issue. Furthermore, Edith was not so much against conversion to Judaism as she was antireligion in general. To Edith, religion was divisive. Look at how it practically destroyed her relationship with her in-laws and her husband!

As a former nurse, I was able to explain to Jeff the exact nature of his father's illness and the dismal prognosis. I implored him to at least ask Edith to visit. My words knocked against a stone wall. He stubbornly tried to cling to the idea that her presence would only be upsetting. I knew he was wrong. I tried to persuade him to reconsider his thinking. I watched his eyes for that moment of understanding, and, I hoped, agreement with me, to no avail.

Back at the bedside, Jeff stared down at his father's blue eyes, which were as wan and as hazy as a cold moon. Mr. Steinman lifted his arm toward his son, fingers shaking. Jeff's right arm reached toward the bony, cold hand, but it just hovered in the air. Their hands did not meet and Mr. Steinman slumped back on his flat pillow. That moment will remain suspended in my memory forever.

Every day, I braced myself against the December winds arriving early in the morning and leaving at sunset. I was angry at Jeff for not staying by his father's side. I wished I could impart Jeff with courage, conviction, and compassion. I had almost lost hope of ever seeing Jeff again. How can hearts be so mute, I wondered. Mr. Steinman had stopped asking me to call Edith and Jeff about conversion.

Occasionally Mr. Steinman would ask me about my work with a sad but kindly smile. On better days he told me the trade secrets of florist shops and where the best tulips and roses could be had.

By the beginning of the second week his condition had deteriorated. There now were wires and tubes all over his body. He was hooked up to machines with dials and switches that measured and recorded each heart beat. The cancer was spreading by leaps, lumps, and bounds. Every time I looked at him I saw that death, not life, was being preserved by the machines.

I felt I owed Mr. Steinman my presence since it seemed I could not provide him with the miracle he craved. I was feeling more sanctimonious than sanctified.

Desperately, I called Jeff and begged him to come see his father before it was too late. I felt as if I was speaking into a dead telephone, but he *did* listen to me.

Late that night, Jeff and Edith entered the room. Mr. Steinman's breathing was shallow but steady. When he saw his son and daughter-in-law, the life force returned to his blood.

I prayed that I had made the right decision to encourage them to come. I prayed that cold words would not be exchanged at death's door. They had to reconcile not just the grief but the guilt, not just the guilt but the racking anguish over something impulsively done that could not be undone. Maybe if the Steinmans had just attended the wedding reception, even if they could not have attended the wedding ceremony, things might have been better between them. Maybe if the Steinmans had tried to get to know Edith as a person first instead of rejecting her for being a gentile, things might have been better between them. Maybe if the Steinmans had been supportive and welcoming, even if they could not be approving and accepting of the son's choice, things would be better. My mind assaulted me with a hundred "maybes." I marveled at the vagaries of human communication and the vulnerability of human relationships.

Jeff moved toward his father and sat on the edge of the bed. He looked into his father's urgent blue eyes, eyes so near to his that he could almost see his reflection through them. But still he kept a distance, as if his father's touch was contagious. They talked about Mr. Steinman's florist business, legal matters, stocks, and funeral plans.

Edith stayed in the shadows of the room surveying the scene. I took her arm and led her outside. Before I could say a word, Edith sputtered, "I know you think I am terrible; you expect me to lie to that old man and tell him that I'm going to convert. Well, I cannot. I feel sorry for him, but I don't even know him and I certainly don't owe him anything."

Edith was right. I wished that she would want to lie to Mr. Steinman, to just tell him that she was going to convert so that he could die in peace, his only wish fulfilled. I knew Mr. Steinman well. Edith did not know him and I did not know Edith. It is wrong to tell a lie, but I knew that Mr. Steinman did not want to hear the truth. I closed my eyes on my confusion. Edith put her hand on my shoulder; we were both crying. She whispered to me, "What should I do?" I understood her dilemma perfectly, completely. I responded, "Do what you can live with."

Edith placed her hands on Mr. Steinman's hands and her eyes went soft with understanding. Edith spoke softly and no one could hear. Jeff and I left the room in search of his father's physicians. When we returned, Edith was smiling and nourishing her father-in-law with spoonfuls of rice pudding and hope.

It was only after Edith and Jeff left Sunday night that I learned from Mr. Steinman that Edith had indeed promised him that she would convert. SHE HAD LIED.

Mr. Steinman told me that he recognized that forgiving and being forgiven are inextricably interrelated. He told me that his son had chosen a fine woman to be his wife. He thanked me profusely for talking to Edith. He asked me to bill him for my "professional fee." In truth, I felt I should be fined, instead. Jokingly I told him that all I wanted was a dozen long-stemmed white roses from his florist shop when he recuperated. He took my hand and solemnly promised that he would send the roses. He has kept the promise.

In the face of death, Jeff and Edith had summoned up the feelings of mercy and forgiveness. Their remaining visits were filled with great kindness, compassion, gentleness, and forgiveness. Even though darkness hovered over Mr. Steinman's life, a healing balm had touched his emotional wounds. By Monday night Mr. Steinman's skin pulled taut over his face like yellow leather. His liver was failing. The nausea pills no longer worked. He retched but never threw up. The diarrhea medication would not stay down. The sleeping pills kept him fitfully awake. Every day brought change for the worse. The brightness in his eyes dulled, and his cheeks had sunken more. I had to turn away every time the needles pierced his fragile skin. He began to slip in and out of consciousness. Jeff and Edith were holding his hands when he died. Even though we embraced each other warmly before they left, I felt that there was a distance between Edith and me. I knew that she had no intentions of converting. Prior to Mr. Steinman's death I hoped that she would lie to him about converting because I wanted him to die with Shalom. But now that he was dead, I felt uncomfortable with Edith's decision, even though it was my idea.

Forgiveness is liberation. Jeff could now remember the past in a way that provided hope and love rather than despair and hate. People's words and actions hurt other people every day. Some of these words and actions bring about anger, hurt, and vengeance that can destroy life. But words and actions can also bring joy, forgiveness, and the promise of wonderful relationships.

Every December first since 1985 the estate of Mr. Joseph Steinman sends me a dozen white roses. The card reads, "Your friend, Joseph Steinman." I look forward to my pearly white roses with mingled emotions of sadness and happiness. I have carried Mr. Steinman in my head and heart, recalling conversations word for word from that previous December.

On December first, 1993, my lovely white roses came accompanied with a letter from Edith informing me of her recent conversion to Judaism. Now I know that Edith and I had each made the right decision, but at different times. May you rest in peace, Mr. Steinman!

*   *   *   *   *   *   *   *   *   *   *   *

The Talmud, on page 16b of *Ketubot*, asks the question, "How do we dance before the bride?" Rashi explains that this question must be understood in the sense of what do we *say* to the bride during the dance. The answers given reflect the differences of opinion between the School of Hillel and the School of Shamai.

The School of Shamai says that one must praise the bride as she actually is. The School of Hillel teaches that every bride is to be told that she is beautiful.

The School of Shamai objected to this answer, asking, what if the bride is disfigured? How is it possible to say in this case that she is beautiful? [Don't we have an obligation to always tell the truth!] After all, does not the Torah explicitly teach in Exodus 23:7, "Keep far from a false statement."

The School of Hillel answered: When a person buys a worthless trifle in the marketplace, do we praise his "find" or do we disparage him [for wasting his money]? Of course we ought to praise him, [so as not to cause him embarrassment. How much more so is it obligatory to praise the bride, even if she is not "beautiful."]

From this our rabbis taught that it is incumbent upon each person to interact properly with the rest of humanity.

I

THE SOURCES

Leo Baeck

The Mission of Judaism

At its Sixth International Conference, the World Union for Progressive Judaism invited Rabbi Leo Baeck to discuss conversion to Judaism. Dr. Baeck chose to present a vision: that Jews were a people with a mission, and that mission was to offer Judaism to the world. Dr. Baeck urged those assembled to understand Judaism as having a purpose, to designate people to carry out that purpose, and to do it all openly. The message stands as an amazing call. Dr. Baeck urges support for the Zionist enterprise while simultaneously energizing American Jewry to take up the responsibility for offering Judaism to the world. He did all this just a few years after the *Shoah*, the Holocaust that had eradicated one-third of the Jewish people. His message here is visionary. He does not connect conversion to intermarriage but to a Jewish purpose.

   Leo Baeck (1873–1956) was a German rabbi and theologian. After the rise of Nazism, Rabbi Baeck determined to fight the menace. He refused many offers to move abroad, declaring his moral obligation to stay with his people, to take part in the last *minyan* if necessary. Rabbi Baeck was deported to the Theresienstadt concentration camp in 1943. His courage and faith served as an inspiration to many. After the war, he moved to London. His best-known book is *The Essence of Judaism*.

Dr. Blank has laid a strong foundation and I feel, and all of us must feel, gratitude for it; the basis is so firm that it is an easy task to build up something upon this foundation. It is the missionary work of Judaism that is to be treated now.

   The greatest historian of the last century, who was also one of the great Europeans, Giuseppe Mazzini, said: "Nation is Mission." Indeed, every nation that is able and willing to be the custodian of a great idea feels impelled

9

to be a teacher, to bring this ideal into the consciousness of other peoples. We see today how the two English-speaking nations are guardians of the ideal of democracy and are prepared and ready to make other peoples learn this sublime idea. All the more a religious people, a nation that was from the beginning the custodians of the greatest ideas, must feel the task to bring these ideas to all mankind. All the principles of Judaism that Dr. Blank has shown today, all the ideals of Judaism aim to this end, to the mission, to work for the great mission of the Jewish people. It was not a barren ideal; it was a fertile thought. Indeed, in the three centuries before the common era and after it, let us see the admirable work of the Jewish mission. Dr. Blank has told us that imagination runs wild, but imagination need not run wild to see the amplitude, the greatness of this missionary work.

It is a conservative estimate if one says that in that time at least one-quarter of all Jews were proselytes, or as the old term runs "God-fearing people"; but one day this work of dissemination promising to reach fruition was discontinued. It was not for the reason that religious energy ceased; it was not by reason of religious weakness, but it was because of political reasons. The battle for liberty, the rebellion of Rabbi Akiba and Bar Kochba was violently suppressed by Rome, and hard oppression followed suppression. It was no longer possible; it was forbidden by the law of Rome that Judaism send out its missionaries. Thus this great work had come to an end, but always and everywhere, when some fresh breeze was given to the Jewish mind, when any possibility was granted, the old missionary enthusiasm awoke. We have many an example, but on the whole the last seventeen centuries were the time when Judaism was not able, was not allowed to do the greater missionary work.

Has the time now come to continue what had been discontinued? We must regard the circumstances of our days. The last centuries, but first and foremost the nineteenth century, were a period of great missionary work on the part of three great religions—Christianity, Islam and Buddhism. The Christian Churches sent out their missionaries to Asia, Africa, and it was a wonderful work, a great success for the sake of mankind that was achieved. Many people, thousands and thousands of people, were given consolation, comfort, help, clearness of mind; their minds were lifted up. One must speak of that with deep respect and also with profound gratitude.

And then the work of Islam in the nineteenth century (work that is not well known, but is one of the greatest religious achievements), the missionary work of Islam met with great success in Africa, South East Asia and Indonesia. A serious crime was committed by Europe against Africa. Three things were brought to Africa: gunpowder, new kinds of alcoholism and some very unpleasant maladies. They were of no benefit to this continent, but the missionary work of Islam was of real benefit. The progress of Islam in Africa was like the triumphal march of prohibition. Many a good thing was done in Africa to many people by this missionary work of Islam.

Buddhism in the same way conquered many parts of China and some parts of Japan. Comfort, consolation, peace of mind and strength of soul were given by Buddhism to many people. We must speak about this with deep gratitude, for all that was done to mankind, a part of which we are. But how is now the position?

Speaking first of Buddhism. The wars in China have ended and will end for a long time the work of Buddhism. Buddhism was not able to give the people in China and Japan what should have been given them — a great self-respect, a moral self-esteem. Buddhism has given peace of mind, but in cruel days, the people in China, this noble old people, has experienced that peace of mind is not enough in these hard times; they need also self-respect.

Islam has been politicised and through being politicised has lost its religious strength. One can see it. The more Islam became politicised, partly by other peoples, the more its religious strength became weakened.

Now Christianity. I speak with some restraint about it, but it is necessary to recall the facts and to speak the truth. There was published six years ago a great book, short in length. I do not know if those here have read it; one reads it time and again with deep emotion; the soul is stirred in reading it. *The Christian Failure*, by Dr. Charles Singer. The book is full of facts, full of truth. The title is not *The Failure of Christianity*. There are two old and new sins of religion. One is the sin of silence — to be silent in the face of crime and oppression. Many a religion has committed this sin. And the other old and new sin of religion is compromising with the powers of earth and thereby procuring a good conscience. Both sins have been committed by the Christian Churches. They have been silent and they have compromised. They have manipulated and lulled their consciences, and therefore the respect for Christianity has diminished.

We who are Jews know what we lack. We must improve many a thing. We must do a new thing, but we have never been silent; we have never compromised. Had we compromised there would have been no Jews. Mankind is hungry and thirsty for that which Judaism can say, what Jews full of Judaism can say. Many an example can be remembered. In the first three decades of our century, I myself have had the experience I am speaking about, and perhaps in other countries it was the same. It was a twofold experience: one, that the children of those who had deserted us returned to us and the second, that Judaism became, so to speak, attractive to the Gentiles, and many a one became a proselyte, educated people, high-minded people. Should we not begin anew? Should we not send out missionaries to Asia, to East Asia and to other places to the people there waiting for us? We are in need of expansion for our own sake.

May I be allowed to repeat what I said on Friday. The totality of Jewish history, the totality of Jewish life and destiny, has never been like a circle, a formation with one focus of strength, with only one centre, but always from the beginning it has been like an ellipse, a formation destined and determined by two focuses of strength, by two dynamic centres. In the old days there was the Northern and Southern realms in Palestine, later Palestine and Babylon, later the Sephardic and Ashkenazic phases of culture, later Western Europe and Eastern Europe, and nowadays the Western world and the State of Israel. Two centres, two focuses, and in the same way there must be two centres of mind and energy. Now one centre is a national centre, the State of Israel, and the other should be, must be, for the sake of equilibrium a missionary centre, so to speak, a centre of internationalism. One cannot do without one or the other. One alone would not be good, and the other alone would not be good. There must be equipoise and equilibrium of the two centres. Many a people, many a Jew is afraid of nationalism in Palestine. There is one help against it, to send our missionaries to mankind. Dr. Blank has rightly said that mission is not assimilation, and a good help against assimilation is the national life in Palestine. Both should be; one not without the other: both must be, missionary work and a strong life in Palestine: a healthy life in Palestine and strong missionary work. Two focuses and equilibrium between them. But missionary work presupposes missionary workers. There must be men fully living their Judaism, going out to other places to speak about our religion, the commandments, the hope, faith and certainty of our religion. They must go out, and in order to go out we must start somewhere a centre where young Jewish people can be educated and instructed to go out to do this work.

Where can this centre be established? It can only be in America. In America there are five million Jews, a Judaism full of dynamic power. Today there are two strong centres, Palestine and America. In America must be the centre, and this centre could be in Cincinnati. There is the right place, not Cincinnati isolated, the Hebrew Union College separated, but together the Hebrew Union College with the Theological Seminary of America, not isolationism but cooperation. To send out young people this way, these men and women must be of course Jews. Judaism is not something to be written in books, something known and forgotten, learnt anew and forgotten again, but the whole of life. They must be men, really men. In order to be indulgent and kind to others they must be earnest with and severe to themselves;

they must be, so to speak, intolerant to themselves so as to be tolerant to others. There must be a trend of asceticism in them. They must be Jewish men, full of Judaism, of the strong Judaism, of the severe Judaism, of the Judaism that does not want a minimum but a maximum. A strong Judaism must live in them and a strong humanity must live in them. They will go out and it will be a wonderful dissemination.

Here again, may I be allowed to speak a special word to our American friends who are here, asking them to take it to our friends who were not able to come. On Friday I appealed to our American friends. I told them that their honour was engaged to help, develop and rouse Liberal Progressive Judaism in Palestine, to help first and foremost the admirable educational work full of humanity that is being accomplished there. I repeat it. Shall our friends in Palestine think that they are abandoned? America is strong; Progressive Judaism there is strong. In Palestine Progressive Judaism is weak. The strong must help the weak.

And now to other work. A place for missionaries must be established. We can no longer live without it. We would not see the signs of the times without seeing this. Our self-esteem, our self-respect ask it of us. The Jews of America can do it. They must do it. Here also their honour is engaged, not the one at the cost of the other, but both belong together. The missionary work will be a help to the national work, and the national work in Palestine will be a help to the missionary work. Begin to help, my friends from America, then others will follow you and hail your help.

But to come to a conclusion. One thing is necessary, one question stands before us. Our destiny puts this question. Are we great enough for it? We must have great thoughts; we must begin to think highly, nobly, magnanimously. All depends on great ideas. One is inclined often to say: let anybody think what he may, if only he thinks in a great manner, if only the thoughts he thinks are great, noble thoughts. That is the future.

There is many an old story in the Talmud that the sanctuary was destroyed by reason of the little-minded, the narrow-minded, the group-minded people. We must free ourselves from the group spirit, from the narrow mind, from the little thought. We must begin to hold the great ideas. Only a people, only a community with great ideas, with the great way of thinking, is able to have a mission, to send out missionaries. All depends on us. We should understand what the present time speaks to us, what it asks from us.

New days wait for us; they expect us. Our God waits for us.

⸲ 2 ⸳

Ben Zion Wacholder

Attitudes Towards Proselytizing
in the Classical Halakah

Dr. Baeck's impassioned call for Jews to see their mission was not based just
on a liberal reading of the faith. He relied as well on classical sources. Dr. Ben
Zion Wacholder considers how traditional Jewish law (*halachah*) handles
questions about actively welcoming converts. Noting the availability of material that lists sources from talmudic writing, Dr. Wacholder focuses on the three
centuries during which a halachic discussion of proselytes was extensive. He is
especially interested in the conflicting views of Rashi and the Tosafists and the
Spanish school. Dr. Wacholder presents the view that the Tosafists believed
that proselytizing was a commandment. This is a crucial observation, for, if
actively welcoming converts and seeking to effect conversions was, in fact, a
divine commandment, Jews would have to perform it independent of the very
real social dangers they faced in doing so. Dr. Wacholder's paper concludes
with the notion that because of the history of *halachah*, the more restrictive
Spanish view became normative. This is a provocative thesis precisely because
Dr. Wacholder allows an interpretation of seeking converts as nothing less than
a divine mission, rather than, for example, a desperate reaction to a contemporary problem such as intermarriage.

   Dr. Wacholder teaches at Hebrew Union College–Jewish Institute of Religion in Cincinnati.

———•—•———

The attitude towards proselytism implied in the Halakah has been the subject of several studies.[1] As the Talmud is the basis of rabbinic law, these studies
have concentrated on the talmudic sources. While this approach is correct
as far as it goes, it does not go far enough. The Mishnah and Gemara, to be
sure, are the basis of Jewish law; Halakah, however, is determined not by the

15

utterances of the Tannaim and Amoraim, but by the interpretation given to them by the medieval scholars. It follows that an analysis of the position of the Halakah towards proselytism must begin not with the talmudic sources, but with the major rabbinic commentators and codifiers.

Analysis of the posttalmudic sources as they deal with proselytes leads directly to the classical period of rabbinics. Few gaonic responsa refer to converts; and the treatment of the question in the *Halakhot Gedolot*, the major gaonic code, contains little from which to draw conclusions. It was not until the first three centuries of the second millennium, when the study of rabbinics experienced unprecedented growth, that the Halakah of proselytes was treated profoundly and extensively. The views expressed by the Tosafists, on the one hand, and by the scholars of Northern Africa and Spain, on the other, became the basis of all subsequent rabbinic law. But as these two schools flourished independently, it is not surprising to find that they differed in their interpretations of the Talmud. This is especially true with respect to laws pertaining to converts, a subject particularly susceptible to emotional and social presuppositions.

Thus a study of the two classical schools reveals fundamental differences of opinion in their treatment of the proselyte Halakah. Although both used the same talmudic sources as the basis of their decisions, the methods of interpretation and the decisions arrived at were sometimes as diverse as if different sources had been used. On the surface it would appear that the divergences arose from the tendency of the Spanish scholars to emphasize codification, while the Franco-German rabbis stressed interpretation. But this cannot be pressed too far, for codification implies interpretation and implicit in interpretation is categorization.[2]

The Franco-German school approached the Talmud by way of the medieval scholastic system, viewing all the tractates as an organic unit. Having assumed this, they proceeded to unify all diverse elements of Halakah, the procedural and the formal, the aggadic and the halakic, the purely historical and the legal precedents, into a oneness that perhaps never was meant to be.[3] The Spanish codifiers, however, emphasized the basic halakic parts of the Talmud. But, as will be shown later, even this diversity fails to explain the fundamental tendency of the Spanish school to be more critical toward the candidate for conversion, while the Franco-German rabbis adopted a more benevolent and less restrictive attitude toward proselyting. It would appear that a more fundamental reason for the divergences of the two schools, as far as the proselyte Halakah is concerned, was the difference in their concept of the meaning of Judaism and its relation to the outside world. The interpretation of Judaism has been influenced by the prevailing religious and philosophical trends of the times, no matter how isolated the Jews have been from their environment.

The chief halakic spokesmen of the Spanish school were Alfasi and Maimonides; of the Franco-German, Rashi and the Tosafists. Actually, however, Maimonides summarizes in his *Yad ha-Hazakah* not only the views of the Spanish scholars but also those of North Africa and the Middle East. And although the center of the Tosafist school was France and Western Germany, it also included prominent members from the British Isles to Kievan Russia, Hungary, and the Balkans.[4] In other words, roughly speaking, the Spanish school represented the Halakah under Moslem rule; the Franco-German, that of the Christian world.[5]

MOTIVE FOR CONVERSION

Based on Ruth 1:15–18, *Yebamot*, 47 a–b, states that a candidate for conversion, before he is accepted, must prove that his motives are entirely sincere. But, says the Talmud, this is only a preliminary requirement. If a candidate's ulterior motives have not been properly investigated, if they are not found out until after conversion, or even if the court flagrantly ignores them, the conversion is valid. Maimonides made this *baraita* the basis of his attitude toward those who want to be converted to Judaism. According to him, the fact that the test of sincerity is only a preliminary requirement enjoins caution in the admission of proselytes. The failure to check the true intentions of the candidates during biblical times explains the negative results of historical proselytism.[6] Interpreting biblical history in the light of Halakah, he says:

> Do not think that Samson, the Savior of Israel, or Solomon, the king of Israel, . . . married non-Jewish unconverted women. But the secret [*sic*] is that when a man or woman wants to be converted, he is investigated lest [his motives are] to gain money, to seek office, or to change his faith because of fear. If a man, it should be investigated whether his eyes are enticed by a Jewish woman; a woman, whether she desires to marry a young man of Israel. But if no such blemish can be found, then we instruct him in the burden of the yoke of the Torah, and how difficult it is for a gentile to observe it. . . . Only when it is evident that the proselyte desires to be converted because of love [of God], is he accepted. . . .[7] This is the reason why no proselytes were accepted during the reigns of David and Solomon: in the days of David their reason for wanting conversion was fear; in the days of Solomon, because of the unprecedented

prosperity. For whoever forsakes the worship of idols merely for vain material advantage is not a righteous proselyte. But, nevertheless, many people were converted in the days of David and Solomon before unordained courts. Toward them the High Court adopted a careful attitude: they [the members of the Court] did not alienate them, for they had already passed through the ceremony of immersion; neither did they draw them near, but waited to see the outcome. And as Solomon converted women and married them . . . and as it was known that their conversion was only for material motives, and as the conversion was not before the High Court, they were considered heathen, and the prohibition to intermarry with them remained.[8]

But because sincerity is only a preliminary requirement, "Samson and Solomon were permitted to retain their wives even after the secret [conversion] became known."[9]

This lengthy passage from *Yad ha-Hazakah* is quoted here to indicate not only Maimonides' historical and legal view, but also his approach to the entire proselyte Halakah. To him conversion to Judaism meant not so much the acceptance of the commandments as the philosophical recognition of the unity of God. It is from the unity of God that the observance of the Torah naturally follows. That is why the proselyte, according to Maimonides, is instructed first not, as the Talmud states, in the practical laws of *leket, shikha*, and *peah*,[10] to leave sheaves to the poor, but in the oneness of God and the futility of idol worship.[11] Those proselytes who are philosophically minded will not find onerous the steep path to the truth of the Torah; others should be excluded anyway.

Now to contrast this with the views expressed by the Tosafists. Commenting on the talmudic statement that proselytes were not accepted during the reign of David and Solomon because they were not sincere, the *Tosafot* attempt to reconcile it with known cases of converts having been accepted even though they had ulterior motives.[12] Thus the *Tosafot* tell of the man who came to Shammai and said that he wanted to be converted in order to become a high priest. Shammai sent him away, but Hillel accepted him.[13] Another case concerns a prostitute who called on R. Meir to be converted in order that she might marry his student and was accepted.[14] These examples were cited to prove that ulterior motives do not necessarily bar from conversion, and the Tosafists modified the rule of sincerity to conform with these precedents. Hillel and R. Meir accepted insincere proselytes because they felt that once converted, these would become sincere. Thus sincerity is judged, not only by present intentions, but also by the probable potential of the convert.[15]

ARE PROSELYTES A PLAGUE?

One of the most unfriendly talmudic passages concerning converts states: "Proselytes are as painful as an itch."[16] Although repeated four times, it is considered by some writers an aggadic statement and omitted in some major codes. Apologists of various periods have attempted to "explain" it.[17] Often the mere inclusion or omission of this passage is a guide to the writer's attitude toward proselyting. The *Tur* and the *Shulhan Arukh* do not quote it, while Alfasi and Maimonides do.

Maimonides' interpretation of this passage is interesting. Legally, he points out, a man who has been converted to Judaism, regardless of motives and whether or not he observes the Jewish ritual, is a Jew. "The sages said, 'Proselytes are as troublesome as a plague,' for the majority of proselytes convert themselves for some unworthy reason and therefore exert adverse influence on the Jews. . . . Remember what happened in the desert: the golden calf, the craving for meat, and most of the trials and tribulations were caused by the אספסוף who showed a bad example."[18]

That the Tosafists felt uneasy about this passage is clearly indicated by the fact that they offered six different interpretations: (1) R. Abraham ha-Ger explains that proselytes, having accepted Judaism voluntarily, observe the commandments more carefully than the average Jew and thereby remind God that born-Jews are sinning while strangers follow His precepts; (2) R. Isaac ben Samuel, one of the leading Tosafists, says that the *Shekhinah* dwells only among those Jewish families whose pedigree is unmingled with alien blood;[19] (3) Rashi states that, as proselytes are not acquainted with the ritual, their influence is adverse;[20] (4) because Jews are responsible for each other's sins, they suffer when a proselyte falters in the law;[21] (5) in twenty-four places the Pentateuch admonishes against oppressing or insulting the convert,[22] but Jews, being merely human, find it difficult not to insult him; (6) the primary reason the Jews have been in exile has been to attract converts, so proselytes have been the cause of the exile of the Jews.[23]

The first explanation is most revealing. This apologetic interpretation is interesting, not only because it is expressed by a convert, but also because it indicates the educational background of the Tosafist, Abraham ha-Ger. Unlike the other interpretations, which are based on talmudic sources, he shows a deep insight into the Bible. His idea that a righteous man reminds God of the evil of sinners is taken from I Kings 17:18. When the son of the woman of Zarephat became ill while Elijah was lodging in her house, she said to him: "What have I to do with thee, O thou man of

God? Art thou come unto me to bring my son to remembrance, and to slay
my son?"

THE PLACEMENT OF PROSELYTE LAWS
IN *YAD HA-HAZAKAH*

In analyzing the major codes it is important to pay attention, not only to the
treatment of the subject matter, but also to the position of a particular topic
as it relates to the general organization of the work. This is especially true in
the case of Maimonides' *Yad ha-Hazakah*, where the importance and relevance of various laws is indicated by their placement. The *Halakhot Gedolot*
and the *Tur* arrange the laws of proselytes among and after those relating to
circumcision, respectively. Why, then, did Maimonides, as Chaim Tchernowitz asks,[24] place the Halakah of proselytes in the thirteenth and fourteenth
chapters of *Issurei biah*? Was Maimonides implying thereby an unfavorable
attitude towards proselytizing?

   Taken by itself the unfavorable location of the proselyte laws is no proof
of Maimonides' personal views. His organization is basically different from
that of other codifiers. His attempt to be comprehensive by including in his
work the laws no longer applicable in his day would have made it awkward
to collect the varied legislation applicable to proselytes in a special section.
Consequently, Maimonides found it more logical to combine the laws pertaining to circumcision of converts with the other laws of *milah*, and to incorporate the prohibitions against the oppression of proselytes into *Hilkhot de'ot*,
which deal with the laws of conduct.[25] The rules for the admission of converts, however, he placed among those relating to prohibited marriages.
Technically, this is correct. Since conversion removes the prohibition against
intermarriage with Jews and sanctions it, these laws properly belong in the
section of *Issurei biah*.[26]

   Granted that the unfavorable placement of the rules for admission of
proselytes by itself offers no proof of Maimonides' personal opinions towards
proselytizing, other circumstantial evidence tends to point in that direction.
Maimonides' unusual departure from purely halakic matter to express his
historical and theological views concerning proselytes in the days of Samson
and Solomon; his statement that "the majority of proselytes have been converted for ulterior motives, having been granted admission by deception,"
together with the placement of the laws for the admission of converts among
those concerned with prohibited marriages, technical reasons notwithstanding, point to bias against proselytizing on the part of the author of the *Yad
ha-Hazakah*.

IS PROSELYTIZING A COMMANDMENT?

R. Shim'on ben Zemah Duran, better known as the Rashbaz, who flourished in the fourteenth century, was the first to ask why the computers of the commandments do not include the admission of proselytes as an obligation. He argues that proselytism should be counted as one of the six hundred and thirteen precepts found in the Torah.[27] Maimonides, Nahmanides and R. Moses of Coucy did not include proselyting as a commandment because there is no provision for the acceptance of proselytes in the Pentateuch. When they are accepted, the manner of their admission, it is implied, is merely an oral tradition.[28] But is there also an oral law to admit proselytes? The Spanish classical rabbis are silent on this question.

The Tosafists seem to have been the first to enunciate the doctrine that Jewish law requires the acceptance of converts. It is interesting to note how they arrived at this conclusion. The Talmud deduces from Leviticus 24:22 the rule that conversion should be performed before a court of three judges. "Ye shall have one manner of law, as well for the proselyte, as for the home-born."[29] *Mishpat*, law, had been interpreted to imply judgment also; there could be no judgment unless three judges were present; these, therefore, must preside at the admission of proselytes. The Tosafists, however, raised the problem, How can proselytes be admitted without a proper court? For a proper court is defined as consisting of three judges who have been ordained in Israel by a person whose chain of ordination goes back to the Sanhedrin.[30] They overcame this objection by invoking two complicated principles: "We fulfill their admission,"[31] and "You shall not bar the door in the front of converts."[32] Although there no longer are proper courts, unordained men have the commission of the ordained judges to convert proselytes. Were not these extraordinary principles invoked, proselytes could not be accepted; and this appeared to the Tosafists as unthinkable, there being a requirement to accept converts.[33]

One of the Tosafists found a more explicit regulation for the admission of proselytes without fulfilling the technical requirements. Numbers 15:15 states: "As for the congregation, there shall be one statute both for you and for the stranger that sojourneth with you, a statute forever throughout your generations." *Throughout your generations* indicates that even if there are some unavoidable technical imperfections in the admission of proselytes, these should not prevent the fulfillment of the main commandment.[34] Further proof is the fact that although there was, during the existence of the Temple, a requirement for the proselyte to offer a sacrifice, after its destruction proselytes were accepted without an offering.

The question whether or not proselytizing is a commandment held more than theoretical interest. If proselytizing is a precept, it must continue despite prohibition by the local government, but if it is merely a voluntary act of the Jews, external law might be binding.[35] The fact that during the Middle Ages Jews jeopardized their lives and property by accepting proselytes seems to prove that they regarded proselytizing as a commandment. A responsum of R. Samson ben Abraham of Sens (1150?–1220?), a leading Tosafist, tells, without comment, of a difficult circumcision performed upon a year-old child converted to Judaism.[36] This certainly violated Church law and perhaps even local legislation. It is reasonable to assume that the conversion of Christian children to Judaism must have involved some kind of a danger.[37]

CIRCUMCISION

Of greater practical importance was the problem of the candidate who had been circumcised before conversion. This question has aroused more controversy than any other in this field.[38] According to one opinion in the Talmud, it had even been debated by the Shammaite and Hillelite schools.[39] Because the Arab and Near Eastern peoples practiced circumcision, it was a live issue. As Mohammedanism spread during the seventh century, the Geonim were often called upon to express their opinion on this subject.[40] *Yebamot*, 72a, indicates that the letting of a drop of blood only is required. *Sabbath*, 135a, differentiates between a child born without a foreskin and a candidate who has been previously circumcised. After an involved debate, in which both tannaim and amoraim participated, the general conclusion seemed to be that even if a boy born without a foreskin needed *hatafah*, the drawing of a drop of blood, it would not be required of a proselyte who had been previously circumcised.

Both Alfasi[41] and Maimonides,[42] following the gaonic decision,[43] rule that the more stringent opinion should be accepted. Nahmanides offers a theoretical explanation for this decision that is not only independent of the Talmud, but seems contrary to it. The talmudic law is more stringent with the one born without a foreskin than with the proselyte; Nahmanides argues that the reverse is true. The reason given by him is that bloodletting is required of a child born without a foreskin as a precautionary measure in case his propuce has been repressed; but for a proselyte it is an indispensable condition to entering into the covenant of Abraham.[44] *Milah* and *hatafah*, according to Nahmanides, assume the character of a sacrificial fulfillment of initiation.

Although the stringent view encountered but little dissent among Spanish scholars,[45] the Tosafists ruled that a candidate who had been previously circumcised needed no operation at all. While it is true that in the texts generally used the position of the Tosafists is somewhat ambiguous,[46] the available digests of the Franco-German school agree that bloodletting should be dispensed with.[47] Perhaps the Tosafists reasoned, as described in the previous section, that the commandment to proselytize supersedes the regulations for carrying it out. Circumcision, a proper court, sacrifice in the temple, are required only when fulfillment is possible.

The two schools also differed as to the rules that applied when circumcision or immersion was witnessed by two men only, or performed at night when no court may sit. Although the Talmud says that a court is required,[48] it also cites the precedent of a proselyte who immersed herself to remove menstrual defilement and was not required to immerse again. Because such immersion is usually done at night in private, it appears to contradict the necessity of a court. In order to reconcile this contradiction, Alfasi and Maimonides rule that such technical shortcomings do not prevent the convert's children from being accepted as full Jews, but the convert himself is not.[49] The Tosafists hold that the presence of a court is indispensable only during the proselyte's acceptance of the commandments, but not for the immersion.[50]

PROOF OF CONVERSION

The differences between the two schools in regard to the admission of proselytes have been documented. Whether a man who claims to be a proselyte needs proof of conversion offers another contrast. In the Babylonian Talmud R. Judah says that only in Israel was proof of conversion needed, while the majority opinion requires proof in Israel or outside.[51] Maimonides, however, seems to agree with the late Palestinian *Gerim*:[52] "Palestine is favored, for the mere presence of the proselyte in the Holy Land qualifies him for acceptance in Israel. If one should say in Palestine: 'I am a proselyte,' we receive him at once. But outside of Palestine, we receive him only when he has witnesses with him."[53]

R. Jacob Tam, the founder of the Tosafot school, interpreted the talmudic sources requiring proof of conversion as referring only to cases where the proselyte had been known when he was still a Gentile. Citing an anecdote of a Gentile who made a pilgrimage to Jerusalem and partook of the Passover sacrifice, he ruled that a person who says he is a convert should be believed if there is no evidence to the contrary.[54] Incidentally, the two schools differ in the relative weight that they accord to legal decision as contrasted with precedents cited in the Talmud. The Tosafot law, like Anglo-Saxon jurisprudence, in the event of a conflict between formal rulings and actual precedents, tends to modify the former to agree with the latter.[54a] The Spanish scholars seem to put more emphasis on formal statements of law. This is true not only concerning the need for proof of conversion, but also in regard to the problem of ulterior motives, whether proselytizing is a commandment, whether bloodletting is always required before acceptance of Judaism, and in the matter of technical deficiencies in the ritual of conversion.

"GOD OF OUR FATHERS"

The rabbis also debated whether a proselyte reciting grace or the *shemoneh 'esreh* is allowed to identify himself with Israel's past by saying: "God of *our* fathers" or "the land that thou has inherited to *our* fathers." Herein lies another difference.[55] Maimonides once again prefers the version found in the Palestinian Talmud, which rules that a convert recites as any other Jew does.[56] R. Tam calls the Palestinian ruling an "error" and advises the proselyte to say, when praying in public, "God of *your* fathers," and in private, "God of Israel."[57] The opinion of the Tosafists is divided. R. Isaac ben Samuel, R. Tam's chief pupil, seems to argue that since there is no decisive *gemara* in the Babylonian text to confirm the *mishnah*, the Palestinian version should be followed.[58] This division of opinion within the Franco-German school probably accounts for the fact that in Würzburg a proselyte was temporarily barred from leading the services in the synagogue, but R. Tam's objections were finally overruled, and the convert continued to lead the prayers.[59]

The ruling of Maimonides in this matter, as well as his moving epistle to Obadiah Ger Zedek, which is too well known to be quoted here,[60] offers another aspect of his views on proselytism. He imposes the full force of the law and advises the utmost caution before admitting a proselyte. But once the convert sincerely accepts the God of Israel and devotedly practices His Commandments, it is as if he had been present at Sinai and Abraham was his ancestor.[61]

ABRAHAM OR OBADIAH

Since the Middle Ages it has been customary for proselytes—Christian, Mohammedan, or Jewish—to change their names upon conversion. Among Jews a uniformity soon developed. In communities under Moslem domination or influence the name Obadiah was preferred. Thus, one of the Khazar princes was named Obadiah;[62] Maimonides wrote epistles to Obadiah Ger Zedek;[63] and a Norman crusader who was converted in the Near East adopted the same name.[64] In Christian countries, however, proselytes were given the name Abraham.[65] Both names are derived from talmudic lore. Abraham, the originator of monotheism and the ancestor of proselytes, needs no explanation here. Perhaps because the Moslems claim that Abraham was the founder of Mohammedanism, the name was avoided in their countries. Obadiah, signifying "servant of the Lord," parallels "servant of Allah," and may have been intended to remove the stigma of the original faith. Ancient sources, moreover, identify Obadiah the Prophet as a proselyte.[66] The phrase found in Obadiah 1:20, "and the captivity of Jerusalem that is found in Sefarad," was believed to be a reference to Spanish Jewry.

PROSELYTES AMONG FRANCO-GERMAN JEWRY

More striking is the fact that in the Tosafist literature references to actual proselytes, named and unnamed, are numerous, while in the Sephardic writings of the period they are but scanty. The correspondent of Maimonides and the Norman convert, mentioned above, are all that we could find. But to enumerate all the proselytes recorded in Franco-German rabbinic sources would require a special study.[67] The Tosafist R. Abraham ha-Ger and two converts who were the subjects of the responsa by Meir of Rothenburg may be mentioned.[67a] The backgrounds of a few others are worth recording here: R. Abraham ha-Ger of Hungary, who wrote biblical exegeses and participated in polemics between Christians and Jews;[68] Abraham ben Abraham, whose practice of studying the Bible by comparing the Hebrew text with that of the Vulgate aroused disapproval and sympathy at the same time;[69] an unnamed proselyte of Pontoise, the subject of a responsum by R. Tam, who studied the Bible and the Talmud "day and night."[70] These were not a group of ignorant or ordinary people, accepting another faith for the sake of wealth or glory, but men who, like the Tosafists themselves, devoted their lives to learning and piety. It may be assumed that some of these converts were former monks and others associated with the Catholic clergy, as very few laypeople knew Latin.

Perhaps the very presence of such dedicated converts among the Tosafists accounts for the tendency of the Franco-German scholars to rule in favor of the proselyte whenever the texts could be interpreted in a liberal manner. In other halakic matter the Tosafists show no definite disposition to leniency in legal interpretation, but are strict or flexible according to the particular case.[71] Actually, however, even in the proselyte Halakah it may be inaccurate to speak of strictness and leniency. It is more correct to say that the rules of admission were somewhat relaxed in order to observe more stringently the commandment to proselytize. There is an eagerness to increase the number of those who observe the laws of the Torah; contemporary extrahalakic sources confirm this impression. The *Sefer Hasidim* recommends tolerant treatment of apostates lest they denounce proselytes to the local authorities.[72] R. Judah ha-Hasid also admonishes those who serve *trefah* foods to proselytes whose conversion has not been completed. He urges that a man shall not postpone his marriage if he can choose a convert, "for Moses realizing that he could not return to Egypt married a proselyte." The talmudic statement that marriages are preordained in Heaven holds true whether one marries a convert or not.[73]

During the second half of the thirteenth century, the Tosafist scholastic style, as well as its interpretive method, was accepted in all centers of Jewish learning. Conversely, the formal rulings of Alfasi and Maimonides were generally accepted everywhere. Nahmanides, Rashba, and Asheri blended the two classical systems into a synthesis that attempted to minimize the divergent opinions of the two schools. In regard to proselyte legislation, the views of Maimonides, if not his underlying philosophy, prevailed. The vigorous campaign against Jewish proselytizing, adopted by the Church and local authorities after the Fourth Lateran Council of 1215, contributed to the prevalence of an unfriendly, or at least an indifferent, attitude toward proselytism. Even a scholar like R. Mordekhai ben Nathan, though of the Tosafist school, reluctantly agreed with the more severe Spanish tradition: "It seems to this writer, a mere layman," he emphasized, "that if a man is known to have an ulterior motive, he should be rejected. . . . I have written what seems to me; but the views of my teachers are different. My understanding, however, is unreliable."[74] If as staunch a follower of the Franco-German tradition as R. Mordekhai ben Nathan had to yield to Sephardic views, later codes naturally followed the Spanish Halakah. The *Shulhan Arukh*, essentially a product of Spanish Halakah, codified the more rigorous halakic laws.[75]

The two branches of classical Halakah differ in their basic approach to the admission of converts. The Spanish school does not recognize any injunction to proselytize. Thus *Yebamot*, 47a–b, stating the principle of purity of motive, became the nucleus of proselyte Halakah. It happens that this principle fits in well with Maimonides' general philosophic ideas. Only candidates with the most lofty aspirations can be admitted, lest they become a plague. Judaism is a spiritual aristocracy, and the ceremonies of circumcision and immersion are indispensable marks thereof. Any doubts in law are resolved against the candidate. But once the proselyte has passed through the severe screening, the glory of being a Jew, of sharing the Jewish past, present, and future, belong to him.

The Franco-German rabbis make the commandment to proselyte their basic premise. The *baraita* requiring purity of motive is viewed by the Tosafists as a mere thread in the tapestry of talmudic proselyte legislation. Once the rulings and particularly the precedents dealing with the subject are analyzed, the proselytizing laws can be arrived at inductively. As there is a command to proselytize, doubts or contradictory passages regarding admission of proselytes must be decided in favor of the convert. A proper court, circumcision, immersion and proof thereof, these are but technical supplements to the injunction to convert. The Tosafists were not less strict than their Spanish colleagues in the observance of the details of the proselyte laws, but such details were superseded by the commandment to proselytize. The scholars of France and Germany put more emphasis on the practical observance of the Torah than on philosophical abstractions like purity of intention and sudden recognition of truth. The Tosafists had direct contact with actual converts who, like themselves, were immersed in the sea of Jewish learning. The learned rabbis felt that the recognition of the beauty of Judaism is but a slow and arduous process to be appreciated only after a lifetime of study. Thus the two schools express well the geographic differences in the intellectual climate of the time. Had the views of the classical Franco-German school prevailed rather than those of the Spanish school, the attitude of traditional Jewry toward proselytism would have been more positive.

NOTES

1. A. Z. Marcus, לתולדות דת נצרת, גרים (Jerusalem, 1937). William G. Braude, *Jewish Proselyting in the First Five Centuries of the Common Era; the Age of the Tannaim and Amoraim* (Providence, RI, 1940); Bernard J. Bamberger, *Proselytism in the Talmudic Period* (Cincinnati, 1939), contain bibliographies.

2. This study adheres to the premise that interpretive passages relating to the laws of proselytes found in *Tosafot*, unless they deal with tentative assumptions or are otherwise implicitly or explicitly excluded, are also meant to be rules of law. Recently the old controversy has been renewed as to whether the Tosafists intended to be mere commentators, as R. Malakhi Hakohen maintained in יד מלאכי, כללי רש"י ותוספות (Przemysl, 1867), No. 14, p. 189, citing R. Bezalel Askenazi, שיטה מקובצת to Khetubot, 4a (Tel Aviv, 1956), p. 87 or legal interpreters, as maintained by the *Piskei ha-Tosafot* (printed at the end of talmudic texts). Ch. Tchernowitz, *Toledot ha-Posekim* (New York, 1947), II, 32–38, agrees basically with the former, but fixes rules by which, he asserts, the Tosefists indicated halakic intent. Tchernowitz's mechanistic system has been forcefully rejected by E. Urbach, *The Tosafists: Their History, Writings and Method* (Jerusalem, 1955), 569, n. 13 (in Hebrew). The latter points

out that R. Malakhi overstates R. Bezalel's opinion. R. Bezalel does not hold that halakic decisions may not be deduced from Tosafist texts, something that he usually does in his *Shitah mekubezet*; all he intends to say is that the halakic intent is not present in *Tosafot* at all times. Be that as it may, this study draws support from the Tosafist digests and works such as R. Jacob Tam, *Sefer ha-yashar* (Vienna, 1811); R. Eliezer of Metz, *Sefer Yereyim hagadol* (Wilno, 1892), and others, which verify the premise as far as the subject of this study is concerned.

3. For a recent and excellent treatment of the Franco-German school, see Urbach, op. cit., 523–574 and passim.

4. Cf. ibid., pp. 191–194.

5. The Provence halakists, R. Abba Mari of Marseille, Rabad, R. Moses of Coucy, and others are treated here only incidentally. As far as the proselyte Halakah is concerned, there is no consistent trend; they differ among themselves depending on the issues involved.

6. Maimonides, *Yad ha-Hazakah, Hilkhot Issurei Biah*, 13, 14–18.

7. Cf. *Yebamot*, 24b, 76a, 79a.

8. Maimonides, *op. cit.*, 13, 14–16.

9. Ibid., 13, 17. For talmudic statements that seem to contradict Maimonides' views concerning Solomon, see *Lehem mishnah* to *l. c.*, which concludes with וצריך עיון; cf. also R. David Kimhi's *Commentary* to I Kings 11:2.

10. *Yebamot*, 47a; *Gerim*, 1, 1.

11. Maimonides, op. cit., 14, 1–5.

12. *Tosafot, Yebamot*, 24b, 109b.

13. *Sabbath*, 31a.

14. In *Minahot*, 44a, the reading is R. Hiya. But the *Tosafot, l. c., s. v. lebeit*, point out that the reading of the *Sifri, Shelah*, 75 (Malbim ed.), is preferable.

15. *Tosafot, Yebamot*, 24b, 109b. J. Karo quotes the *Tosafot* in his *Bet Yoseph, Tur Yoreh De'ah*, 268 (Wilno, 1924), p. 215b, but omits it in his code. S. Cohen restores it in his *Siftei Kohen, Shulhan Arukh, Yoreh De'ah*, 268, 23.

16. *Yebamot*, 47b, 109b; *Kidushin*, 70b; *Niddah*, 13b.

17. The *Zohar* (Wilno, 1911), I, 214b, explains this passage as referring to messianic times when the proselytes will be so numerous that no breathing place will be left in Israel for native Jews. For a modern treatment of R. Helbo's statement, see Braude, op. cit., pp. 42–45.

18. Maimonides, op. cit., *Hilkhot Issurei Biah*, 13, 17–18.

19. *Kidushin*, 70b.

20. *Pesachim*, 91b.

21. *Sotah*, 37b.

22. Cf. *Baba Mezia'*, 59b; Malbim, *Kedoshim*, 82, enumerates the passages.

23. *Pesachim*, 87a. *Rashi, Tosafot, Yebamot*, 47b; *Kidushin*, 70b–71a; *Niddah*, 13a; *Pesachim*, 91b.

24. כמו כן קשה לישב על פי סדר הגיוני את סידורן של ה' גרים בהלכות איסורי ביאה אלא Tchernowittz, op. cit., I, משום שה' גרים תלויות בל"ת של חיתון וכך הן מסודרות בספר המצוות.

224. I have, however, been unable to find the Halakah of proselytes in the place indicated by Tchernowitz. Perhaps Tchernowitz is referring, not to Maimonides' *Sefer ha-mizvot*, but to the *Sefer Mizvot Gadol* by R. Moses of Coucy, *lo ta'aseh*, No. 116, where the rules for the admission of converts are treated together with the prohibition against Jews intermarrying with Ammonites and Moabites. But the system of R. Moses of Coucy is based on that of Maimonides and could not have been the basis of the organization of the *Yad ha-Hazakah*.

25. Maimonides, op. cit., *Hilkhot milah*, 1, 6–7; *Hilkhot de'ot*, 6, 4. Positive proof that Maimonides treats, in *Issurei biah*, only the rules for admission can be shown by the laws of slavery. Although he devotes a special section to slavery legislation, the admission of slaves, like that of proselytes, is arranged with *Hikhot Issurei biah*.

26. Prof. Samuel Atlas, commenting on this paper. I would like to take this opportunity to thank him for his perusal of this article and for his helpful comments and suggestions.

27. Simon ben Zemah Duran, *Zohar ha-Raki'a* on *Sefer Azharot* (Wilno, 1879) '*esin*, 40; *Encyclopedia Talmudit* (Jerusalem, 1954), VI, col. 426.

28. הלכה למשה מסיני.

29. Except for necessary elucidation of the text, the Jewish Publication Society translation is used in this paper for all biblical references.

30. *Tosafot Yebamot*, 46b–47a, *Kidushin*, 62b.

31. Ibid.; *Gittin*, 88b, שליחותייהו קא עבדינן.

32. *Tosafot*, 47a, וכמו שהשו לנעילת דלת בפני לווין חשו נמי לנעילת דלת בפני גרים. Cf. ibid., 109b, where the command to accept proselytes is treated.

33. *Tosafot Yebamot*, 47b; *Kidushin*, 62b.

34. *Tosafot Kidushin*, 62b.

35. Cf. *Mordekhai*, Yebamoth, *Hagahot ha-Holez*, No. 110; and B. Wacholder, *Historia Judaica*, XVIII (1956), 105, regarding slaves who could not be Judaized because of prohibition by local authorities.

36. R. Moses of Vienna, *Or Zaru'a* (Zitomir, 1862), II, 26a, No. 99.

37. The Halakah sanctions the conversion of minors, but with the option, upon reaching manhood, of leaving Judaism (Ketubot, 11a). According to Rashi, *l. c.*, the consent of at least one of the parents is required. The Tosafists, however, regard the conversion of minors as a violation of a Torah law. The reason given is that it is assumed that to be converted to Judaism is a favor to the child, the court acting as proxy for the minor's future welfare. But, *Tosafot* ask, as there is no provision in Jewish law for minors to appoint proxies, how can the court claim to act as such? To avoid this technical difficulty, the Tosafists hold that to act for the welfare of the child, the Rabbis modified the Torah law to make it possible for the child to be converted: דיש כח ביד חכמים לעקור דבר מן התורה בקום ועשה. *Tosafot* to *l. c.*

38. *Sabbath*, 135a; *Yebamoth*, 467b, 71a, 72b; *Nedarim*, 31b; *Abodah Zarah*, 27a. Arabs, Gibeonites, as well as Egyptians, practiced circumcision in antiquity; Herodotus, II, 37.

39. *Sabbath*, 135a. For a recent treatment of these sources, see Bamberger, op. cit., 42–52.

40. B. Lewin, *Ozar ha-Geonim* (Jerusalem, 1936–1940), II, 127–128; VII, 366; *Halakhot Gedolot* (Berlin, 1888), p. 107; Abba Mari of Marseille, '*Itur* (Lemberg, 1860), 22a.

41. *Alfas, Sabbath*, 54a (Wilno, Rome editions).

42. Maimonides, op. cit., *Hilkhot Milah*, 1, 7.

43. See note 40.

44. Nahmanides, *Milhemet ha-Shem* on *Alfasi*, 53b f. (Rome edition), defending the views of Alfasi from R. Zerahiah ha-Levi's arguments in *ha-Maor ha-Katan*, *l. c.*; and Nahmanides' Commentary on *Sabbath*, 135a.

45. R. Hannanel, the eleventh-century Gaon of Kiruan, on *Sabbath*, 135a, ruled that a circumcised candidate requires no operation, his children are converted, but he himself is not allowed to intermarry if he should request permission. See *Tur, Yoreh De'ah*, 268, beginning.

46. *Tosafot Sabbath*, 135a, *Yebamot*, 46b. On the one hand, the Tosafists defend the *Halakhot Gedolot* position that bloodletting is required, and on the other hand, they seem to rule that no operation is necessary.

47. V. Aptowitzer (ed.), *Sefer Rabiah* (Berlin, 1918), I, 355; Eliezer of Metz, *Sefer Yereim ha-Gadol*; *Shiltei ha-Gibborim* on Alfas, 35b; R. Moses ben Isaac of Vienna, *Or Zaru'a* (Zitomir, 1862), II, 99, quotes responsum by R. Samson of Sens.

48. *Yebamot*, 46b; *Kidushin*, 62b.

49. *Alfas, Yebamot*, 15a–b; Maimonides, op. cit., *Hilkhot Issurei Biah*, 13, 9.

50. *Tosafot, Yebamot*, 45b; *Kidushin*, 62b.

51. *Yebamot*, 46b–47a.

52. Maimonides, op. cit., 13, 10. The *Migdal 'Oz* on *Yad, l. c.*, was the first to point out the Palestinian source of Maimonides.

53. M. Higger (ed.), *Gerim*, 4, 5.

54. *Tosafot, Pesahim*, 3b; *Yebamot*, 47a; J. Tam, op. cit., 31a.

54a. *Tosafot Yebamot*, 45b, 109b; cf. also *Berakhot*, 2a; *Sanhedrin*, 36b.

55. *Mishnah, Bikkurim*, 1, 4; *Makkot*, 19a; Rashi on *Deut.* 26:11.

56. *Yer. Bikkurim*, 1, 4; Maimonides, op. cit., *Hilkhot Bikkurim*, 4, 3; cf. Bamberger, op. cit., pp. 65–68.

57. *Tosafot, Baba Batra*, 81a.

58. Ibid. *Makkot*, 19a, does support the majority opinion of M. *Bikkurim*, 1, 4, but *Yer. Bikkurim*, 1, 4, is emphatic.

59. *Mordekhai, Megillah*, No. 786.

60. A. Freimann (ed.), *Teshubot ha-Rambam* (Jerusalem, 1934), No. 42; *Mordekhai*, op. cit.

61. The two schools follow their respective trends in other differences: whether a proselyte who had children prior to conversion has fulfilled the commandment to bear offspring. Maimonides, *Hilkhot Ishut*, 15, 6; *Tos. Yebamot*, 62a, *Hagigah*, 2b. Their divergence on *Ger Toshab* is too extensive to enter into here; Rashi, and the

Tosafists and the Spanish school differ on whether a proselyte may judge a native Jew in criminal cases.

62. A. Harkavy, in Graetz, *Dibrei Yemei Israel* (Rabbinowitz tr., Warsaw, 1893), III, 345, note 10.

63. Freimann, op. cit., No. 42, p. 40. It would seem that Maimonides draws a sharp distinction between converts in general and those whose sincerity cannot be questioned. In addressing Obadiah he calls him *ger zedek*; R. Akiba's father, Yoseph, was a *ger zedek*, as was the father of R. Meir, according to the Introduction to the *Yad ha-Hazakah*. The phrase וכן שמעיה ואבטליון גרי־צדק היו in the Introduction to the *Yad ha-Hazakah* may be an answer to the problem raised by R. Yom Tob Lipman, *Tosafot Yom Tob* to Abot, 1, 10: If, according to Maimonides, Shemayah and Abtalion were converts, how were they permitted to preside over the Sanhedrin (*Yad, Hilkhot Sanhedrin*, 11, 11)? Perhaps Maimonides took the position that the rule barring converts from presiding over a court applied to ordinary converts only, and not to great scholars. For a similar interpretation, see R. Shimon ben Zemah, *Magen Abot* (Leipzig, 1855), 1, 10.

64. J. Mann, *ha-Tekufah*, XXIII (1925), 253–261; R. E. J., LXXXIX, 235–259; S. D. Goitein, "Obadyah, a Norman Proselyte," *Journal of Jewish Studies*, VI (1956), 74–84.

65. R. Asher ben Yehiel, *Teshubot ha-Rosh* (Wilno, 1881), 15, 4, however, indicates that *peloni*, X, ben Abraham is the correct version. Cf. *Zohar*, 1, 96a.

66. *Sanhedrin*, 39b; Bamberger, op. cit., 204, has a good treatment on Obadiah as a proselyte.

67. The writer is preparing a list of converts mentioned in the Tosafist writings. So far the list exceeds a score. But as cases of conversion are referred to only when unusual halakic problems are raised, it must be assumed that the actual number of converts during the twelfth and thirteenth centuries was relatively high. For nonhalakic sources, cf. Carmoly, "Wanderungen im Gebiete der jüdischen Geschichte," *Ben Chananjah*, IV (1861), 205; A. Berliner, *Aus dem Leben der deutschen Juden im Mittelalter* (Berlin, 1900), p. 108; S. Grayzel, *The Church and the Jews in the XIIIth Century* (Philadelphia, 1933), pp. 198–199. The halakic sources would seem to substantiate Pope Gregory's charges, rejected by Grayzel: "*Nonulli etiam non re, sed solo nomine Christiani sponte se transferentes ad ipsos, et eorum ritum sectantes circumcidi permittunt, et Judeos se publice profitentur.*"

67a. *Sheelot u-Teshubot* Meharam (Cremona, 1595), No. 54; (Prague, 1608), No. 103.

68. Urbach, op. cit., p. 194, attempts to identify Abraham ha-Ger of Hungary with Abraham ha-Ger the Tosafist, *Kidushin*, 71a. But since Abraham was commonly used as a name for proselytes, identification is doubtful.

69. Aptowitzer, op. cit., II, 253–256; *Mordekhai*, op. cit., No. 786.

70. J. Tam, op. cit., 76a; Urbach, op. cit., p. 112.

71. Urbach, op. cit., 78 and passim.

72. Judah ha-Hasid, *Sefer Hasidim* (Berlin, 1924), p. 73, No. 189.

73. Ibid., p. 77, No. 114; p. 291, No. 1150; p. 285, No. 1128.

74. *Mordekhai, Yebamot, Hagahot* to *ha-Holez*, No. 110.

75. The *Shulhan Arukh, Yoreh De'ah*, 268–269, mostly quotes Maimonides. On the differences cited in this paper, Karo agrees with the Spanish school: (1) only present motives should be considered (268, 12); (2) a candidate who has been circumcised prior to conversion needs *hatafah* (268, 1); (3) Karo cites Maimonides that proof of conversion is needed outside of Israel (268, 10); (4) a proselyte fulfills the commandment to bear children only if both he and his children have been converted (*Eben ha-'Ezer*, 1, 7); (5) the proselyte may say "God of our fathers" (*Orah Hayim*, 199, 4). But Karo, like the *Tur*, (1) places the proselyte laws in a more favorable light; (2) does not quote the statement that proselytes are a plague; (3) cites the Tosafist opinion that the presence of three judges during circumcision or immersion is only a preliminary requirement (*Yoreh De'ah*, 268, 3).

⊰ 3 ⊱

Martin Goodman

Proselytising in Rabbinic Judaism

Many scholars, most particularly Dr. Louis H. Feldman (see especially his book *Jew & Gentile in the Ancient World* [Princeton, NJ: Princeton University Press, 1993], have argued that the theoretical interest in proselytizing discussed by Dr. Baeck and Dr. Wacholder found expression in Jewish history with an enormous and successful effort to integrate new Jews especially during the era of the Second Temple. This was a widespread view, not only among Jewish scholars like Rabbi Bernard Bamberger and Rabbi William Braude but also among many Christian scholars as well. However, this view has not gone unchallenged. Scholars, again Jewish and Christian, have suggested that welcoming is not the same as actually searching for converts. This is the thesis Martin Goodman explores.

Indeed, it is crucial to understand as a background to this paper that the semantics are very tangled. Jews do not seem to have had any organized, centralized missionary efforts, and if that is the definition of proselytizing, then their efforts were simply of the welcoming variety. However, if we understand proselytizing to include: (1) creating literature aimed at attracting converts; (2) making synagogue services available; (3) marrying gentiles who became Jews; (4) adopting gentile children and raising them as Jews; and, most particularly, (5) seeing mission work in everyday activity (so that, for instance, a merchant would explain Judaism to gentiles as part of his daily activity, not thinking of himself as a missionary but just fulfilling a religious obligation as part of his life), then Jews were active.

Martin Goodman considers the evidence and concludes that Jews did not actively seek converts until the Rabbinic period, not, as often assumed, during the Second Temple Period.

Dr. Goodman is Reader in Jewish Studies at the University of Oxford. His book *Mission and Conversion: Proselytizing in the Religious History of the Roman Empire* was published by Clarendon Press in 1994.

Members of a community who accept that suitable outsiders should be welcomed into their society do not imply by their acceptance that a positive search for such newcomers is appropriate. The notion of a proselyte was well established in Judaism long before the end of the Second Temple era,[1] but the impetus for conversion was expected to come from the worthy gentile concerned, not from the Jews whom he or she wished to join. Jews were often eager to change the general attitudes of gentiles both to God and to each other;[2] they liked non-Jews to admire and respect Jewish customs;[3] they encouraged the spread of monotheism;[4] and they speculated with some interest on the eventual status of gentiles in the last days.[5] But a mission to gain converts, a phenomenon most familiar from the history of Christianity, requires an attitude rather different from any of these. In this article I shall examine the emergence of such an attitude in rabbinic Judaism.[6]

Prior elucidation of the stance of prerabbinic Jews would be desirable, but the evidence is complex and ambiguous and it must suffice here to note that the belief in some modern scholarship that Jews before A.D. 70 were eagerly committed to the conversion of gentiles seems to me at best unproven.[7] I have given reasons elsewhere for upholding the somewhat contentious proposition that it was extremely unusual for any Jew in the first century A.D. to view the encouragement of gentiles to convert to Judaism as a praiseworthy act. There is room here only for a brief sketch of the evidence.[8]

No early source holds gentiles morally guilty for not being full Jews. Gentiles had no share in the covenant between God and Israel. If in their own lands they wished to continue to worship their pagan divinities, there could be no objection. Both Josephus and Philo follow the lead of the Septuagint translators in interpreting Exodus 22:27 as an injunction to Jews not to revile the gods of other nations.[9] The exceptions to this liberalism prove the rule: pagans living among the Jews in the holy land could not be allowed to pollute the sanctified people with idolatry and were compelled either to espouse Judaism or depart elsewhere.[10] In the diaspora Jews were not much concerned whether particular outsiders joined them or not. This lack of concern is reflected in the vagueness of Jewish terminology about the status of gentiles who accreted to their community. To the convert it was doubtless crucial to know whether he was or was not included within the covenant between Israel and God, but native Jews in this period do not seem even to have agreed on publicly recognisable criteria for such inclusion.[11]

Some of these attitudes can be found also in the rabbinic texts, all of which were redacted in the early third century or later. The biblical notion that God rules over all peoples but that his name rests specifically on Israel still predominated (e.g. *MdRi Mishpatim*, p. 334). The rabbis assumed that it is a good thing for Jews to persuade gentiles to be monotheists, just as Abraham told all Babylon to acknowledge that there is only one God.[12] Many texts continue to take it for granted that prospective converts will normally offer themselves and that it is not part of a good Jew's role to try to increase their number. According to the second-century tanna R. Yose, it will eventually come about that idol worshippers will offer themselves as proselytes (bAb. Zar. 3b), but the hard line taken in the anonymous baraita reported at bYeb. 24b precludes any assumption that such pagans will always be accepted, for in that passage opportunist conversions in (for?) the days of the messiah are treated with disdain (אין מקבלין גרים לימות המשיח). It is notorious that R. Helbo argued that proselytes actually delay the coming of the messiah and are therefore, it must be presumed, to be turned away, or at least not actively to be sought (bNidd. 13b; bYeb. 109b, and parallels).[13]

Alongside this continuation of older ideas some curious changes can be traced in statements attributed to rabbis who taught between the second and fifth centuries. On the one hand there was a trend to codify the behaviour that would classify as righteous a gentile who has *not* converted to Judaism. On the other hand there emerged among some rabbis, perhaps for the first time among any non-Christian Jews, a belief that Jews have a duty to win proselytes.

The first trend is bound up with the codification of the theoretical Noachide Laws, a subject that can be discussed here quite briefly since it has been treated at length in recent years by Novak.[14] The first explicit evidence for such rules being drawn up can be found in the third-century text tAb. Zar. 8:4, but since the tannaim there are portrayed as debating the number and content of the laws, but not the concept of such a code in itself, it can be assumed that the principle that gentiles could be righteous without conversion was generally accepted in rabbinic circles. At first sight it is rather surprising that in a contemporary passage, tSanh. 13:2, it is asserted by some rabbis that no gentile will be admitted to the next world (עולם הבא) but, given the cheerful inconsistency of the rabbis on the hypothetical question of entry to the next world even by Jews, perhaps these views were not regarded as contradictory; alternatively, it may be thought that the rabbis who believed all gentiles to be excluded from the world to come accepted the idea of the Noachide Laws but claimed with characteristic rhetorical exaggeration that no gentile in fact lived up to the Noachide requirements.

This latter claim was gradually rendered more plausible by a novel insistence that good gentiles who had no desire to convert to Judaism nevertheless had a duty to abstain from idolatry.[15] At tBer. 7 (6):2 it is argued that Jews should extirpate idolatry only from the land of Israel, and it seems likely that the godfearers who attended the synagogue at Aphrodisias probably in the early third century had no suspicion that continued adherence to paganism was reprehensible — included within their number were city councillors who, by virtue of their office, could not avoid involvement with civic cults.[16] This liberalism continued among some amoraic rabbis — thus at *bHull.* 13b it is stated explicitly that gentiles should be allowed to practise paganism so long as they are outside the holy land (see also the parallel at *yBer.* 9:2, 13b). But in the expansion of the Tosefta passage mentioned above (*tBer.* 7 (6):2), the tannaitic rabbis cited in the Babylonian Talmud assert that idolatry will eventually be rooted out not just from Israel but from the whole world (*bBer.* 57b), and it is alleged at *bMeg.* 9a–b that the Septuagint translation of Deut. 4:19 and 17:3 implied that all humanity was forbidden to worship the heavenly bodies; such an interpretation is not actually found in any extant Septuagint text and is most likely to have been the invention of the amoraim themselves.[17] The prohibition on returning runaway slaves to a heathen master, found in *Sifre Deut.* 259, seems to presuppose the undesirability of even gentile slaves practising paganism. The commentary on Ps. 50:20 found at *Deut. R.* 6:4 (Soncino 6:9) urges Jews to show respect for gentiles, but it shows no trace of the respect for the gentiles' gods that had been advocated in earlier times by Philo and Josephus (see above, p. 34). This new attitude of some rabbis towards gentile paganism had quite considerable potential consequences, for pagan cults flourished in the centuries before Constantine as much as at any previous time in classical antiquity.[18]

But the same attitude that made it harder for gentiles to live up to the standard in theory required of them by the rabbis might be expected to make the achievement of such recognition all the more significant. The second trend in rabbinic thought about gentiles in this period — and the main subject of this paper — becomes increasingly hard to explain. If rabbis reckoned that keeping the Noachide Laws was all that gentiles had to do to be considered virtuous, why seek to convert any of them to Judaism? It may be that the lack of direct statements in rabbinic texts about the desirability of proselytising is due to uneasiness about precisely this paradox. At any rate, the evidence for rabbinic approval of the winning of converts is, as will be seen, extremely indirect and allusive; but I hope that when it is laid out below it may be seen to have some cumulative force.

The most persuasive evidence seems to me to lie in the common rabbinic depiction of Abraham as a missionary. Approving reference is made in many rabbinic passages (e.g. *ARNB*, ch. 26; *Num. R.* 14:11; *Pes. R.* 43.181a, etc.) to the activities of Abraham and Sarah in Haran where, according to Gen. 12:5, they "created souls." How, asked the rabbis, could humans create life? Already in the earliest extant reference to this problem, in the tannaitic midrash *Sifre Deut.* 32, the response is given that the expression "created souls" (עשו נפשות) means that Abraham and Sarah "brought men and women under the wings of the Shekhinah (תחת כנפי השכינה)"; this latter phrase possessed a semitechnical meaning, derived from its use in Ruth 2:12, of converting someone to Judaism. In this passage in Sifre thc implications of the actions of Israel's ancestors for contemporary Jews are made explicit. The words of Deut. 6:5 (ואהבת את ה' אלהיך) are interpreted by a shift of vowels to mean not "you should love" but "you should make the Lord your God be loved [by humanity]"; the reason given for this injunction is that this is what Abraham and Sarah did when they made proselytes (מגיירם) in Haran. Since what they did was praiseworthy, all Jews should try to follow suit.

Nor is the image of Abraham as missionary confined to discussion of his behaviour in Haran. Gen. 12:8, which reads, "And he [Abraham] called upon the name of the Lord (ויקרא בשם ה')", is interpreted at *Ber. R.* 39:16 as "he summoned people to the name of the Lord"and taken to signify that he began to make converts. In *Mid. Tanhuma Lekh Lekha* 12 (ed. Buber, p. 70), it is asserted not only that the Egyptians converted when Abraham came to their country but that this was the same pattern as was later followed when the children of Israel arrived in Egypt.

This new status of Abraham as the great missionary is all the more striking because he lacked the role in the eyes of Philo and Josephus. According to the latter he went down to Egypt intending either to learn about the gods from the natives or to teach them if he found his own knowledge superior (*A.J.* 1.161). Discovering that the Egyptians were comparatively ignorant, he imparted to them his wisdom. But that wisdom turns out to have consisted in neither the teachings of Judaism nor even ethical monotheism, but the sciences of arithmetic and astronomy (*A.J.* 1.166–167). Artapanus in the second century B.C. had an even odder notion. According to him, Abraham instructed the Egyptians in astrology (Euseb., *Praep. ev.* 9.18), and Moses introduced them to their idolatrous animal cults.

Other figures from the Bible are similarly portrayed in rabbinic texts as missionaries, evidently with approval. R. Hoshaya, a third-century amora from Palestine, cited R. Judah b. Simon's reading of Gen. 37:1 ("And Jacob dwelt in the land of his father's sojournings (מגורי אביו) as מגירי אביו, with the implication that Isaac had made proselytes in that area—but whether this implies that he had undertaken deliberate proselytising, I am not sure. In his interpretation of the Joseph story the late-third-century Palestinian amora R. Abba b. Kahana alleged that Joseph inspired the Egyptians with a longing to be circumcised (*Ber. R.* 90:6). In the same passage a certain R. Samuel (pre-

sumably some rabbi other than the great Mar Samuel?) is said to have interpreted the reading החיתנו in place of the grammatically possible חיתנו to mean
that Joseph gave the Egyptians life not only in this world but also in the world
to come; in the eyes of the redactor of *Bereshit Rabbah* at least, if not necessarily in the opinion of Abba b. Kahana, Joseph's insistence that the Egyptians be circumcised (cf. *Ber. R.* 91:5) was intended to lead to their conversion to Judaism. Numerous texts portray Jethro as a missionary. Exodus 18:27
(וישלח משה את חתנו וילך לו אל ארצו) is glossed in the version of Ps. Jonathan
with the assertion that Jethro went home to convert all the inhabitants of his
country (לגיירא כל בני ארעיה); the same interpretation of this incident is found
also at *MdRi Amalek* 106–8 and *Sifre Zuta* to Num 10:30. In *Sifre Num.* 80
it seems that Jethro's ability to gain proselytes is given as a reason for *not* leaving the children of Israel, but here too proselytising is seen as a self-evident
good.

Apart from such commendation of alleged missionary figures from the
past, other evidence for rabbinic approval of positive proselytising is all implicit rather than stated. The behaviour attributed without reference to Rabbah
bar Abbuha by Urbach,[19] of whom "it is related that he said to those who
came before him . . . 'Go, sell all that you have and come and be converted
(זילי זבינו כל מה ראית לכו לתו איתגיירו)'" turns out on inspection of the context
(*bAb. Zar.* 64a) to have been not an echo or parallel of Jesus' missionary call
in Matt. 19:21 and parallels, but a practical injunction to gentiles who *already*
intended to convert to sell before conversion those of their possessions that
were connected with idolatry so that after the ceremony they might benefit
with a good conscience from the purchase price. But the more indirect evidence that is to be found is not without value. For instance, according to the
fourth-century Rabin, citing the third-century Palestinian teacher Resh Lakish,
the winning of converts is so desirable that one may buy a heathen slave from
a gentile for this purpose (*bAb. Zar.* 13b); Resh Lakish even taught that such
purchases could be made at pagan fairs despite the danger of contact with
immorality at such events (*yAb. Zar.* 1.1, 39b). The ritual bath marking the
conversion of a woman proselyte in Laodicea was an occasion of sufficient
importance for the third-century patriarch R. Judan Nesiah to detain R.
Joshua b. Levi in the town overnight for its sake, according to a rather incon-
sequential story attributed to R. Isaac b. Nahman (*yYeb.* 8.1, 8d).

More tenuous is the implicit appeal to altruism for any Jew who might
accept the tenet expressed at *bYeb.* 48b by an anonymous group of rabbis
(probably of the third century, since R. Abbahu, who lived late in that century, provided a scriptural proof for their view), that the sufferings of proselytes after conversion are a punishment for their delay in entering under

the wings of the Shekhinah, if such a Jew also accepted the opinion of the fourth-century amora, R. Bun, that in practice converts come over only because the righteous go to seek them, as Joseph went to Asenath, Joshua to Rahab, Boaz to Ruth (!) and Moses to Hobab. Altruism is in the forefront at *bNed.* 32a, where R. Yohanan takes Abraham to task for his behaviour, as described at Gen. 14:21, in allowing the king of Sodom to take the captives after their victory while he took the goods: such a decision was reprehensible, according to Yohanan, because הפריש בני אדם מלהכנס תחת כנפי השכינה. It is not clear whether the sin with which Abraham is charged by an unspecified R. Judah at *Ber. R.* 40:14 (Soncino 41:8) — his failure to make his nephew Lot cleave to God despite his success in persuading others — was seen by R. Judah as a failure of altruism or of duty to God.

All this adds up to quite strong implicit approval for an active mission to win converts to Judaism. But the reluctance to be more explicit is striking, and it is worth noting how little of the extensive rabbinic literature on conversion even alludes to the topic. Thus, for instance, the two great homilies on proselytes at *MdRi Nezikin* 18 and at *Num. R.* 8 do not even refer to the problem of how converts come to consider becoming Jews in the first place.

This reticence should be contrasted to the numerous texts that advise Jews that proselytes who offer themselves should be accepted. These texts have been collected by Braude and Bamberger, and I do not wish to challenge their conclusions that the rabbis often welcomed those who sought them out. But in contrast to them I want to stress that a willingness to accept is quite different from a positive desire to acquire.[20] I do not think that there is justification for the assumption, found quite widely in modern scholarship, that the existence of numerous converts in itself reveals a mission to win them.[21] Rabbis did in general assume that a gentile living within a Jewish community (in the land of Israel?) is a potential convert (in halakhic terms, that a גר תושב is a potential גר צדק, cf. *bAb. Zar.* 65a), but this did not imply any onus on Jews to take any action with regard to gentiles who lived elsewhere. As doves scent the food given to their fellow doves and come to partake, so proselytes are converted "when the elder sits and preaches" (*Cant. R.* 1:63 (Dunsky, p. 143; Soncino, IV 1, 2, p. 177)), but it is not suggested that such attraction of proselytes is the reason for the teaching in the first place. The remarkable assertion that God brought about the exile as a way of increasing the number of proselytes is found both in the name of the tanna R. Eliezer at *bPes.* 87b and, ascribed to a Jewish acquaintance, in the writings of the third-century Christian writer Origen (c. *Celsum* 1:55), but no rabbi even hints that a deliberate prolongation or extension of the exile would be desirable to further this mission to the nations.

In sum, despite the hints outlined above that some rabbis assumed the desirability of a proselytising mission, such a notion does not appear to have been explicitly formulated in any rabbinic text and did not ever become a general rabbinic doctrine. It remained the common assumption that the normal impulse to conversion would be and should be that of the prospective proselyte. Thus, for example, it is reported at *Sifre Deut.* 354 that the sight of Israel worshipping at the Temple will eventually lead the nations to wish to convert *en masse*. It is on the gentiles that the onus rests, for in the last days they risk punishment for failing to become proselytes as they could have done (*Lev. R.* 2:9; but it is worth noting that in the parallel version at *Pes. R.* 35.161a, in the name of R. Hanina b. Papa, the reproach to the gentiles is only their failure to forsake idolatry; cf. also *yR.H.* 1.3, 57a). At *yYeb.* 8.1, 8d R. Isaac b. Nahman even reported a ruling in the name of R. Joshua b. Levi that seems to imply that in certain circumstances even the commonly accepted duty of Jews to convert gentile slaves in their ownership may be waived: הכל כמנהג המדינה. The only duty to the gentile world that the rabbis blazoned forth explicitly was the need to be a light to the nations, to sanctify the name of God and proclaim his existence and glory to all men: thus *Lev. R.* 6:5 interprets Lev. 5:1 (אם לוא יגיד ונשא עונו) as "if you will not proclaim me as God unto the nations of the world, I shall exact penalty from you."

The paradox should not be shirked. On the one hand it was taken for granted that conversion to Judaism is an advantage to the proselyte which it was desirable that a Jew should help him acquire. Thus, according to R. Huna, a minor incapable in law of giving consent may nonetheless be converted by a court on the grounds that a court has an absolute power to confer a benefit (*bKet.* 11a). On the other hand this view, despite its momentous potential consequences, was only implied rather than explicitly formulated in rabbinic texts, and it ran a risk of being undercut by the rabbis' simultaneous espousal of precise requirements for pious gentiles who remained gentiles, since Jewish acceptance that such requirements are sufficient might appear to make conversion to Judaism irrelevant and any mission to win proselytes otiose. The paradox can be seen at its clearest in the statement of the third-century Palestinian amora R. Yohanan, reported at *bMeg.* 13a, that any gentile who spurns idolatry is called a Jew. Yohanan's assertion is rightly branded by Braude as a homiletical conceit, but his ability even to propose such a notion suggests a remarkable unawareness of the conflicting implications of the rabbinic attitudes of his time.

It is tempting to assume that such contradictory attitudes must have been originally espoused either at different times or in different places, but it is not possible to be certain whether in fact this was so. It is possible, but not provable, that the Noachide Laws were formulated by the rabbis rather earlier than a positive attitude towards proselytising emerged. It has been noted above that the principle of the Noachide Laws seems to have been already accepted by the tannaim, although insistence on abstention from idolatry appears not to have been universally held even in the amoraic period. In contrast all of the comments that imply approval of proselytising are ascribed, when they are ascribed at all, to Palestinian rabbis of the third or early fourth centuries *(Ber. R.* 84:4 (R. Hoshaya, in the name of R. Judah b. R. Shimon); *Ber. R.* 90:6 (R. Abba b. Kahana); *Pes. R.* 43.181a (R. Eleazar b. Pedat, in the name of R. Yose b. Zimri); *Mid. Tanh. Lek Lekha* 12 (R. Yehoshua of Sikhnin, in the name of R. Levi); *bAb.* Zar. 13b (Rabin, in the name of Resh Lakish); *bNed.* 32a (R. Yohanan); *yYeb.* 8.1, 8d (R. Isaac b. Nahman, with a story about amoraim of the first generation); *yAb. Zar.* 1.1, 39b (Resh Lakish); *Eccl. R.* 8:10 (R. Bun); *bYeb.* 48b (R. Abbahu; some say R. Hanina (b. Abbahu?))). No amoraic text seems to ascribe approval of a proselytising mission to any second-century tanna apart from *ySanh.* 2.6, 20c, where R. Yose b. Halafta, of the mid-second century, is credited with the implausible view that Solomon multiplied his wives not from voluptuousness but to bring them under the wings of the Shekhinah. On the contrary, the key teaching in *Sifre Deut.* 32 (see above, p. 37) is ascribed in *Pes. R.* 43.181a to the third-century amoraim R. Eleazar b. Pedat and R. Yose b. Zimri. It is therefore *possible* that the anonymous references to Abraham and Jethro as missionaries in the tannaitic midrashim and Ps.–Jonathan were composed by the last generation of the tannaim in the early third century, and that the notion that proselytising is desirable was only first espoused by rabbis at that time; but I am aware that any claim that such midrashic stories were already traditional by that time cannot be disproved.

Wherever and whenever they *originated,* these contradictory notions seem to have been *held* in conjunction by later rabbis in both Palestine and Babylonia, for both ideas appear in both talmuds. How had the rabbis come to commit themselves to such conflicting ideas?

Most who have tried to answer this question have started from the premise that proselytising is a natural religious instinct and that what needs to be explained is therefore only the caution displayed by the rabbis in its espousal. For those who begin thus an answer is readily to hand: Jews were constrained from openly proselytising first by Roman imperial legislation against the circumcision of non-Jews after Hadrian, and then by further laws against the conversion of Christians to Judaism after Constantine. The conversions that did occur, it is alleged, must have been carried out in secret. Active proselytising would risk the ferocity of the state.[22]

This explanation is consistent, but it has flaws. State opposition might have been expected to spur on missionaries to greater efforts rather than dampen their enthusiasm, as in the history of early Christianity and, even more strikingly, third- and fourth-century Manichaeism.[23] Inscriptions on which the status of *proselytos* is openly displayed, such as that recently published from Aphrodisias, suggest that state legislation on this topic as on others may often have remained theoretical and in practice disregarded.[24] More important, the presumption in favour of proselytising rests on Christianising presuppositions about the nature of religion and ignores the rarity of missionary behaviour in other religious movements in the ancient world. Many religions and philosophies spread throughout the Roman world during the early empire, but in almost all cases apart from Christianity this was through the travel of existing adherents from one place to another for secular purposes and the imitation of such people by interested outsiders: the notion that existing worshippers should put effort into attracting others to their cult was rarely, if ever, found outside Christianity before the third century.[25]

It seems to me that the problem is best tackled from the other end. Since there is so little to suggest that Jews in the first century had an interest in a proselytising mission, why did such a notion emerge, albeit only as an implicit and occasional assumption, in the sayings of some rabbis of third-century Palestine?

No direct answer to such a question is likely to be provided by the rabbinic texts themselves: the rabbis' espousal of contradictory notions about gentiles suggests that they never tried to probe the reasons for their particular attitudes, and it is worth bearing in mind how small a proportion of rabbinic discourse concerns the status of non-Jews.[26] The explanatory model proposed below is only a hypothesis.

The impetus for Jews to encourage non-Jews to take a respectful interest in Judaism may have been increased after A.D. 70 when the attraction of gentiles to Judaism might help to bridge the gulf that separated Jews' belief in their election with the reality of their defeat and exile. But whereas non-Jews before A.D. 70 accreted to Jewish communities in all sorts of loose ways, without the Jews concerned showing any real interest in whether such newcomers be defined as full converts or just adherents (see above, p. 34), Jews from about A.D. 100 began to delineate much more precisely who was, and who was not, Jewish.

The reasons for this new interest of Jews in the precise boundaries of their communities can only be surmised. It is possible that Jews were keen to differentiate themselves from the burgeoning Church and, in particular, Judaizing Christians, but such an explanation may exaggerate the influence of Christianity on Jews at so early a date. A more mundane reason may have been the need to establish who was liable to pay the *fiscus Judaicus* to the Roman state.

The *fiscus* was a two-drachma tax on Jews originally imposed as a punishment for rebellion after A.D. 70.[27] Its collection was reformed under Nerva in A.D. 96, apparently in such a way as to exclude those born as Jews who had forsaken Jewish customs (hence *calumnia sublata*) but at the same time recognising, probably for the first time, the existence of proselytes whose religious affiliation alone was sufficient to make them liable to the tax.[28] The tax was still being collected in the mid-third century (Origen, *Ep. ad Africanum* 20 (14)) and perhaps later. It was no longer possible for the status of gentiles sympathetic to Judaism to be left ambiguous: either they paid the tax (and were presumably considered Jews) or they did not.

It may be assumed without undue cynicism that most of the gentiles sympathetic to Judaism preferred when pressured in this way to be considered by the Roman state—and therefore also by the Jews among whom they lived—as non-Jewish. The semijuridical title "godfearers" found on the early third-century inscriptions from the Aphrodisias synagogue reveals the willingness of some Jews to give a formal status within the Jewish community to such gentiles.[29] It is possible, despite the lack of evidence for any direct link, that rabbinic interest in the second and third centuries in the formulation of the theoretical Noachide Laws for the definition of righteousness among gentiles (see above, p. 35) was spurred on by the existence of such sympathisers, who were now clearly defined as gentiles but who presumably sometimes still participated in some Jewish communal activities, as they appear to have done at Aphrodisias.

Some sympathisers, presumably a minority, opted for full conversion to Judaism. There was no reason in the second century for Jews to encourage this process by looking for more such proselytes, and there is no firm evidence that they did so. It is only in the third century that we can be certain that some rabbis began assuming the desirability of a mission to proselytise. One new factor that may have encouraged this novel attitude is that rabbis in Palestine were by now aware of the success of some Christians in winning pagans. If the rabbis paid any attention at all to the spread of the Church they will have known that it had succeeded thus far not by positing good behaviour for non-Christians but by an energetic mission to win outsiders into the Christian fold.

What I am suggesting is that the effectiveness of the Church's methods may have gradually changed the religious assumptions of some non-Christians in the ancient world. Even if such non-Christians were not themselves tempted to convert to Christianity, it may have become more common for them to take it for granted that, for their faiths too, a mission to convert was a natural corollary of religious belief. If this hypothesis is correct, it would be unsurprising to discover that, as with much religious and intellectual change in late antiquity, the rabbis were not immune from trends in the wider society of the Roman Empire.

NOTES

1. See e.g. references in E. Schürer, rev. G. Vermes et al., *The History of the Jewish People in the Age of Jesus Christ*, vol. III.1 (1986), pp. 170–171.

2. Cf. Schürer, op. cit., III.1, pp. 155, 160.

3. Cf. Schürer, op. cit., III.1, p. 615.

4. Cf. Schürer, op. cit., II.1, p. 154.

5. Cf. P. Frederiksen, *From Jesus to Christ: The Origins of the New Testament Images of Jesus* (1988), pp. 149–150.

6. No study specifically on this subject has been written, but there is much relevant material in B. J. Bamberger, *Proselytism in the Talmudic Period* (2nd ed. 1968); W. G. Braude, *Jewish Proselyting in the First Five Centuries of the Common Era* (1940); E. E. Urbach, *The Sages: Their Concepts and Beliefs* (E.T. 1975), pp. 541–554.

7. On the question of a Jewish proselytizing mission before A.D. 70 there is a huge bibliography. See for instance J. Jeremias, *Jesus' Promise to the Nations* (E.T. 1958), pp. 11–18; for a contrary view, see e.g. J. Munck, *Paul and the Salvation of Mankind* (E.T. 1959).

8. "Jewish Proselytizing in the First Century," in J. Lieu, J. North, and T. Rajak, eds., *The Jews among Pagans and Christians in the Roman Empire* (New York: Routledge, Clagsman & Hall, Inc., 1992), pp. 53–78.

9. Jos., A.J. 4.207; Philo, *De Spec. Leg.* 1.51–53.

10. Jos., A.J. 13.319, 397.

11. I take the vagueness, noted e.g. by S. J. D. Cohen, "Respect for Judaism by Gentiles According to Josephus," *HTR* 80 (1987), p. 411, as evidence not of Josephus' apologetic but of the general Jewish lack of interest in the status of gentiles; cf. similarly J. J. Collins, "A Symbol of Otherness: Circumcision and Salvation in the First Century," in J. Neusner and E. S. Frerichs, eds., *To See Ourselves as Others See Us* (1985), p. 184.

12. The relevant midrashim are collated in L. Ginzberg, *The Legends of the Jews*, vol. I (1909), p. 193.

13. On R. Helbo's dictum see Bamberger, op. cit., pp. 163ff.; Braude, op. cit., pp. 6–7 and n. 15, and pp. 42ff.

14. D. Novak, *The Image of the Non-Jew in Judaism: An Historical and Constructive Study of the Noachide Laws* (1983).

15. See Novak, pp. 114–126. I shall discuss elsewhere the possible significance in this regard of the destruction of pagan temples in Cyrene during the Trajanic revolt.

16. J. Reynolds and R. Tannenbaum, *Jews and God-Fearers at Aphrodisias* (Cambridge Philological Society, suppl. vol. 12) (1987), p. 58.

17. See Novak, pp. 121–122.

18. See R. Lane Fox, *Pagans and Christians* (1986), esp. pp. 69–82.

19. Urbach, op. cit., p. 553 n. 17 (p. 938 n. 17).

20. *Contra* Braude, op. cit., pp. 3, 18; Bamberger, op. cit., p. 290.

21. E.g. L. H. Feldman, "The Omnipresence of the God-Fearer," *BAR* 12.5 (1986), p. 59.

22. J. Juster, *Les Juifs dans l'Empire Romain* (1914), vol. I, pp. 259–263; Braude, op. cit., p. 23. For criticism, see M. Simon, *Verus Israel: A Study of the Relations between Christians and Jews in the Roman Empire* (135–425), trans. H. McKeating (1986), pp. 272–273.

23. W. H. C. Frend, *Martyrdom and Persecution in the Early Church* (1965); S. N. C. Lieu, *Manichaeism in the Later Roman Empire and Medieval China: A Historical Survey* (1985), pp. 60–90.

24. Reynolds and Tannenbaum, op. cit., pp. 43–45.

25. R. MacMullen, *Paganism in the Roman Empire* (1981), pp. 94–130.

26. Cf. W. S. Green, "Otherness Within: Towards a Theory of Difference in Rabbinic Judaism," in J. Neusner and E. S. Frerichs, eds., op. cit., pp. 49–69.

27. On the *fiscus* in general, see *Corpus Papyrorum Judaicarum* I, pp. 80–88; II, pp. 119–136, 204–208.

28. Cf. L. A. Thompson, "Domitian and the Jewish Tax," *Historia* 31 (1982), pp. 329–342. See now my article, "Nerva, the *Fiscus Judaicus* and Jewish Identity," *JRS* 79 (1989).

29. Reynolds and Tannenbaum, op. cit., pp. 48–66.

⇥ 4 ⇤

Jochanan H. A. Wijnhoven

The Zohar and the Proselyte

Most of the written material about proselytism in sacred literature deals with talmudic or midrashic texts. In this important essay, Jochanan H. A. Wijnhoven (author of such works as *Sefer ha-Mishkal: Text and Study*) examines how the kabbalistic classic, the *Zohar*, treats converts. Prof. Wijnhoven's conclusion, that the differences between born Jews and converts are stressed more than the similarities, shows how Judaism's evolving feelings about proselytism were congealing during the time of the *Zohar's* composition by those who followed its teachings. As Professor Wijnhoven notes, there had been, at least from talmudic times on, an ambivalence about embracing converts, but the positive attitude toward welcoming converts far outweighed the relatively small number of negative comments in the Talmud. By the time of the *Zohar's* composition, in the last third of the thirteenth century, Jews had suffered intense persecutions, in part because they accepted converts and were so successful in attracting them.

The anti-Jewish persecutions combined with the Christian transformation of the role of conversion. The Jewish sense of conversion was that of a voluntary act that was done independent of the fate of one's soul. Christianity changed conversion into a frequently involuntary act that often included violence or a threat of violence and that determined the fate of one's soul. These and related facts made Jews begin to see themselves as on one side of a profound gulf between themselves and the non-Jewish world. The ambivalence about conversion began to change from mostly favorable to mostly unfavorable.

Interestingly, one important psychological problem the Jews still faced was that, as Dr. Wacholder pointed out, many prominent thinkers had seen embracing converts as a *mitzvah*, a required commandment. As *halachah* developed, this *mitzvah* got transformed. Over time, the view that welcoming converts was a religious obligation incumbent upon Jews became transformed into a view that welcoming converts was not a requirement and endangered Jewish communities. The Jewish view, slowly and subtly, came to be that conversion was somehow un-Jewish. What a strange view this would have been to a talmudic rabbi or a Tosafist, but it was a view that was to remain part of modern Jewry until first challenged by the Reform movement in the nineteenth century and later by many other Jewish thinkers as well.

———•———

Two major streams of thought on the proselyte coexist in Jewish literature. One stresses the equality of the convert and the born Israelite, the other views the convert as of lower status. Only his children's children can be considered equal to born Jews. Both streams of thought are found in Talmud and Midrash, as well as in medieval philosophical literature. In so far as the Zohar is a reflection of this literature, it contains the same ambivalence. If we look, however, at which theme can be considered the dominant one, one has to say that the Zohar stresses inequality. In this respect, the Zohar continues the tradition of the nonrationalists rather than that preserved in talmudic literature and Maimonides.[1]

In Talmud and Midrash the rabbis are by no means unanimous in welcoming proselytes. Some very beautiful as well as some very nasty sayings about converts can be adduced. Thus R. Simeon ben Lakish (3rd cent.) states:

> The proselyte is more beloved unto God than all those multitudes who stood at Mount Sinai. For if those multitudes had not seen the flash of lightning and not heard the sound of the thunder and the blast of the horn, they would not have bowed unto the kingdom of God. But this one (the proselyte) beheld no miracles and yet made his peace with God and accepted the kingdom of God. Can anyone be more dearly beloved than he?[2]

In the passage of the Babylonian Talmud where the process of conversion is described, the proselyte, having undergone circumcision and immersion, is considered in all things equal to the born Israelite.[3] This equality is also stressed by R. Abbahu, a third-generation Amora from Palestine, in a saying quoted in *Midrash Leviticus Rabbah*:

> They (the proselytes) become the root just like Israel, even as thou sayest . . . "And they shall blossom as the vine" (Hos. 14:8), even as thou sayest, "Thou didst pluck up a vine out of Egypt; Thou didst drive out the nations and didst plant it" (Psalm 80:9). The Holy One, blessed be He, said: "The names of the proselytes are as dear to me as the wine of libation which is offered to me on the altar."[4]

Other rabbis, however, were less enthusiastic about proselytes. In the tractate b. Yebamot, a warning is given that "evil upon evil will befall those who receive proselytes," to which R. Helbo adds that "proselytes are as annoying to Israel as scabs."[5] Elsewhere in the same tractate the reasons why converts are problematic are enumerated and discussed: proselytes are not as conversant with the Torah as the born Jew; they do not become Jews out of love, but out of fear; it takes them too long to decide to convert.[6] In the tractate b. Niddah the proselytes are blamed for delaying the advent of the Messiah.[7] In a controversy as to whether a proselyte can recite the blessing of the first fruits (Deut. 26:3) in which the formula "our fathers" occurs, R. Judah ben Ilai (2nd cent.) decided that the proselyte could speak of the patriarchs as "our fathers," though in general R. Judah ben Ilai is not favorably inclined towards converts.[8] Despite the presence of negative views and caution towards proselytes, the prevailing theme in talmudic literature is more likely that of the tractate b. Shabu'ot, wherein it is stated that the souls of the future proselytes were present together with the preexistent souls of all Jews at the lawgiving on Mount Sinai.[9]

Philosophical medieval literature is less ambiguous about the status of the proselyte than rabbinical literature. The distinction between the born Israelite and the convert is strongly emphasized in the *Kuzari* of Judah Halevi. There is a metaphysical *super additum* in the Israelite, to whom the gift of prophecy alone belongs, which is lacking in the proselyte, and a *fortiori* in the Gentile. "Those who become Jews," writes Judah Halevi, "do not take equal rank with born Israelites, who are especially privileged to attain to prophecy, whilst the former can only achieve something by learning from them, and can only become pious and learned, but never prophets."[10] As will be seen, this distinction between born Jew and proselyte, rather than Maimonides' defense for equality, suited the Zohar, though the Zohar interprets this metaphysical difference in its own symbolic way.

For the Kabbalists, Scripture, history, events, ritual, and numbers, in short, every aspect of reality reflects the mysteries of the supernal world where the mystery of the divinity is contained in the life of the ten *sefirot* (divine emanations). A hidden mystery is therefore contained and symbolized by the convert who joins the community of Israel. The ritual of conversion, the lives of the great proselytes, in particular the first proselyte Abraham, the rabbinical sayings on the proselytes, and the philosophical discussions on the difference between proselytes and born Jews serve as so many elements to weave a kabbalistic theology of the proselyte. In so far as the proselyte is a reality, he provides a special dimension, perspective, and opportunity to understand the richness, dynamism, and complexity of the divine emanation in the life of the *sefirot*. How far the reality of the proselyte was a historical reality in the time of the author of the Zohar is difficult to determine. Moses de Leon

(1250–1305), its reputed author, lived before Christian Europe renewed its assaults on the Jews on occasion of the Black Death (middle 14th century) and the decrees against the Iberian Jewry (from the last quarter of the 14th century until the expulsion in 1492). Perhaps the quiet and prosperous times for the Jews under Alfons the Wise (d. 1284) and Alfons XI (d. 1350) provided a climate in which conversions to Judaism were life issues. If so, the Zohar not only opened kabbalistic pastures to revive, relive, and rethink ancestral heritage but also serves as a historical comment on the relations between Jews, converts, and Gentiles in the days of Moses de Leon.[11]

The following is an analysis and commentary upon ten passages in the Zohar dealing with the proselyte. Together they form, as one could say, Moses de Leon's "theology of the proselyte."

UNDER THE WINGS OF THE *SHEKHINAH*

The prologue of the Zohar contains a discussion of fourteen commandments (cf. Maimonides' fourteen books in his *Yad-ha-Hazakah*), interpreted in a kabbalistic way. The seventh commandment deals with the circumcision of the male Jew and centers on the mystery of Israel's election. The eighth commandment is to love the proselyte and presents the relationship of the convert to the chosen people. Both commandments serve to understand the mysteries of the divine *sefirot* and are basic for the Zohar's approach to the proselyte.[12]

The fact that the Israelite is circumcised on the eighth day is taken as an allusion to the origin of the Israelite soul from the eighth *sefirah*, called *Binah* (Understanding). One has to start counting from the last, tenth *sefirah* (*Malkhut*, or Kingdom), to arrive at *Binah* as the eighth. The *sefirah Binah* is, according to the Zohar, the place of origin for the soul of the born Jew. *Binah* is the fountain of life where the mystical depth of the first two *sefirot*, *Keter* and *Hokhmah* (Crown and Wisdom), become apparent and visible. In *Binah*, the source of the "life-giving waters" comes to the surface. The river of life, which flows through the *sefirot*, and in which "swarm living souls," wells up from *Binah*. The souls that originate in *Binah* are stored in the *sefirah* of *Tiferet* (Beauty), which is the center of the sefirotic system where the strength of the divine emanation is concentrated. The sixth *sefirah* (*Tiferet*) is thus the "storehouse of souls" waiting to be lodged in the human body. *Tiferet* is also called "Bridegroom," or "Lord." The "Lord" unites himself with the "Bride," the tenth *sefirah*, called *Shekhinah* (the community of Israel), or more often, *Malkhut* (Kingdom). The holy souls that came from *Binah* are conveyed to the community of Israel by mystical intercourse between the "Groom" and the "Bride." The ninth *sefirah*, *Yesod* (Foundation), links *Tiferet* and *Malkhut*.

In light of this sefirotic drama, the Zohar stresses how the life of the community of Israel is holy by virtue of its origin in the eighth *sefirah*, *Binah*, so that the circumcision of the Jew on the eighth day "sacramentally" expresses this divine mystery. The Hebrew letter that represents the *sefirah* *Hokhmah* is *Yod*, while the letter *Heh* stands for *Binah*. *Yod* and *Heh* together form the divine name *YaH*, which the Zohar compares to the symbolic imprint left by circumcision upon the male organ. The act of separating the foreskin is Israel's separation from the *Sitra Ahra* (Evil Side), visualized outside and to the left of the *sefirot*. While the souls of the Gentiles find their origin in the impure region of the *Sitra Ahra*, Israel proceeds from the "pure part" of God's creation. This mystery is acted out by the Jews observing the laws of purity and by making distinction between pure and impure animals and fowl, a law that the Gentiles do not observe.

After the Zohar has explained the different origin of souls of Jews and Gentiles, it interprets the eighth commandment "to love the stranger," to further explain the peculiar status of the proselyte. Since the proselyte was not circumcised on the eighth day, his soul does not originate in *Binah*, but in "the region of impurity" and comes from there under the "wings of the *Shekhinah*." From the *Sitra Ahra* the soul of the proselyte finds refuge in the vicinity of the tenth *sefirah* (*Malkhut*). While the born Jew stands in a special relationship to *Binah*, the proselyte stands under the aegis of *Malkhut*. The Zohar observes that in the litany of names, attributed to the *sefirot*, both *Binah* and *Malkhut* are referred to as "mother of souls," the first being the "upper mother," and *Malkhut* being the "lower" one. Both are principles of spiritual fertility, and the mystery of life flows from the "Source" (*Binah*) to the "Sea" (*Malkhut*). The ontological status of holiness between the souls of born Jews and proselytes is therefore different.

The Zohar indicates further what is meant by the "wings of the *Shekhinah*." The passage stresses "wings of" and "not further than the wings." What it seems to suggest is that the proselyte soul comes close to the realm of the *sefirot*, in this case the tenth one, but does not fully participate in it. The same passage stresses the great variety of proselytes. Adjacent to *Malkhut*, or "under the wings of the *Shekhinah*," are various compartments. Under the right wing are Ishmael and Edom, Islam and Christianity, the two great monotheistic religions. It would seem that the Zohar is only discussing here the *ger toshav* (resident proselyte) and not the *ger zedek* (righteous proselyte). Placing both religions under the right wing of the *Shekhinah*, the Zohar reflects a common notion among many rabbis in medieval times that the adherents of monotheistic religions, if they lead an ethical life, can be considered "resident proselytes" (*ger toshav*). Similarly Judah Halevi, who made such a point of the metaphysical difference between an Israelite and a proselyte, was quite willing to regard Christians and Moslems as "proselytes" if they abstained from idolatrous practices and led a moral life.[13] As for the Ammonites and Moabites who swell "under the left wing of the *Shekhinah*," closer to the *Sitra Ahra*, it is not clear what they stand for. The Zohar seems to side with R. Joshua, who accepted them as proselytes, against the opinion of R. Gamaliel, who refused their admission on biblical grounds (cf. Deut. 23:4).[14]

In its treatment of the commandment to love the proselyte, the Zohar shows that belonging to *Malkhut* is not unique to the born Jew. The divine action that produced Jewish souls for the Kingdom and that stems from the marrow of the holy *sefirot* spreads the wings of *Shekhinah* to provide shelter for the souls escaping the impure region. They join *Malkhut* "varying in kind as befitting," as the Zohar indicates.

ABRAHAM, THE PROSELYTE IN THE *SEFIROT*

In commenting upon the *parashah* of "*Lekh Lekha*" (Gen. 12:1–17, 27), the Zohar again deals with the mystery of the proselyte.[15] The difference between a born Jew and a proselyte is seen alluded to in the two kinds of altars mentioned in Exod. 20:24–25:

> An altar of earth you shall make for me and sacrifice on it. . . . And if you make me an altar of stone, you shall not build it of hewn stones; for if you wield your tool upon it you profane it.

The stone altar refers to the proselyte, the unhewn stones to the uncircumcised Gentiles. The stones bear no imprint; they belong to the Evil Side where the Holy Name is absent. By circumcision, the covenant sign replaces the *Sitra Ahra* with the Holy Name. The altar of earth refers to the born Jew because the circumcision of the newborn Jew is performed over a vessel filled with earth.

After this introduction the Zohar proceeds with a homily on the first proselyte, Abraham. All ninety-nine years before Abraham's circumcision were counted as one year because the Bible has "ninety-nine year" in the singular (Gen. 17:1). In that year "the Lord appeared" (ibid.). On previous occasions God had "spoken to" Abraham only, but now He "appeared." This indicates that no "holy seed" could be begotten by Abraham until he was circumcised. Before the impression of the holy seal of the covenant, Abraham was "closed" and the source of life in him concealed. Until then Abraham belonged to the *Sitra Ahra* as can be seen from the fact that when God (SH-D-Y) appeared, a letter *Yod* was added to the word "SH-D," meaning devil. The letter *Yod* was, as we saw previously, seen as the imprint left by the circumcision.[16]

Abraham is also a name for the fourth *sefirah*, *Hesed* (Mercy). In the line of emanation it follows *Binah*. This indicates that the proselyte is a son by adoption (Mercy), whereas Isaac, symbol of the fifth *sefirah*, *Din* (Justice), is a son by right, birth, and heritage. To illustrate this the Zohar quotes Isa. 5:1: "Let me sing for my well-beloved (*Yedid*) a song of my beloved (*Dod*)." That *Yedid* refers to Isaac can be seen from the talmudic passage that Isaac was "beloved (*Yedid*), from the womb."[17] This is interpreted to mean that by birth was Isaac well beloved, whereas his father, Abraham, came to be sanctified in his old age. At the time of Abraham's circumcision both he and his wife, Sarah, received the additional letter *Heh* into their names, Abra*Ham* and Sara*H*. The two *Heh*'s refer respectively to *Binah* and *Malkhut*.[18] Thus, whereas his parents were grafted into the life of the *sefirot* by virtue of conversion, Isaac was a holy "by right." This is further demonstrated by the verse "Thus will be your seed" (Gen. 15:5). The word "Thus" in Hebrew is *KoH*, but the letters *Kaf* and *Heh* can also be read: "As a (letter) *Heh* will be your seed," which means that Isaac is the product of the supernal letter *Heh*, *Binah*.

While *Yedid* refers to Isaac, the fifth *sefirah*, the sixth *sefirah*, Jacob, is alluded to in the word *Dod* (Isa. 5:1). In the arrangement of the *sefirot*, Jacob occupies a middle position between the right and the left, between Mercy and Justice, between Abraham and Isaac. Jacob represents the perfect blending and concentration between the attributes of mercy and justice. Jacob is called Israel to indicate that only the grandchild of the proselyte, or the third generation, can be called "Israelite" in the full sense. All the fullness is concentrated in Israel, the *sefirah* of *Tiferet*. In Hebrew, the names Isaac and Jacob begin with a letter *Yod*. This signifies, the Zohar says, that the proselyte begets children with souls of a higher origin than his own. The *Yod*, which is the first letter of the *tetragrammaton*, is connected with Abraham's children. He and his wife, Sarah, had to be satisfied with the second and fourth letters of the divine name, the two *Heh*'s of YHWH. Further, the verse "In Isaac thy seed will be called" (Gen. 21:12) was taken to mean that not in Abraham, but only in his son Isaac, would the holy seed be manifest to full perfection. Thus Isaac begot Jacob "in truth," as stated: "Thou givest truth to Jacob" (Micah 7:20). The Hebrew word "truth" is spelled with the letters *aleph, mem*, and *tav*. The letters successively present the first, middle, and last letter of the Hebrew alphabet, thereby symbolizing the fullness of revelation.

From this second passage on the proselyte we see both a similar stress on the distinction between the born Jew and the proselyte, and the viewpoint of the Zohar, that the children of proselytes will gradually become fully equal with born Jews. This was deduced from the function of the sefirotic proselyte, Abraham, who begot souls of a higher origin so that Jacob, the supernal Israel, achieved the fullness of the divine blessing promised to Abraham.

THE GUESTS AT THE BANQUET

Another commentary on the proselyte is found in the explanation to the verse: "Then Joseph could not refrain himself before all who stood near him and he cried: Let every man go out from me. And there stood no man near him while Joseph made himself known to his brethren" (Gen. 45:1).[19] The Zohar introduces four rabbis, R. Hiyya, R. Eleazar, R. Jesse, and R.Hizkia. Each in turn gives his commentary on this passage. In the Zohar, Joseph is the symbol for the ninth *sefirah*, *Yesod*. Another name for *Yesod* is *Zaddik* (Righteous), in the biblical sense of "righteous" in which the "giving" element is more prominent than the English implies. This aspect of free giving is characteristic of *Yesod*, here introduced as Joseph.

Joseph and his brethren symbolize the giving and receiving that takes place between the groom and the bride by means of sexual intercourse. The *sefirah* of Joseph, then, stands for the act of love and intimacy. Joseph's brethren symbolize the community of Israel, *Malkhut*. The aspect of intimacy between the Lord and the community of Israel is seen in the words "all who stood near him," and Joseph's request that "every man go out from me," so as to be alone with his brethren. From these words the Zohar derives the exclusion of the idolatrous nations from the life of the *sefirot*. The proselyte, however, neither belongs to the idolatrous nations nor is fully identified with the "bride," *Malkhut*. As R. Hizkia explains, the proselytes will be admitted to the banquet after the bride, the community of Israel, has first been satisfied "by the dainties of her husband."

JETHRO THE PROSELYTE, BRINGER OF WISDOM

Like Abraham, the figure of Jethro is treated as a prototype of the proselyte. When the Zohar deals with Jethro, it naturally focuses on the status of the stranger who wants to join Israel.[20] Besides stressing the same distinction between the born Jew and the proselyte, which we noticed earlier,[21] this passage adds two new aspects. Jethro, being a non-Jew, comes from the *Sitra*

Ahra but is presented in Scripture as a "wise man." He is, furthermore, described as an adviser to Moses, the lawgiver. This fact leads the Zohar to
discuss the problem of how wisdom can be found outside the realm of the
sefirot. As the passage explains, the *Sitra Ahra* borders on the left of the sefirotic
precinct. But wisdom can originate only in the world of the *sefirot.* Thus we
learn that the light of wisdom that illuminates the divine realm is so strong
that it even shines "into the world of the *Sitra Ahra*." Like Job, Balaam, and
the wise men of Pharaoh's court, Jethro is, so to speak, a borderline case. His
knowledge and prophecy come from the light of the *sefirot* as it diffuses
beyond the limits of the divine realm. But it is imperfect, like "the light that
a man can perceive through his closed eyelids." The *Sitra Ahra*, on the left
of the divine sphere, borders directly on the *sefirah* of *Din* (Justice), also called
Elohim (God). The Gentile who lives in the *Sitra Ahra* can have *yir'at Elohim*
(fear of God), i.e., knowledge of the *sefirah* of *Din*, if he turns towards the
light. Although he can know *Elohim*, he can never know the intimate revelation of the holy name YHWH, which concerns the inner life of the *sefirot*
and is reserved for Israel. Standing outside, the non-Jew can only perceive
the fractured light, filtering through the left of the divine sphere.

The second point of interest in this passage is the stress on the function
of support that the proselyte provides the community of Israel. Jethro's wisdom contributed to the perfection of the holy people by bringing back "the
sparks of holiness that fell into the realm of evil." As long as Evil and Good
are not neatly separated and distinct, the proselytes are those who bring back
the stray sparks of the divine light. Jethro came to Moses in the desert. The
word desert, *MiDBaR*, the Zohar explains, can also be read *MeDaBbeR*, pre-
serving the same consonants. So "coming to the desert" signifies "coming to
the one who speaks." The one who speaks, *MeDaBbeR, is* another symbol
for the *sefirah* of *Malkhut.* Thus Jethro came to Moses in the desert as a proselyte comes to *Malkhut.* Further, the desert evokes the image of mountains.
Just as the desert is a "free land," so is the mountain elevated from its surroundings and free on all sides. Becoming a proselyte is not only going to
"free land," the desert, it is also the ascent of a mountain, i.e., climbing from
a lower status to a higher. Abraham ascended the mountain (Moriah) and
Jethro went into the desert. Both are prototypes of the proselyte. Here the
Zohar quotes Isa. 2:3, "And many nations will come and say: Let us go to the
mountain of God, to the house of the God of Jacob." "Mountain" and "house"
are contrasted: "mountain" is where the proselyte meets God; "house" is
where Israel dwells with God. The house conveys the intimate togetherness
of Israel with God, the mountain the nomadic quest of the proselyte pilgrim.

THE SOUL OF THE CONVERT AND THE DISCOURSE
OF THE DONKEY DRIVER

The old donkey driver, the *Saba*, who often astounds and baffles the rabbis by cryptic sayings and puzzling explanations of the secrets of Torah, is introduced by the Zohar with two discourses on the proselyte.[22] The theme of both passages is the provenance of the proselyte's new soul after his conversion. As we have seen, the origin of the proselyte is like that of the Gentiles in the *Sitra Ahra*. Once the proselyte is circumcised and brought under the wings of the *Shekhinah*, where does his new soul come from? The preexistence of souls is a well-known notion in rabbinic literature and is accepted without question in the Zohar. The matter becomes complicated when preexistence has to be explained together with the medieval philosophical notion of man's tripartite soul: *neshamah, ruah,* and *nefesh.* The *Saba* keynotes his discourse with two parallel passages: Lev. 22:12 ("And if a priest's daughter be married unto a common man . . .") and Lev. 21:9 ("And if the daughter of a priestly man . . ."). Why, he asks, is *bat kohen* used in one case, and *bat 'ish kohen* in the other? In the *sefirot* the name "priest" is used for the *Hesed.* The daughter of the priest then would mean that the soul (daughter) is drawn from *Binah* by the priestly *sefirah, Hesed.* This corresponds with the previous notion that the *neshamah* of the born Jew originates in *Binah.* The *'ish kohen,* or priestly man, is not to be identified with any of the *sefirot,* but is applied to the archangel Michael. The angelic world is a replica of the sefirotic world on a lower scale. In the angelic system Michael occupies the same place and parallel function to the *sefirah* of *Hesed.* Michael is the angelic counterpart to the priest. But if the *neshamah* that comes from *Binah* is only allotted to born Jews, the *nefesh* that stems from the angelic world has the same origin for Jew and proselyte. But the question remains how the *neshamah* comes to the proselyte.

The *Saba* continues his explanation from the continuance of the biblical verse (Lev. 22;12). "and the daughter of a priest allied to a stranger . . ." and explains that this "daughter of a priest," i.e., higher, *neshamah,* enters into the proselyte "in a mysterious manner." What this "mysterious manner" is remains untold. I. Tishby explains it to be another kind of *neshamah,* not coming from *Binah* but begotten by the matrimony of holy *neshamot* in the garden of Eden, *Malkhut.*[23] The mysterious *neshamah* that the proselyte receives is portrayed as a mixed marriage between the daughter of a priest and a stranger. One cannot be wholly satisfied with this explanation of the *Saba.* What, for instance, happened with the *ruah*? Besides pointing to the fact that the three souls *neshamah*, *ruah* and *nefesh* correspond to the three different orders of priests, no further explanation is given. One has the feeling that the Zohar fails in its tour de force to reconcile the many traditions concerning the soul and to lead them all into kabbalistic channels. Even the great acrobatic dexterity of *Saba's* cryptic allusions does not achieve this.

What remains clear from the foregoing discourse is that the proselyte and born Jew take equal parts in angelic souls (*nefesh*); but as far as his *neshamah* goes, the proselyte marries into the sefirotic nobility as a stranger. From the discussion the complexity of medieval "psychology" is clear. Souls and spirits were such a vivid reality that kabbalistic "psychology" easily added one more dimension to it.

One more notion of importance in the discourses of the *Saba* should be mentioned. The preexistent souls, be they of the born Jews or of the proselytes, all come into the body naked. By living a virtuous life the souls receive a garment of merits. Man weaves a trousseau for paradise. In this respect no difference is made between born Jew and proselyte. Personal merit has caught up with ontology, and the proselyte may appear in paradise more beautifully attired than the born Jew.

THE GOLDEN CALF AND THE PROSELYTE

A kind of moralistic, rather than kabbalistic, commentary on the proselyte is found in an exposition on the idolatry of the golden calf.[24] No secret mysteries are extracted from Exodus 32, where the "mixed multitude" who accompanied Israel from Egypt seduced the people into idolatry. We find here a straightforward moralistic sermon on the danger of proselytes. The absence of "mysteries" may perhaps point to a concrete historical situation in Moses de Leon's time. As the Christian Church and kingdom in Spain realized the dangers of fraternizing and started on its course of hunting down what it believed to be the pernicious effects of Jews upon Christian life, it may well be that the Jews were concerned about similar dangers on the moral life of the Jewish community. Hence, perhaps, Moses de Leon's singular moral stress on the curse that the alien element can bring to Judaism. The "mixed multitude" were the strangers who had attached themselves to Israel and followed them into the desert for hope of booty. They are the prototype of the false proselyte who joins Israel for ulterior motives. To this kind of proselyte the Zohar applies the talmudic saying that "proselytes are as annoying to Israel as scabs";[25] for the heart of the false proselyte still clings to the *Sitra Ahra. His* idolatrous practices were a stumbling block for Israel on the eve of the Lawgiving. Dishonest proselytes are the breach whereby the *Sitra Ahra* invades the community of Israel.

THE PROSELYTE AND THOSE WHO STOOD AT SINAI

One of the strongest passages in the Zohar stressing the essential difference between the born Jew and proselyte is similar to the earlier discussion on Gen. 17:12, where the commandment is given to circumcise the male child on the eighth day.[26] To this verse the Zohar cites Jer. 33:20, "Thus says the Lord: If you can break my covenant with the day and my covenant with the night, so that day and night will not come at their appointed time . . ." R. Simeon explains that just as day and night are "two crowns that fit together," so do the two *sefirot*, *Hesed* and *Din*, belong together; white and red, male and female. Circumcision also reveals the mystery of the great covenant in the *sefirot*, between the right and the left, male and female. Of the duality in the *sefirot*, that between *Hesed* and *Din* is central. The proselyte is called *ger zedek* (righteous proselyte) because he has a special relationship to the tenth *sefirah*, *Malkhut*, which bears also the name *Zedek* (Righteousness). As we have already seen, the proselyte bears only a special relationship to this last *sefirah*.

But how, the Zohar asks, does the proselyte have access to the great duality of the *sefirot*, to both *Hesed* and *Din*? "One cannot compare," R. Eleazar says, "that which comes from the Holy Root (*Binah*) and from the Stem of Beauty (*Tiferet*) with those that come forth from the tree of evil forces and abomination (*Sitra Ahra*)." Whereas Israel is "wholly of pure seed" (Jer. 2:21), those who are of gentile origin are like "flesh of asses and issue of horses" (Ezek. 23:20). Unlike Israel, the nations did not stand at Mount Sinai and are still contaminated with the impurity of their origin. This impurity cleaves to the proselyte until the third generation. In addition to stressing, in no uncertain terms, the lower pedigree of the proselyte, this passage points to the importance of the Sinaitic experience as the purifying element. Through Mount Sinai, Israel as a whole was liberated for all future generations from the *Sitra Ahra* and was introduced to the inner life of the divine world. The proselyte does not share this "sacrament" of holy birth. It is clear that the Zohar does not associate itself with the talmudic view that, together with those who stood at Mount Sinai, are "the coming generations and proselytes who were later to be proselytised . . . because it is said, 'and also with him who is not with us this day' (Deut. 29:15)."[27] The answer to the question whether the proselyte has access to the duality of *Hesed* and *Din* is not answered explicitly, but is implied in the dual character of *Malkhut* to which the convert bears a unique relationship.

THE HEAVENLY SCHOOLMASTER AND
THE SOUL OF THE PROSELYTE

A special discourse in the Zohar is devoted to a visionary journey of a group of sages to *Gan Eden*, where they are lectured to by the *Rav Methivta*, the Master of the Heavenly Academy.[28] In this discourse the subject of the destiny of souls is discussed. Elaborating further on what the *Saba* (cf. *supra*)[29] hinted at, the *Rav Methivta* explains that the preexistent souls of the proselytes are begotten out of matrimony of holy souls of righteous people. He adduces, to this effect, Prov. 11:30: "The fruit of the righteous is the tree of life." Since the *sefirah* of *Yesod* (Righteous) is called the "Life-Spending-Tree" in the divine world, the righteous person in this world is similarly a producer of life and souls. This idea is also deduced from Gen. 11:30, where it is noted Sarah was barren, while in Gen. 12:5 it says that Abraham took Sarah his wife, and "the souls they had begotten in Haran." The *Rav Methivta* explains that the souls begotten there were the souls of future proselytes. In this context Abraham does not serve as the sefirotic prototype of the proselyte but rather illustrates the power of righteous men to produce souls that will be stored in *Gan Eden* to provide future converts with a *neshamah* at the moment of their circumcision. The "mysterious way" to which the donkey driver only alluded becomes clear in this lecture by the schoolmaster of the Heavenly Academy.

THE PROSELYTES IN THE DAYS OF THE MESSIAH

This present section is of quite different nature than those previously discussed.[30] While all previous passages consistently stressed the lower status of the proselyte to the born Jew, this section suggests his complete equality. It should be noted that doubt has risen as to whether this section belongs to the original Zohar or constitutes a later interpolation.[31] The verse that introduces the discourse is Gen. 48:6, "And thy posterity which thou begets after them shall be thine and shall be called after the name of their brethren in their inheritance." R. Simeon explains this verse as referring to the proselytes of the latter days. The "second-rate posterity" of Joseph will, in those days, be ranked equal with their brothers, the born Jews. The verse, as R. Simeon explains, speaks of Jerusalem after the time of dispersion, i.e., the days of the Messiah. Then "the strangers shall be joined with them, and they shall cleave to the house of Jacob" (Isa. 14:1). In the days of return the proselyte will be named "son of Israel," and no longer called after his place of provenance, such as "proselyte of Kapotkia" (the "Cappadocia" of the Zohar!). In other words the place of origin will no longer be relevant. No longer will the proselyte dwell "with" the Jews: but he will be counted among them, joining their tribes and participating in their heritage.

Rachel weeping over her lost children (Jer. 31:15) will be consoled by her new sons. Rachel stands for the *sefirah* of *Malkhut*. Three successive connections with biblical passages are culled: Gen. 48:6–8, Jer. 31:15, and Isa. 44:5. Gen. 48:6 speaks of the "posterity which you will beget after them . . ." and refers to the proselytes of messianic times. Gen. 48:7 mentions Rachel's death and serves as a link with Jer. 31:15, Rachel weeping over her lost children. Gen. 48:8 "And Israel beheld Joseph's sons and said: 'Who are these?'" This provides R. Abba with the opportunity to expound on Isa. 44:5, which speaks of the influx of the nations to the community of Israel in the days of the Messiah. Like the astonished Israel seeing the sons of Joseph, the Israel of the eschatalogical times will ask; "Who has begotten me these? Behold I was left alone, and these, where were they?" (Isa. 49:21). These new sons that will populate Israel are the proselytes, the "strangers (that) shall be joined with them and shall cleave to the house of Jacob" (Isa. 14:1). Once the "cleaving" of the proselytes is mentioned the famous dictum of R. Helbo is adduced: "Proselytes are as annoying to Israel as scabs" (l.c.). But whereas we previously saw it quoted in a context dealing with the danger of proselytes, causing wounds (clefts, *sapahat*) to Israel, the "cleavage" in this context is not taken in the sense of "cleft" but in that of "adherence" or "attachment." The "scabs" (*sapahat*), to which R. Helbo compared the proselytes is reinterpreted here as a cause of joy on account of the "adherence" (the English homonym "cleave—cleavage" can be maintained) of the vast multitude of proselytes.[32] Again one might ask whether we can see in this section any historical allusion. The use of Rachel as the name and symbol of *Malkhut*; the historical-eschatological concern; the absence of any speculation about the sefirotic provenance of souls so typical for the other passages discussed suggest a later climate of authorship than the Zohar. The great toll taken from the community of Israel in the times of the Black Death and the Spanish persecutions would even suggest a late date for this passage, when messianic restoration outweighed the theosophic speculations on the *sefirot* in the discussions of the kabbalists.[33]

RUTH, THE PROSELYTE

A second passage that seems "out of step" with the ordinary views on the proselytes expressed in the Zohar is found in the *Midrash ha-Ne'elam* on Ruth.[34] The *Midrash ha-Ne'elam* is a part of the Zohar that reflects an earlier stage in the development of Moses de Leon's thinking.[35] This stage bears

the imprint of an author who is still interested in philosophy and is now turning to Kabbalah. The hostility of Moses de Leon towards philosophy and
philosophers increases as he grows older, as one can frequently notice in his
later Hebrew writings.[36] The section to be discussed here shows a great interest
of the author in the doctrine of tripartite souls: *neshamah*, *ruah*, and *nefesh*.
The verse, "See, I have set before thee this day life and good, and death and
evil" (Deut. 30:15), becomes the clue to a parallel drawn between the souls
of Jews and Gentiles. Life and God refer to the *sefirot*, more specifically to
Tiferet, from which, according to this passage, the *neshamah* of the Jew
derives. It is worth noting that in the later passages of the Zohar *Binah* is
stressed as the origin of the *neshamot*. The two lower souls of the Jew, *ruah*
and *nefesh*, are called "Adam." Is this, perhaps, a reference to "natural man"
without the specific Jewish, i.e. sefirotic, dimension?

The Gentiles have an evil *neshamah*. Just as there was an angelic replica of the *sefirot*, there also exists a mirror image of the ten *sefirot* in the *Sitra
Ahra*. This counterpart to the ten *sefirot* is referred to in Deut. 30:15, as "Death
and Evil." The demonic opposite to *Tiferet*, which in this text is the place of
origin of the holy *neshamah*, is Samael. Samael, the angel of death, the prince,
lord, and chief of demons is a well-known figure in aggadic lore. He is the
serpent who planted the forbidden tree in paradise, who seduced Adam and
Eve, and who is the great antagonist of Israel. When the author in this section makes a comparison between Israel, Ishmael (Islam), and Edom (Christianity), he stresses the point that whatever "kinship" exists between Israel,
Ishmael, and Edom is of a physical nature. Spiritually, however, they are far
apart. The Jewish soul stems from YHWH, *Tiferet*; the Gentile soul from
Samael, Lord and Prince of the *Sitra Ahra*. When a Gentile converts, what
happens? Here we encounter a completely different "psychology" of the proselyte than we saw in the previously examined texts on this subject. To the
proselyte a holy *ruah* and a holy *nefesh* is granted, but not a *neshamah*. On the
basis of this holy *ruah* and holy *nefesh* the proselyte will have a share in
the world to come. But even this share in the afterlife will be different from
the born Jew, for even in the world to come the souls of the proselytes will
still be "smeared by the dregs of an unholy body." Following G. Scholem,
who considers the *Midrash ha-Ne'elam* to be an earlier stage in Moses de
Leon's development, we may conclude that Moses de Leon toned down his
previous views on the proselytes considerably. We may also conclude that
while his views on the tripartite soul (*neshamah*, *ruah*, and *nefesh*) also underwent considerable changes, a theory of three souls, and three categories of
people—Jews, proselytes, and Gentiles—were too many elements to maneu-
ver harmonically into his kabbalistic theology of the soul.[37]

A question that was left unexplained in a previous section concerning the mixed nature of *Malkhut*[38] is fully answered in this section. Ruth the Moabite woman, another prototype of the proselyte, is an ancestor of David. She illustrates the mixed nature of "David's house," *Malkhut*. In the *sefirot*, *Malkhut*, the tenth and last *sefirah*, receives the emanation from the right and the left equally. *Malkhut is* a combination of mercy and sternness, of love and punishment. This double line of divine activity is associated with the male (*Hesed*) and female (*Din*) elements. Ruth represents the female elements, namely, that of stern judgment and harshness. She is the symbol of the left strain in *Malkhut*. How else could David have manifested both hardness and mercy? the Zohar asks. How else could a king rule unless he displays both qualities? From this image of ancient kingship and the biblical account of David, the Zohar derives the dual characteristics of *Malkhut*. Ruth, the proselyte, represents the motherly line from which David inherited his harshness; his merciful side was received through the paternal line. The Zohar does not reflect upon the meritorious deeds of Ruth, but only upon her ontological status as a Moabite woman, and thus is symbol of the left in *Malkhut*.

Another symbol of the dual strain in *Malkhut* is the two trees that grew in paradise: the "tree of life" (*Tiferet*) in the midst of *Gan Eden* (= the *sefirot*) and "the tree of the knowledge of good and evil" by which man sinned. The "tree of life," *Tiferet*, bears the fruit of the souls, the *neshamot*, for Jews. The "other tree," the "tree of the knowledge of good and evil" is not a fruit tree and only provides "shade." This shade-providing tree reminds the author of the green and shady trees under which acts of idolatry were performed.[39] The biblical associations of sinning under such trees set the context for new warnings against the stranger and the false proselyte, who trap Israel into acts of apostasy. The theme resembles the sermon on the golden calf that we discussed earlier. Ruth, however, by becoming a true proselyte, was that element among the nations that "gave sweet odor to the Lord," and compared to her surroundings she was "the rose among the thorns." By her conversion Ruth became symbolic for the seed of the nations that gives "delight to the Lord," while being at the same time that element and contribution to the community of Israel (*Malkhut*) by which it will be able to have the harshness "to execute vengeance among the nations."

CONCLUSION

If we add up the elements that appear from the preceding ten passages in the Zohar, we can see that the dominant theme (with the exception of the one, possibly later, text) is the emphasis on the unequal status of the born Jew and the proselyte within the Jewish community. As we saw, this reflects Judah Halevi's thinking rather than that of Maimonides. This difference between the born Jew and the proselyte finds its origin (or, rather, is projected into) the sefirotic system. The emanation of the *sefirot* differs in each. The circumcision is, for the kabbalist, a mystery rite, and has a different "sacramental" effect when performed on the eighth day, as is the case of the newborn Jew, or in later life, such as is the case of the proselyte. It connects the newborn Jew to the upper world of the *sefirot*, specifically to the eighth *sefirah*, *Binah*, while it brings the proselyte "close to *Malkhut*," the lowest *sefirah*. The *sefirot* also manifest the absorption process of the "alien element" into Israel, for good and for ill. Abraham, the proselyte, is blessed in his seed. But only the posterity of the proselyte will possess the sefirotic fullness of the born Jew. Jethro, a proselyte, restores the sparks of holy light from the realm of darkness to the holy people. Ruth, also a proselyte, brings as representative of the left, female, side the element of stern judgment to *Malkhut*, by which the royal realm will stand. The born Jew has access to the intimacy of "nuptial delight," which is the secret of love and life as portrayed in the *sefirot*. In contrast, the proselyte has to wait to receive his due, "afterwards." While the Jew dwells in Jacob's house, the proselyte receives the call from the desert and ascends the mountain. Under "the wings of the *Shekhinah*" are many mansions, signifying the various degrees of closeness of proselytes and "pious" among the nations to *Malkhut*.[40]

The medieval preoccupation with origin, nature, and destiny of the soul is worked out in the Zohar in a complex manner. The *sefirot*, the *Sitra Ahra*, angels and demons, and *zaddikim* (holy men) played a role. The proselyte is crossing sides. That which is "evil" in him because of his origin places him ontologically lower than the born Jew. But this same element also contributes to the life of Israel. Perhaps man is greatest where he overcomes fate. The doctrine of merits provides the proselyte with the opportunity to cover the nakedness of his origin with a garb of virtue.

Was the theology of the proselyte in the Zohar a theoretical issue only? Even if the faint hints to life situations, reflected in the vehemence with which the author at times sermonizes against false proselytes, are not borne out by historical data, the treatment of the proselyte in the Zohar reflects how the kabbalist thought about the complexities of life, about the reality of good and evil, about the relationship between Jews and Gentiles. He tried to understand these aspects of life through the Jewish tradition and enrich it with the poetic creativity of kabbalistic myth and symbolism. Theoretical issues in Judaism have always remained practical issues too, because the vital interest in theory has provided the Jew with the means to deal with the issues of his time in the perspective of his tradition.

NOTES

1. Maimonides in his letter to Obadiah the Proselyte encourages him by saying: "Do not consider your origin as inferior. While we are the descendants of Abraham . . . you derive from Him by whose word the world was created." Translated in Isadore Twersky, *A Maimonides Reader* (New York, 1972), pp. 475–486. Original in *Kovetz teshuvot ha-Rambam ve-iggerotav*, B. A. Lichtenberg, ed. (Leipzig, 1859), vol. I, 33 c, d. For Maimonides on the status of the proselyte see also his *Mishneh Torah*, Book V, treatise 1, ch. 13–14.
2. *Tanh.* ed. S. Buber (Wilna, 1885), *Lekh lekha*, no. 6 (p. 63).
3. *b. Yeb.* 47a–b.
4. *Midrash Rabbah, Lev.* I, 2 (Soncino trans., London, 1951), vol. IV, pp. 3–4.
5. *b. Yeb.* 109b; cf. ibid., 47b, and *b. Kid.* 70b. This statement is softened by Maimonides to mean the proselytes with ulterior motives. Cf. *Mishneh Torah* V, 1 ch. 13, no. 8.
6. *b. Yeb.* 48b.
7. *b. Nid.* 13b.
8. *j. Bik.* 64a; segregation of proselytes *b. Kid.* 73a (R. Judah). The blessing of the *bikkurim* and the permission for the proselyte to recite the formula "God of our fathers" is also the subject of Maimonides' letter to Obadiah (cf. note 1).
9. *b. Shebu'ot* 39a.
10. *The Kuzari*, I, 115, trans. H. Hirschfeld (New York, 1964), p. 79. On Judah Halevi's attitude towards the proselytes cf. Jacob Katz, *Exclusiveness and Tolerance* (New York, 1961), pp. 146–147.
11. The authorship of the Zohar by Moses de Leon (1250–1305) from Spain, as shown by Scholem, is assumed here. Cf. G. Scholem, *Major Trends in Jewish Mysticism* (New York, 1965), pp. 156ff. A basic acquaintance with the sefirotic system of the reader is also assumed. Cf. Scholem, op. cit., pp. 213–214. On proselytism in the 13th cent., cf. Katz, op. cit., p. 75 and note.
12. Zohar I 13a–b (*Hakdamah*); the edition of R. Margoliouth (Jerusalem, 1940) was used.
13. *Kuzari* IV, 10–11; English transl., op. cit., pp. 215–217.
14. *b. Ber.* 28a; for a discussion on the medieval Jewish attitude towards Christians and Moslems, cf. Katz, op. cit., pp. 115ff.
15. Zohar I, 95a–b (*Lekh lekha*).
16. The resemblance of the letters *Yod* and *Heh* to the seal of the covenant in the circumcision, curious as it may seem, is an aggadic motif.
17. *b. Shabb.* 137b.

18. The tetragrammaton as applied to the ten *sefirot* was seen in the following way:

Keter and *Hokhmah* = *Yod*
Binah = *Heh*
Hesed, Din, Tiferet, Nezah, Hod, Yesod the "six" sides = *Vav*
Malkhut = *Heh*

19. Zohar I, 208a–b (*Wayigash*).
20. Zohar II, 69a–70b (*Jethro*).
21. Zohar I, 13a–b (*Hakdamah*).
22. Zohar II, 95a–b; 98a–b (*Mishpatim*); on the *Saba*, cf. Scholem, op. cit., p. 161.
23. I. Tishby, *Mishnat ha-Zohar* (Jerusalem, 1957), vol. I, pp. 48–49; ibid. 62–54; cf. *infra* section to be discussed, Zohar III, 14a–b.
24. Zohar II, 192a–b (*Ki Tissa*).
25. Cf. *supra*, note 5.
26. Zohar III, 14a–b (*Wiyakra*).
27. *b. Shebu'ot* 39a.
28. Zohar III, 168a (*Shelah Lekha*).
29. See the section of Zohar II, 95a–b; 98a–b and notes 22–23.
30. Zohar I, 215a–b (*Wa Ychi*).
31. Scholem, op. cit., pp. 244ff. on the change of kabbalistic concerns after the expulsion from Spain. Doubt about the authenticity of this passage in the Zohar, cf. English trans. by H. Sperling and M. Simon, London, 1956, vol. II, p. 301 note 1.
32. Seven interpretations on this dictum of R. Helbo are given in the *Tosafoth* to *b. Kid.* 70b. As J. Katz notes, op. cit., 81, three of them change the meaning of this saying into its opposite, like the passage of the Zohar under discussion.
33. On the climate of this passage and a possible resemblance to the character of the *Raya Mehemna*, posterior to the Zohar, cf. Scholem, op. cit., p. 234.
34. *Zohar Hadash* 78b–79a. On the *Midrash ha-Ne'elam on Ruth* and the character of the *Midrash ha-Ne'elam* in general, cf. Scholem, op. cit., pp. 162; 181–185.
35. Ibid., p. 188.
36. So e.g., in Moses de Leon's *Sefer ha-Mishkal*. See the unpub. Ph. D. dissertation of the writer, Brandeis, 1964.
37. Scholem, op. cit., pp. 240–241, where the "three souls" are discussed.
38. *Supra*, Zohar II, 192a–b.
39. E.g., Jer. 3:13, "And hast scattered thy ways to the strangers under every leafy tree." Ibid., 2, 20; Isa. 57:5; Ezek. 6:13, etc.
40. Katz, op. cit., pp. 119ff.

II

THE CONTEMPORARY DEBATE

◄ 5 ►

Alexander M. Schindler

Presidential Address

The Reform movement's embrace of modernism made it the first to see that the post-Emancipation, postreligiously dominated world would transform the relationship between Jews and Christians. Part of this transformation led to tragedy, as Jews were no longer seen as religious strangers capable of being saved by baptism but as racial strangers incapable of being saved at all, or so the Nazis claimed. The other part of the transformation led to closer, warmer contacts between Jews and Christians. Reacting to this latter development, the Reform movement, starting in the nineteenth century, began to explore how Judaism could be seen as a universal religion, attractive to all.

These explorations did not go very far, however, and the number of actual conversions to Judaism was relatively small—to the point of being insignificant.

Intermarriage changed all that. Accelerating at a rapid pace during the second half of the twentieth century in the United States, intermarriage today is a significant issue in the Jewish community.

It took Rabbi Alexander M. Schindler, president of the Union of American Hebrew Congregations, a Reform group, to bring this issue into contemporary focus. Rabbi Schindler forged a link between the moribund ancient Jewish tradition of welcoming converts, the nineteenth-century liberal reading of that tradition, and the rise in intermarriage. In a bold speech in December 1978 to his organization's board of trustees gathered in Houston, Texas, Rabbi Schindler proposed a series of steps designed to welcome converts. He went further, however, in suggesting that an outreach program be launched aimed at "unchurched" Americans who were seeking a spiritual home. This last suggestion, to be institutionalized through such means as establishing information centers, having courses in synagogues, and developing appropriate publications, brought Rabbi Schindler considerable conflict. This proposal, it was suggested, smacked of proselytization, an activity that many Jews closely identified with Christian persecutions.

Rabbi Schindler, though, had irrevocably brought conversion to Judaism into, if not the center of modern Jewish consciousness, at least finally to its periphery. His continuing examination of the issue, and the reality of Jewish life, eventually did bring it into the center.

———•———

It is good to be here, my friends, good to be reunited with the leaders of Reform Jewry, with men and women from many congregations and communities but of one faith, bound together by a common sacred cause. Your presence here gives us much strength, as does your work throughout the year. We are what we are because of you, a product of those rich gifts of mind and heart you bring to our tasks.

It is good to have our number enlarged by the presence of leaders and members of our Southwest congregations. We are grateful for your hospitality. You are true sons and daughters of Abraham whose tent, so the Midrash informs us, had an opening on each of its sides so that whencesoever a stranger might near he would have no difficulty in entering Abraham and Sarah's home.

We are grateful for the sustaining help which you have given us over the years, your material help, and the time and talents and energies of your leaders, who have always played an indispensable role in our regional and national councils. I hope that you will participate in our deliberations, in any event, that you will listen most carefully if only to give you the assurance that that which you have given was well applied.

It is not my intention this night to give you a comprehensive report of the Union's activities—as I do at these board meetings from time to time—but rather to offer a resolution and to place it in its proper context. It is a resolution which recommends the creation of an agency within our movement involving its every arm which will earnestly and urgently confront the problems of intermarriage in specified areas and in an effort to turn the tide which threatens to sweep us away into directions which might enable us to recover our numbers and, more important, to recharge our inner strength.

I begin with the recognition of a reality: the tide of intermarriage is running against us. As a rabbi committed to the survival of the Jewish people, it pains me to say so, but the statistics are undeniable. We heard them from Dr. Fein last night. Between the years 1966 and 1972 the rate of Jewish intermarriage in the United States was 31.7 percent, that is to say, one out of three of our children chooses a non-Jew as a life mate, and this percentage is steadily rising. We do not really need these figures to instruct us. Our own experience teaches us: we see it in our communities, we feel it in our families. We know it with the knowledge of a heavy heart that there are more and more of these marriages each and every day. Indeed, a survey published in the *New*

York Times only this past week shows that there is increasing acceptance of such marriages, even of interracial marriages, and that the degree of this acceptance has risen most dramatically among Jews.

However much we deplore it, however much we struggle against it as individuals, these are the facts: the tide is running against us. This is the reality, and we must face it.

Now facing reality does not import complacent, fatalistic acceptance. It does not mean that we must prepare to sit *shiva* for the American Jewish community. Quite the contrary! Facing reality means confronting it, coming to grips with it, determining to reshape it.

Jewish education is usually held forth as the healing balm, and to a certain extent this is true. Those self-same statistics which brought us the bad news also gave us proof of that: the incidence of intermarriage is in inverse proportion to the intensity of Jewish rearing. The more Jewish education, the less the likelihood of intermarriage. But it isn't always so, alas. As the Mishnah long ago averred: "Not every knowledgeable Jew is pious," not every educated Jew is, perforce, a committed Jew.

The Union justly boasts of its program of formal and informal education. The bulk of our resources and energies are expended in this realm: We run camps and Israel tours and youth retreats. We conduct college weekends and kallahs and teacher-training institutes. We create curricula and texts and educational aids.

More to the point, no less than forty-five thousand youngsters participate in Union-led programs each and every year. Forty-five thousand sons and daughters of Reform congregations, their Jewish literacy enhanced, their Jewish commitments deepened. Among them are your rabbis and leaders of tomorrow; among them, the guides and scholars of our future.

Among them are also many who will intermarry — hundreds, if not thousands, of them. We live in an open society. Intermarriage is the sting which comes to us with the honey of our freedom.

Yet even when our children intermarry, Jewish education remains a crucial factor, because all the studies agree that in the preponderance of such marriages it is the JEWISH partner who ultimately determines whether or not there will be a conversion to Judaism and whether the children will or will not be reared as Jews. It is the Jewish partner whose will prevails . . . provided, of course, he or she chooses to exercise that will.

To put the matter differently: the fact of intermarriage does not in and of itself lead to a decline in the Jewish population. "That decline, if a decline there be, depends on what the Jews who are involved in the intermarriage actually do." (Massarik)

Jewish education is important, then, but important as it is, tonight I do not make a plea for its extension and intensification, although I might well make it to stem the tide of intermarriage. But rather it is the plea that we as a movement can and should be doing far more than we are, once having been touched by the tide, to turn it around in our favor.

The conversion of the non-Jewish partner-to-be is clearly the first desideratum, and we make a reasonable effort to attain it. The Union offers "Introduction to Judaism" courses in most major communities, and congregational rabbis spend countless hours giving instruction. Jewish ideas are explored, ceremonies described. History and Hebrew are taught. But there, by and large, our efforts come to an end. Immediately after the marriage ceremony between the born Jew and the newly converted Jewish partner, we drop the couple and leave them to fend for themselves. We do not help them to make a Jewish home, to rear their children Jewishly, to grapple with their peculiar problems. More serious still, we do not really embrace them, enable them to feel a close kinship with our people.

If the truth be told, we often alienate them in a kind of reverse discrimination. We question their motivations (as if to say that only a madman would choose to be a Jew and so there must be an ulterior motive), or we regard them as being somehow less Jewish (what irony in this, for they know more about Judaism than most born Jews); and unto the end of their days we refer to them as "converts," if not worse.

Don't for a moment think these whispers-behind-the-back aren't heard and do not hurt. Listen to these lines written to a colleague recently:

Dear Steve:
I know that I personally resent being referred to as a convert–a word that by now is alien to my heart. My conversion *process* was nearly ten years ago–I have been a *Jew* for a long time now. I think, eat and breathe Judaism. My soul is a Jewish soul, though I am distinctly aware of my original background and birthright. This does not alter my identity as a Jew. If one is curious about whence I come or if, indeed, " I am really Jewish," the answer is categorically "Yes, I'm really Jewish–a Jew by choice."
I shall continue to grow and to search as a Jew. My "conversion process" was just that–a process which ended with the ceremony. From then on I was a Jew.
Yours,
Jane

Jews-by-choice have special needs, and we need special guidance on how to meet them. There is the problem of how to *deal* with the *Jewish*-born partner who is *indifferent* to his or her faith.

Then there is the matter of the *past*. The new Jews may have broken with it, but in human terms they cannot forget their non-Jewish parents or families and at certain times of the year, on Christmas and Easter, they are bound to feel ambivalence. Finally, those who choose to become Jews quickly learn that they have adopted something far more than a religion; they have adopted a people, with its own history, its way of life.

We certainly need them to be a part of this people, for they can add no strength to us if they are only individuals who share our beliefs rather than members of our *community* of faith. Newcomers to Judaism must embark, in effect, on a long-term naturalization process, and they require knowledgeable and sympathetic guides to help them along the way.

Let the newly formed commission show us how we can provide this special and sensitive assistance, how these couples can be made to feel that the Jewish community welcomes them and *that they are fully equal members of the synagogue family*.

This point merits the emphasis of repetition. Jews-by-choice are Jews in the full meaning of the term. Thus Maimonides wrote in answer to a convert's query:

> You ask whether you, being a proselyte, may speak the prayers: "God and God of our Fathers" and "Guardian of Israel who hast brought *us* out of the land of Egypt," and the like.
>
> Pronounce all prayers as they are written and do not change a word. Your prayers and your blessings should be the same as any other Jew. . . .
>
> This above all: do not think little of your origin. *We* may be descended from Abraham, Isaac and Jacob, but *your* descent is from the Almighty Himself. . . .

Now not all non-Jewish partners of an intermarriage convert to Judaism, as we so well know. The majority, in fact, do not. Statistics are hard to come by, but what we have suggests these facts: A preponderance of intermarriage involves Jewish husbands and non-Jewish wives, and upward to 40 percent of these women formally accept our faith. In that smaller grouping involving non-Jewish husbands and Jewish wives, the rate of conversion is not much more than 3 percent. However, something extremely interesting has come to light. Social scientists have uncovered a "Jewish drift," the phenomenon of a "turning" to our faith. Their research has established that *"nearly 50 percent of non-Jewish husbands"* though not *formally embracing Judaism*, *"by their own description, nonetheless regard themselves as Jews."* (Massarik)

This brings me to my second proposal: I believe that our Reform congregations must do everything possible to draw into Jewish life the non-Jewish spouse of a mixed marriage. The phenomenon of the "Jewish drift" teaches us that we ought to be undertaking more intensive Jewish programs which will build on these already-existing ties of identification. If non-Jewish partners can be brought *more actively* into Jewish communal life, perhaps they themselves will initiate the process of conversion or, at the very least, we will assure that the children issuing from these marriages will, in fact, be reared as Jews.

We can begin by removing those "not wanted" signs from our hearts. I am in substantial agreement with Dr. Fein here: we reject intermarriage—not the intermarried. If Jews-by-choice often feel alienated by our attitudes, we can imagine how, unwittingly or not, we make the non-Jewish spouses of our children feel.

We can also remove those impediments to a fuller participation which still obtain in too many of our congregations. Even the most stringent approach to Halacha offers more than ample leeway to allow the non-Jewish partner to join in most of our ceremonial and life-cycle events. Thus the Halacha permits a non-Jew to be in the Temple, to sing in the choir, to recite the blessing over the Sabbath and festival candles, and even to handle the Torah. There is no law that forbids a non-Jew to be buried in a Jewish cemetery.

As for the children born of such a marriage, if the mother is Jewish the child is regarded as fully Jewish. But if she is not, then even Orthodoxy, providing consent of the non-Jewish mother is obtained, permits the circumcision of the boy, his enrollment in religious school, and his entitlement to be called to the Torah on the occasion of his Bar Mitzvah and to be considered a full Jew everlastingly thereafter.

All this is possible under Orthodoxy. How much the more so under Reform! Reform Judaism has never been chained by the Halacha; we insist on its creative unfoldment. If we put our best minds to it, we will find many other ways which can bolster our efforts in this realm.

As a case in point, why should a movement which from its very birth hour insisted on the full equality of men and women in religious life unquestioningly accept the principle that Jewish lineage is valid through the maternal line alone? Some years ago, I heard a learned paper by Dr. Wacholder of our College-Institute, a man most knowledgeable in rabbinic sources and heedful of their integrity, who argued that there is substantial support in our tradition for the validity of Jewish lineage through the paternal line. I discussed his paper with one of Israel's foremost rabbinic authorities, who found much weight in Dr. Wacholder's argument.

By way of illusration: a leading member of the United States Senate is not a Jew, although he was born a Jew. His father was Jewish. His mother converted from one of the Christian denominations. He was circumcised, reared as a Jew, and attended religious school. When the time of his Bar Mitzvah approached, the rabbi refused to recognize the validity of his mother's conversion and did not allow the boy to recite the blessings over the Torah. Embarrassed, enraged, the entire family converted to Christianity. This is why a leading United States solon is not a Jew today.

Now I am not about to propose a resolution of this maternal/paternal line issue. I lack sufficient knowledge. I merely insist that there is a possibility of the harmonization of tradition with modern need and that the Task Force for whose creation I call should include representatives of our Rabbinic Conference's Responsa Committee or enlist its effort in toto as we pursue our delicate tasks.

It may well be that in our collective wisdom and mindful of the needs of a larger Jewish unity, we will ultimately determine that certain privileges simply cannot be extended to non-Jews. If we do, then I am certain that the thoughtful non-Jew, who is favorably disposed to Judaism, will recognize that only through conversion can these privileges be won.

It is the inertia which I want to overcome. It is the indifference that I mean to master.

Let no one here misunderstand me to say that I am accepting of intermarriage. I deplore it, I discourage it, I will struggle against it. Rhea and I have five children, and we are as ardent as all other Jewish parents in our desire to stem the tide. But if our efforts do not suffice, why, then, we do not intend to banish our children, we will not say *shiva* over them. Quite the contrary, we will draw them even closer to our hearts, and we will do everything we humanly can to make certain that our grandchildren will be Jews, that they will be a part of our community and share the destiny of this people Israel.

I have a third proposal to make on the subject of our declining Jewish population in America and it is this: I believe that it is time for our movement to launch a carefully conceived Outreach Program aimed at all Americans who are unchurched and who are seeking roots in religion.

Let me not obfuscate my intent through the use of cosmetic language. Unabashedly and urgently, I call on our members to resume their time-honored vocation and to become champions for Judaism. Champions for Judaism—these words imply not just passive acceptance but affirmative action.

I sense those images which flash through your mind. Let me therefore enter the substance of my proposal by correcting their distortions.

I do not envisage that we conduct our Outreach Program like some kind of travelling religious circus. I envisage rather the unfoldment of a dignified and responsible approach: the establishment of information centers in many places, well-publicized courses in our synagogues, and the development of suitable publications to serve these facilities and purposes. In other words, I suggest that we respond openly and positively to those God-seekers who voluntarily ask for our knowledge.

Nor do I suggest that we strive to wean people from religions of their choice and, with the boast that ours is the only true and valid faith, engage in eager rivalry with all established churches. I want to reach a different audience entirely, the unchurched, those reared in nonreligious homes or those who have become disillusioned with their taught beliefs, the seekers after truth who require a religion which tolerates, nay encourages, all questions, and especially the alienated and the rootless who need the warmth and comfort of a people well known for its close family ties and of an ancient, noble lineage.

The notion that Judaism is not a propagating faith is wide of the truth. That may have been true for the last four centuries, but it is not true for the four thousand years before that.

Abraham was a convert and our tradition lauds his missionary zeal. Isaiah enjoined us to be a "light unto the nations" and insisted that God's house be a "house of prayer for *all* peoples." Ruth of Moab, a heathen by birth, became the ancestress of King David. Zechariah forsaw the time when men of every tongue will grasp a Jew by the corner of his garment and say, "Let us go with you, for we have heard that God is with you."

During the Maccabean period, Jewish proselytizing activity reached its zenith . . . schools for missionaries were established and by the beginning of the Christian era they had succeeded in converting 10 percent of the population of the Roman Empire—or roughly four million souls.

True, the Talmud insists that we test the sincerity of the convert's motivations, by discouraging them, by warning them of the hardships which they will have to endure as Jews. But the Talmud then adds that while we are "to push converts away with the left hand" we ought to "draw them *near* with the right."

After Christianity became the state religion of the Roman Empire and, later, again, when Islam conquered the world, Jews were forbidden to seek converts or to accept them. The death penalty was set for the gentile who became a Jew and for the Jew who welcomed him. Many were actually burned at the stake. This served to cool our conversionist ardor somewhat. Still, it was not until the sixteenth century that we abandoned all proselytizing efforts and our rabbis began their systematic rejection of those who sought to join us.

But we live in America today. No repressive laws restrain us. The fear of persecution no longer inhibits us. There is no earthly reason now why we cannot reassume our ancient vocation and open our arms wide to all newcomers.

Why are we so hesitant? Are we ashamed? Must one really be a madman to choose Judaism? Let us shuffle off our insecurities! Let us recapture our self-esteem! Let us demonstrate our confidence in those worths which our faith enshrines!

Millions of Americans are searching for something. Tragically—as the grisly events of the past week have established—many of these seekers have fallen prey to mystical cults which literally enslave them.

Well, Judaism offers life, not death. It teaches free will, not surrender of body and soul to another human being. The Jew prays directly to God, not through an intermediary who stands between him and his God. Judaism is a religion of hope and not despair, it insists that man and society are perfectible. Judaism has an enormous amount of wisdom and experience to offer this troubled world, and we Jews ought to be proud to speak about it, frankly, freely, and with dignity.

Aye, there is something different in the world today, and we all can feel it. The very air we breathe is tense, a wind blows through space, and the treetops are astir. Men and women are restless, not with the restlessness of those who have lost their way in the world and have surrendered to despair, but with the hopeful questing of those who want to find a way and are determined to reach it. It is a searching after newer and truer values, for deeper, more personal meaning. It is a purposeful adventure of the spirit. These men and women are in the grips of a great hunger, which, like all "great hungers feeds on itself, growing on what it gets, growing still more on what it fails to get."

The prophet Amos spoke of such a hunger when he said;

> Behold the Day cometh saith the Lord God that I will send a famine in the land not a famine of bread nor a thirst for water but of hearing the words of the Lord.

Can you find a more vivid limning of the very body and spirit of our age? Can you paint a more striking portrait of the Great Hunger which has seized us?

My friends, we Jews possess the water which can slake the thirst, the bread which can sate the Great Hunger. Let us offer it freely, proudly—for *our* well-being and for the sake of those who earnestly seek what is ours to give.

⊰ 6 ⊱

Dennis Prager

Judaism Must Seek Converts

As the subject of conversion to Judaism was explored and excavated, the original sources became better known, as did the fact that many more than just Reform rabbis and thinkers believed in the merit of actively welcoming converts. Rabbi Robert Gordis, one of Conservative Judaism's great thinkers of the twentieth century, had endorsed a program to welcome converts, as had other Conservative thinkers. Orthodox thinkers were found whose views were at least welcoming to converts, even converts who became Jewish because of an impending marriage to a born Jew.

Also, the rate of intermarriage continued to rise. The loudest call to the Jewish community came from the Council of Jewish Federations 1990 National Jewish Population Survey. One of the startling statistics that emerged from the survey was that in marriages since 1985, 52 percent of people born Jewish were married to an unconverted gentile. In the years since that study, there have been many recommendations, including methods to prevent intermarriage.

Interestingly, Dennis Prager, one of the most energetic and passionate contemporary Jewish voices, focuses much more on what he sees as Judaism's lost sense of mission rather than on simply the number of intermarriages. Prager, a radio and television host and publisher of the journal *Ultimate Issues*, is the author of many excellent works, including, along with Joseph Telushkin, the highly influential *Nine Questions People Ask About Judaism*. He included his views on conversion in *Ultimate Issues*. Prager is noted for his clear, direct, memorable style, and these characteristics are evident in this dramatic call for Judaism to seek converts.

Prager's assertive approach includes advertising for converts, and he concludes his article with an example of such an advertisement.

I

One of life's most ironic and important lessons is that our greatest weaknesses usually come from our greatest strengths — and this is as true for religions as it is for individuals.

One of Judaism's greatest strengths, for example, is that, unlike some other religious traditions, Judaism has always held that God judges people of other faiths by their deeds. Jews have therefore never held that non-Jews need to adopt Judaism in order to attain divine rewards.

Among the positive consequences of this attitude have been a tolerance of non-Jewish faiths and noncoercive behavior toward non-Jews. Jews, even those who may be described as fundamentalists, leave members of other faiths alone to practice their respective faiths. No religious group has to worry about Jews trying to convert their children to Judaism, let alone trying to coerce them to adopt Judaism.

This Jewish attitude has been very noble, particularly compared to non-Jewish attitudes that believe that people of other faiths are eternally damned or that regard all people as constant targets of conversion.

But one of the consequences of this attitude is not noble, nor is it even good for the Jews themselves: Jews have ended up ignoring non-Jews, who happen to make up 99.99 percent of mankind.

This has led to a most ironic situation.

The noble Jewish attitude that good non-Jews of all faiths "have a portion in the world to come" has contributed to an *ignoble* end — Jewishly committed Jews ignoring the world. On the other hand, the Christian belief in the damnation of non-Christians — a uniquely intolerant belief that has led to terrible suffering — has contributed to a highly *noble* end: a great reaching out by religious Christians to the rest of the world. Maimonides, the great Jewish philosopher and codifier of Jewish law, noted at the end of his great compilation of Jewish law, the *Mishneh Torah*, that while it was the Jews who introduced God into the world, Christians have imparted knowledge of God *and even of the Torah* to the world.

Adding to this irony is that while Catholics no longer hold that non-Christians are necessarily damned, and while many (though by no means all) Protestants have modified their theology about the damnation of all non-Christians, Jews have yet to confront a question of overwhelming importance: What is Judaism supposed to say, if anything, to non-Jews?

We have not devoted a moment to rethinking our old answer, that we have nothing Jewish to say to non-Jews, and that all we want is that they be good people. Yet, this answer is as intellectually vapid as it is un-Jewish and, as we shall see, self-destructive. There is nothing more important for the Jewish future than rethinking it.

Even those few Jews who do feel that Jews have a mission to non-Jews have not really confronted the issue. Chabad chasidim, for example, believe that Jews must articulate the "seven Noahide laws" (prohibitions against murder, theft, incest, eating the limb of a living animal, blasphemy, and idol worship, and a law to set up courts of justice). This is a major departure from other Orthodox and Conservative groups that generally say nothing Jewish to non-Jews. The Reform movement has come out, in theory, for encouraging unchurched non-Jews to convert to Judaism, but it does little about it. Moreover, since its decision to count children of non-Jewish mothers and Jewish fathers as Jews, the number of Reform converts has declined.

But advocating the seven Noahide laws hardly deals with the question.

First of all, most of the non-Jews with whom Jews come into contact already have these laws. Teaching them will only have an impact if we do so as one component of our greater obligation to teach ethical monotheism. Otherwise, going around telling people not to murder, commit incest, or eat limbs of living animals is not likely to compel people to take Judaism seriously.

Second, and more important, non-Jews want more than seven basic ethical laws. It is extraordinarily condescending for religious Jews to say that it is enough for non-Jews to observe the seven laws of Noah. Religious Jews thank God daily for giving them hundreds of laws to enrich their lives—and then posit that the rest of the world can get by on seven. How are non-Jews supposed to fulfill *their* religious, spiritual needs? Do non-Jews have fewer religious aspirations than Jews? Do non-Jews yearn less than Jews to touch the divine? Of course not.

What then are non-Jews to do?

The answer is obvious. Since Jews do not offer Judaism to non-Jews, non-Jews have developed, and will continue to develop, their own religions.

REASON ONE: NON-JEWS WILL GO ELSEWHERE

This, then, is the first reason why Jews must offer Judaism to unchurched non-Jews. If we do not, non-Jews will simply go about adopting or developing other religions.

Now, depending on how Jews view a given religion, the fact that non-Jews will develop other religions may not pose much of a problem. For example, any Jew who regards Christianity as a potential vehicle to ethical monotheism for non-Jews—which is the normative Jewish view of Christianity—has little problem today with that particular alternative to Judaism.

Jews, then, must either publicly acknowledge the ethical monotheist credentials of Christianity and work with Christians "to repair the world under God's kingdom," or begin seeking converts to Judaism — including from among Christians. Jews cannot deny Christianity as an ethical monotheist option for non-Jews and then offer Christians and other non-Jews nothing.

Of course, since Judaism regards Christianity as a vehicle to ethical monotheism for non-Jews, I see no reason to seek Christian converts to Judaism (though Christians who leave Christianity must be made aware of the welcome that they would receive if they should decide to become Jews).

But Christianity is hardly the only alternative available to non-Jews. In fact, for many individuals in the Western world today, Christianity is the last place they are likely to look for spirituality. Go, for example, to any popular American bookstore, and you will probably find a far larger "New Age" section than a Christian one. And both Islam and Mormonism are growing faster than Christianity in the United States.

Non-Jews are either developing spiritual alternatives to Christianity, joining Islam or the Mormon church, or remaining secular. From a Jewish perspective, none of these, except Mormonism, can be regarded with equanimity. The spiritual alternatives to Christianity are usually neopagan, (e.g., the New Age equation of the self with God) and sometimes outright dangerous (e.g., satanism and Jim Jones-like cults). Islam, though at one time a great civilization, is, in our time, increasingly a world of moral darkness and religious backwardness.

The third alternative, secularism, breeds hedonism, moral relativism, and political substitutes for religion. This century has offered a very rich, and very evil, smorgasbord of secular alternatives to Christianity. Hundreds of millions of people have believed in Marxism, Nazism and fascism with no less fervor than religious Jews and Christians have believed in their respective religions. Furthermore, with the collapse of leftist totalitarian regimes, many true believers of the left have avoided a sorely needed self-examination as to how they could have believed in something so foolish and evil, and have either remained leftists or adopted new forms of nihilism. They have substituted the trinity of Race, Gender and Class for moral and religious values, or have replaced green symbols (extreme environmentalism, radical animal rights) for the discredited red ones.

If Jews do not seek converts, they must make peace with the fact that the rest of mankind will either remain where it is, adopt other religions, or invent new ones.

Given these alternatives — and how much Jews have suffered because of many of them — it boggles the mind that Jews do not offer Judaism to non-Jews. Or, to put it bluntly, any Jew who does not fear the steady increase in Muslim fundamentalism, both in the Muslim and Western worlds, the erosion in the West of the Judeo-Christian ethic and a corresponding steady march toward neopaganism, and increased antisemitism in many places is a fool.

But it is not enough merely to recognize negative trends. Jews ought to do something about them. Yes, *do* something about them. While many individuals who were born Jewish have deeply influenced the world, for two thousand years the Jewish people and Judaism have been reacting to the world, not acting upon it—at a cost of terrible suffering to the Jews and non-Jews.

In order to influence the world, Jews can and must do two things: teach ethical monotheism and offer Judaism. Or the world will go its own unmerry way, and the Jews once again will be victims of a world they did nothing to influence.

REASON TWO: THE MORE JEWS THE BETTER

We lost one out of every three Jews during the Holocaust. Today we continue to lose about the same percentage to assimilation. Obviously, we are in terrible need of more Jews. With more Jews every Jewish problem comes closer to solution.

More Jews means far more Jewish resources—more Jewish schools, more Jewish institutions of all types, more resources to resettle Soviet and Ethiopian Jews, to help poor Jews, to fight antisemitism, and to build Israel. Conversely, the fewer Jews there are, the more impotent and irrelevant to the world Jews become. With small numbers, an increasingly large percentage of which is composed of *kharedi* (ultra-Orthodox) Jews who shun the outer world, Jews will become little more than a religious sect, much better known, but not much more influential, than the Amish. While large numbers do not ensure great influence, nations surely do not increase their influence while their already small numbers dwindle.

And, of course, more Jews means more Jewish security. Small groups invite big bullies. If Jewish numbers are great enough, antisemites will think twice before attacking Jews. That is why Arab countries that want to see Israel disappear fear Jewish immigration to Israel more than they fear any weapons given to Israel.

There are only two ways of increasing our numbers—through a very high birthrate and by gaining converts.

The first method, however, is not working. Many of the Orthodox (especially the *kharedim*, the ultra-Orthodox) are reproducing in very high numbers, but that will not even make a dent on the overall demographic problem. Given the low birthrate among other Jews, and given the high rate of Jewish assimilation, the surging Orthodox birthrate will only mean that the ultra-Orthodox will constitute a significantly higher percentage of Jews.

The only method of increasing the number of Jews is by gaining new Jews.

REASON THREE: DECREASED ANTISEMITISM

Seeking converts to Judaism will also dramatically increase antisemitism.

The most obvious reason is that greater Jewish numbers reduce the like-lihood of antisemitic violence. But there are two additional reasons.

It Will Force Jews to Relate to Non-Jews

First, Jews should never forget what the great German rabbi and hero of Ger-man Jewry, Leo Baeck said: "If all Germans had had a Jewish relative, the Shoah [Holocaust] could not have happened."[1] People do not generally slaughter members of their family, or that person's friends and relatives. Furthermore, people are simply more disposed to liking those whom they trust, and they are more likely to trust those whom they know well.

This is further borne out by Professors Samuel and Pearl Oliner, authors of the most extensive study ever done of non-Jews who rescued Jews during the Holocaust (*The Altruistic Personality*, Free Press, 1989). The Oliners, in an interview with me, stated that one of the few traits that seemed to typify rescuers was having had a relationship with individual Jews prior to World War II.

To put it in understated terms, Jewish seclusion does nothing to dimin-ish antisemitism.

It does not take an advanced degree in social psychology in order to appreciate that the more and better that identifying Jews relate to non-Jews, the more positive non-Jews' reactions to Jews will be. And nothing will induce Jews to relate more and better to non-Jews than a sense of mission to them. We are not living in the Middle Ages when Jews were unable to relate to non-Jews as equals or were forcibly confined to ghettos. Historical circum-stances under both Christian and Muslim rule rarely enabled Jews to think about relating normally with non-Jews, let alone about advocating Judaism. For nearly 2,000 years Jews *have had* to turn inward. Today Jews have a choice, but many religious Jews continue to live as if the ghetto is the Jewish ideal.

Freedom means opportunity, and for Jews opportunity means the chance to finally reembark on their mission to humanity.

That mission is first and foremost to teach the world ethical monotheism, which is the affirmation of the one God whose primary demand is that people treat each other justly. There is much more to ethical monotheism, especially in our age of resurgent paganism (for example, the growing worship of nature), and this will be fully developed in a future issue of UI. But that is not the Jews' only calling. Part of the Jews' mission is also to offer Judaism to those who do not already affirm a religious tradition consonant with Judaism's ethical monotheist values. Even though most Jews think otherwise, seeking converts is very Jewish, as we will see in Part II of this article.

Not Seeking Converts Causes Resentment

Outreach efforts to non-Jews will also reduce antisemitism because *not* seeking converts actually causes resentment among many non-Jews. This is something of which very few Jews are aware. It is the very opposite of what they believe, which is that not seeking converts makes us admirable and lovable to non-Jews. That belief is wrong.

Many non-Jews see in the lack of Jewish proselytizing a disregard for them. They see it not as an affirmation of non-Jews' religious values but as an affirmation of Jewish purity of blood. They see our ignoring them as a desire not to have non-Jews join us, lest our clan be polluted by non-Jewish blood.

Are they wrong? Not very. There *is* a clannishness that pervades much of Jewish life. How could it be otherwise? Secular Jews have no religion to share, so their entire Jewish identity is ethnic. And, sadly, even many religious Jews feel similarly.

By seeking new Jews, Jews can undo this perception of a clan that doesn't care about outsiders. We would be announcing that our values, not our blood lines, are sacrosanct, that we seek anyone of any racial or ethnic background to become one of us.

Seeking Converts Neutralizes Non-Jewish Jews

Jewish outreach would also dramatically improve non-Jews' views of Jews.

By and large, the only Jews who are known by the general public are those with no religious identity and frequently with no Jewish identity of any sort. The only Jewish Jews whom many non-Jews ever come to know lived 3,000 years ago, in the Bible.

Moreover, the most prominent Jews are frequently antagonistic to Judaism, Christianity and to most traditional values. There are few radical organizations without a membership roster that includes many Jewish family names. As a result, the public frequently identifies Jews with hostility to religion and to a God-based value system—in effect, to Judeo-Christian civilization itself. From the Jewish lawyers of the American Civil Liberties Union who wage war upon any hint of religion in the public sphere, and the Jewish professors who teach moral relativism and who cast Judeo-Christian civilization in the role of history's villain, to the radical Jewish writers and activists who are seen as enemies of Western values, the best known Jews in America are nearly always the Jews most alienated from Judaism.

How refreshing it would be if Jews affiliated with Reform, Conservative and Orthodox Judaism would reach out with Jewish values to the non-Jewish public: Look, America, there are Jews who do want the Ten Commandments posted in America's schools. Look, West, there are Jews who welcome your joining with us in fighting for the concepts of the holy and the transcendent. Look, world, at us and at our religion.

Such an attitude would transform many non-Jews' thinking about Jews.

We Can Be Sure of Converts' Values

The final reason why more new Jews will diminish antisemitism is so obvious that it is rarely noted. The more people who live by Judaism, the fewer the antisemites. Could anything be clearer? Not all converts will keep Shabbat punctiliously, but none of them will join a pogrom, argue that Jews are inferior, teach that the Jews killed Christ, or organize an anti-Israel group on a college campus (though many born Jews do precisely that).

That is the *least* that we can expect from new Jews. More likely, Judaism will attract some of the finest people in the world. People do not become Jews in order to attain salvation (they can attain it, according to Judaism, without converting). People certainly do not become Jews in order to become popular. Jews are hardly the most popular people on earth. Anyone who moves from a majority culture to Judaism is usually doing so for idealistic reasons, even if marrying a Jew is the original impetus.

In the past, the motives of some Reform converts—especially female converts marrying Jewish men—were regarded with suspicion. Many Jews suspected that they had converted solely in order to have their children considered Jews. But with Reform Judaism's decision to count the children of non-Jewish mothers and Jewish fathers as Jews, this ulterior motive for conversion has been removed (and, indeed, there has been a decline in Reform conversions ever since that decision).

REASON FOUR: A BETTER WORLD

Even if seeking converts did not lessen antisemitism by one iota, Jews should be passionately pro-conversion. Could any committed Jew argue that if there were millions more people living Judaism, the world would not be a better place?

Imagine a world in which a hundred million Jews were trying to lead lives in accordance with Jewish values. Imagine a world that set aside its preoccupation with money one day each week. Imagine a society in which tens of millions of its members really believed that gossiping was wrong, where a sex ethic lying between hedonism and sexual repression became the norm, where people consulted Jewish laws before entering business deals. Imagine a world that read Isaiah weekly, that studied biblical and other Jewish texts a few hours each week during office hours.

A committed Jew who is not moved by such a dream is not committed to Judaism's dream.

And if such a dream seems too romantic, I will pose the question in a more down-to-earth manner: Would the world be better or not if many of its inhabitants took up Judaism? Would America (not to mention black-Jewish relations) be better or not if blacks looking for an alternative to Christianity had become Jews rather than Black Muslims? Would Jews prefer that non-Jews searching for religious or spiritual meaning read Maimonides or Shirley MacLaine?

REASON FIVE: IT WILL BE GOOD FOR JUDAISM

A major reason to seek converts is the positive effect of many new Jews on Judaism.

Go to almost any Jewish community in America today, and you will find that a disproportionate number of that community's most dynamic Jews are new Jews. Having spoken in virtually every Jewish community in North America, I no longer even react upon being told that the women's division is headed by a Jew by choice, or that the chairman of the day school's board became a Jew 10 years ago, or that the leading voice on behalf of Israel is a convert. I simply respond, "So what else is new?"

Jews by choice bring something else into Jewish life—freshness. We have become too inbred, too much like each other (even when we thoroughly dislike each other). New Jews bring healthy attitudes toward Judaism, toward the world. True, they don't come with childhood memories of Shabbat, but neither do the vast majority of born Jews anymore, and they also don't come with unhealthy Jewish emotional baggage from childhood. They bring an attitude of joy of being Jewish, not just the "shver zu sein a Yid" ("It's tough to be a Jew") attitude that many Jews have.

In fact, this joy at being a Jew often confuses born Jews. "We were stuck

with it, but they chose it," many incredulous Jews exclaim in response to the
enthusiasm of new Jews.

New Jews challenge us—and we certainly need to be challenged. They
keep asking why. And telling them that this is the way it was done in our
parents' home doesn't quite answer their questions. Nor should it. Jews are
supposed to live according to authentic Judaism, not according to the patterns of behavior, speech, dress and cuisine of Eastern European Jews. To
cite a simple example, it is Eastern European tradition, not Judaism, that
calls for eating chicken on Friday nights.

Being around new Jews forces born Jews to think about their religion
and identity, not just assume it.

Between the Holocaust and the never-ending need to fight for Soviet
Jewry and for Israel's survival, we are a somewhat weary people. New Jews
invigorate us, give us hope. In fact, they may be our best hope.

Moreover, nothing will persuade born Jews to take Judaism seriously
better than converts to Judaism. Assimilated Jews tend to assume the values
of the non-Jewish majority among whom they live. What, then, could possibly be as Jewishly influential on these Jews as the sight of non-Jews choosing
to become Jews?

REASON SIX: NON-JEWS ARE MORE OPEN
TO JUDAISM THAN MOST BORN JEWS

After I spoke recently at the University of Alabama, Richard Cohen, the professor of Judaic Studies there, despaired at how few students show up at Jewish events or enroll in Jewish classes. "It's odd," he lamented, "in my classes
on basic Judaism, the non-Jews show much more interest than do the Jews."

In fact, it is not odd, and it points to an extremely important lesson.

We Jews are making a terrible error in thinking that we should focus
our outreach efforts exclusively on those who happen to have been born as
Jews. I am as aware as anyone of the numbers of Jews who have "returned"
to Judaism. I have, after all, devoted much of my life to bringing Jews to
Judaism, and have developed proficiency at it.

But the numbers are still infinitesimally small. Most Jews remain Jews
by last name, not by any volitional act of Jewish commitment. And while we
must continue to work to acquaint them with Judaism, we should not focus
on them exclusively.

There are at least three reasons for this:

First, there is no possible way to communicate only with nonaffiliated
Jews. Nonaffiliated Jews are thoroughly integrated into the general public,
living with, working with and marrying non-Jews. How can any message be

directed to them and not to others? Are we going to take out radio ads announcing: "The following message is only for people who were born Jews"?

Second, any message directed solely to Jews is likely to be dismissed. Nonaffiliated Jews want to hear why Judaism is worth living by anyone, not only by people who happen to have a Jewish parent. Either Judaism has something to say to everyone, these Jews feel, or it has nothing to say to them. And they are absolutely right.

Third, most Jews take seriously what their non-Jewish friends take seriously. Therefore, a message inviting non-Jews to take Judaism seriously will elicit far more credibility among nonaffiliated Jews than a message aimed only at born Jews. Indeed, I can imagine few things more likely to attract alienated Jews to Judaism than the sight of many quality non-Jews taking Judaism seriously.

The very best way to attract Jews is to have them see Judaism touching the world, and the world responding positively. One of the reasons that so many Jews ignore Judaism is because of their perception that it is insular and provincial—that it only relates to Jews. When we demonstrate that Judaism relates to *anyone*, unaffiliated Jews will begin to look seriously at it.

Unlike many born Jews, untold numbers of non-Jews would love to be part of the Jewish people and to live a Jewish life. They would love a religion that stresses right behavior over right faith, that teaches one how to incorporate the holy into everyday life, that stresses a life of the intellect, that makes one a member of a people as well as a religion, that is the oldest ongoing civilization in the world, that gave the world God and the Ten Commandments, and that, through involvement with the Jewish people, keeps one passionately involved in the great moral issues of the day—from the Middle East to Eastern Europe to relations with Christians and Muslims.

Untold numbers of non-Jews need Judaism. And Judaism needs them.

II

It comes as a surprise to many Jews that Judaism reveres and deeply desires converts. But the evidence for this is overwhelming.

To begin with, the first Jew was a convert, an extremely important fact that Jewish sources repeatedly stress: "Said the Holy One, 'I cherish the convert. Abraham was a convert'" (*Tankhuma B.* and *N. Lekh Lekha*).

"If a man wishes to convert to Judaism but says, 'I am too old to convert,' let him learn from Abraham who when he was ninety-nine years old, entered God's covenant" (*Tankhuma B, Lekh Lekha* 40).

"Every Jew should endeavor to actively bring men under the wing of God's presence just as Abraham did" (*Avot de Rabbi Nathan*, chapter 12).

Not only was the first Jew a convert. The *Tanakh* (Hebrew Bible) holds that the Messiah will come from a convert, Ruth. Could Judaism have made a more powerful statement on behalf of converts?

In the Talmud, Rabbi Eleazar ben Pedat held that the Jewish temple and the Jewish state were destroyed, and that the Jews were exiled from their land—the greatest Jewish catastrophes until that time—so that the Jews would be able to gain converts!: "The Holy one, Blessed be He, exiled Israel among the nations in order to increase their numbers with the addition of converts" (*Pesachim* 87b).

As Bernard Bamberger wrote in his book *Proselytism in the Talmudic Period*, "That the tragedy of the exile . . . should be interpreted even by a few teachers, as a method used by Providence for the increase of proselytes, indicates how great was the importance attached by the rabbis to the missionary movement."

According to Judaism, God not only loves converts—"Converts are beloved; in every way God considers them as part of Israel" (*Mekhilta Nezikim* [*Mishpatim*] 18)—some rabbis even held that God holds them in greater esteem than born Jews! "Said Resh Lakish: the convert is dearer than the Jews who stood before Mount Sinai. Why? Because had they [the Jews at Sinai] not seen the thunder and the lightning and the mountains quaking and the sounds of the horn, they would not have accepted the Torah. But this one, who saw none of these things, came, surrendered himself to the Holy One and accepted upon himself the kingdom of heaven" (*Tankhuma B, Lekh Lekha* 6).

As for how to receive prospective converts, the generally accepted rabbinic attitude is, "When a person comes to be converted, one receives him with an open hand so as to bring him under the wings of the Divine presence" (*Leviticus Rabbah* 2:9). Even Rabbi Eliezer ben Hyrcanus, who was quite suspicious of converts, probably because of bad experiences with converts to the new sect of Christian Hebrews, said: "When a person comes to you in sincerity to be converted, do not reject him, but on the contrary encourage him" (*Mekhilta Amalek* 3).

Moreover, while Judaism wants people to come to Judaism out of love for God, Torah and Israel, the Halakha accepts those who were converted "in order to marry, to advance themselves, or out of fear" (*Yevamot* 24b).

The Rambam (Maimonides) wrote: "Toward father and mother we are commanded honor and reverence, toward Prophets to obey them, but toward converts we are commanded to have great love in our inmost hearts" (Response no. 369, edited by Freimann, cited in *Encyclopaedia Judaica* [*EJ*]).

Later, in the mid-thirteenth century, Moses ben Jacob of Coucy argued that Jews must always act nobly among gentiles because "so long as Jews act deceitfully toward them, who will attach themselves to the Jews?" (*Semag, Asayin* 74, cited in *EJ*).

Against a massive pro-convert, pro-missionizing body of literature, there are just four ambivalent statements in the rabbinic literature. Considering the wide variety of views on almost any subject in the Talmud, this minimal number is impressive proof of the pro-convert views of traditional Judaism. Moreover, the little ambivalence that exists relates to those converts who proved less than loyal during times of persecution. The likelihood, however, is that at least as many born Jews proved to be equally disloyal, and as noted in Part I, while it is common to find born Jews participating and even leading anti-Israel activities, it would be shocking to find a convert engaged in any anti-Jewish activities.

JEWS SOUGHT CONVERTS WHEN POSSIBLE

As a result of Judaism's attitude toward convert-seeking, *Jews vigorously sought converts whenever possible.* In the ancient world, Jews were such active missionaries on behalf of Judaism that by the time of Jesus, 10 percent of the Roman Empire was Jewish. According to the dean of Jewish historians, Salo Baron, Jews numbered 8,000,000 in the Roman Empire (A *Social and Religious History of the Jewish People*, Vol. I, p. 170)—largely as a result of active convert-seeking. The New Testament Book of *Matthew* correctly describes the Pharisees as "crossing seas to make one convert." The Jewish historian Josephus wrote at the time, "Proselytism was widespread among the ordinary people." As a result, he wrote, the inhabitants of both Greek and Barbarian cities evinced great zeal for Judaism (*Contra Apion* 2, 39).

The results were also qualitatively impressive. Among the notable rabbinic converts to Judaism was Onkelos, whose Aramaic translation of the Bible is studied by religious Jews to this day. A listing of the rabbis in the Talmud who descended from converts includes the greatest names: Rabbi Meir, Rabbi Akiva, as well as Shemaiah and Avtalyon. Maimonides notes in his introduction to the *Mishneh Torah* that Akiva's father was a convert.

It was Christianity, not Judaism, that stopped a likely massive movement of people to Judaism. When Christianity became the Roman state religion, the state immediately prohibited conversion to Judaism, and by 407 of the Common Era, it became a capital offense for a Christian to convert to Judaism. Both the convert and the Jew facilitating the conversion were put to death. Such prohibitions, along with the gradual deterioration of the Jews' condition, and the ascent of Christian Jew-hatred, are what prevented the Jews from continuing to seek converts. *Jew-haters, not Judaism, stopped Jewish convert-seeking.* Those Jews who believe that Judaism should not seek converts have adopted the attitude of the Jews' oppressors, not of Judaism.

Despite these persecutions, Jews continued to seek converts whenever possible. But the consequences were frequently horrific.

In 1012, Father Vicilinus, a Catholic priest in Mainz, Germany, converted to Judaism, and scholars consider this a cause of the subsequent expulsion of the Jews from Mainz.

In Poland in 1539, Catherine Weigel, an 80-year-old woman, was burned at the stake for having converted to Judaism (*EJ*, Vol 5, p. 1190).

All of this had a terrible impact on the Jews' psyche. Constant fear of persecution, and the forced segregation of Jewry, resulted in the Jews seeing themselves as inherently, almost racially, different. One consequence was a disinterest in, even antipathy toward making converts. Thus, the sixteenth-century Polish legal scholar, Rabbi Solomon Luria, the Maharshal, could write, "Would that the seed of Israel continue to stand fast and hold its own among the nations throughout the days of our exile and no stranger be added to us who is not of our nation" (*EJ*, Vol. 5, p.1191).

Despite the growing belief in inherent Jewish distinctiveness, some conversions continued—and so did the persecutions. In 1716, two Christian women who became Jews were put to death in Dubno. In 1738, a naval officer, Alexander Voznitsyn, was publicly burned to death in Russia for converting to Judaism, along with the Jew who persuaded him to convert. In Vilna in 1746, the same thing happened to Count Valentine Potocki. But, in the main, the attitude of apathy toward converts, born of centuries of repression, remained.

WHY MOST JEWS DON'T SHARE JUDAISM'S ATTITUDE TOWARD CONVERTS

Centuries of Persecution

Thanks to centuries of antisemitism, of enforced segregation from all non-Jews, of the killing of converts and of the Jews who supported them, the attitude expressed by the Maharshal came to be widely held among Jews. Jew-haters forced Jews to ignore the world, against the wishes of Judaism. When a Jew today expresses ambivalence toward convert-seeking, he or she is expressing a non-Jewish attitude, which while indefensible, is explicable. It is time to return to Judaism's true aims and to break away from the isolation and insularity forced upon us by antisemites.

It is ironic that many of the Jews most ambivalent or even opposed to convert-seeking are those who most deny that Jewish religious attitudes have been shaped by historical events. For here is a very clear case of Jews holding a non-Torah attitude solely as a result of historical forces. For a religious Jew to be ambivalent about convert-seeking is to let antisemites and historical events, not Judaism, determine his *hashkafa* (religious outlook).

The Lost Sense of Mission

A second and related reason why many Jews are ambivalent about convert-seeking is that most Jews involved in Judaism have lost any sense of mission to the world. The insularity and self-obsession forced upon us by Jew-haters has come to be accepted as the normal state of Jewish affairs. One result is a situation wherein the Jews who feel a mission to the world and who communicate with it are usually those Jews who know nothing about Judaism, while the Jews who are most immersed in Judaism feel no mission to the world and communicate nothing to it.

When religious Jews ignore the world they sin against both God and Judaism. As we have seen, the Bible and the Talmud could not have been clearer as to the desirability of influencing humanity and of bringing non-Jews under the wings of the *shekhina* Divine Presence). Yet these goals remain thoroughly neglected among religious Jews. Indeed, if anything Jewish religious energy seems ever more preoccupied with further isolation from non-Jews and further development of Halakhic concerns within ever narrower boundaries. The only Jews who feel a sense of mission to humanity are secular Jews of the left who for nearly two centuries have laboriously worked to bring the world under the wings of their ideologies. Thus every day Jews do not offer Judaism to unchurched non-Jews, more of them will be approached by Scientology, leftism, pacifism, and New Age thought, not to mention other religions, especially contemporary Islam.

Negative Associations with Convert-Seeking

A third reason why Jews disregard convert-seeking is that they identify it with the often offensive missionary efforts of other religions. The moment you mention convert-seeking, most Jews recoil in horror—they think of the historical Christian missionizing efforts to save others' souls, and they imagine Jews knocking on non-Jews' doors, handing out tracts.

Yet, saving souls has nothing to do with Judaism, and knocking on doors has nothing to do with the sophisticated outreach explained below.

Judaism does want converts, and it does demand that non-Jews become ethical monotheists, but *it never held that non-Jews must become Jews.* This is one reason why Jews would never feel as driven as Muslims or Christians to seek converts. To the classical Christian, not seeking converts has been the equivalent of consigning some poor soul to hell. The only thing preventing the non-Christian from eternal fire and damnation is the individual Christian proselytizer. Jews do not have these views of non-Jews or of themselves as the non-Jews' key to salvation. Judaism holds that every decent non-Jew has a portion in the hereafter. In fact, unlike other faiths, Judaism holds that coming to Judaism actually makes it *harder* for the individual to go to heaven.

Judaism wants non-Jews to become Jews for the sake of the world, not for the sake of the non-Jew's soul. For this reason, Jews should think of bringing people to Judaism in the way that Democrats and Republicans think of bringing people to their parties and candidates. People try to influence other people's political views not for the sake of those individuals' souls, but for the sake of the greater good. The more people who share their values, liberals and conservatives believe, the better the world will be. That is the primary reason why Judaism wants non-Jews to adopt Judaism: the world will be a better place (not to mention better for Jews—see Part I). Period.

As for Jews' negative associations with the concept of seeking converts, we are dealing with a certain element of hypocrisy here. For in the last 200 years, Jews have probably been the most active missionaries in the world—just not to Judaism

Whether it has been socialism, feminism, Marxism, or liberalism, Jews have played an utterly disproportionate role in these movements' seeking of converts. It may be that the only ideology to which modern Jews have not sought converts is Judaism. This has often been bad for the world, and it has often been suicidal for the Jews—in terms of the numbers of Jews lost to these ideologies, and in terms of the destruction that some of these ideologies have wrought upon the Jews.

It is quite hypocritical for Jews who take out newspaper and magazine ads, support door-to-door canvassing for political candidates and environmental movements, and who engage in and support all other forms of social action, to become squeamish when it comes to doing anything on behalf of Judaism. It can only be explained by Jewish insecurity or by a contempt for Judaism, not by a contempt for seeking converts.

If most Jews regarded Judaism with the same respect that they regard many secular ideologies, they would advocate that others adopt it.

Jewish Insecurity

A major reason why Jews have been active in so many liberal and leftist ideologies has been Jewish insecurity—specifically, fear that an illiberal world will kill Jews again. Jews active in liberal or radical social movements rarely mention this, and many are probably not even fully conscious of it, but it is undoubtedly so. Jews are scarred deeply by the Holocaust and by nearly two millennia of religious antisemitism. Jews are a very small people who greatly fear recurrences of massive anti-Jewish violence.

Many Jews, especially those on the left, believe that the solution to antisemitism lies in Jews ceasing to be Jews (while, they hope, non-Jews also relinquish their distinctive identities).

Therefore, the last thing that fearful Jews want—whether they are on the left or not—is that Jews be publicly Jewish. And nothing seems as aggressively public as seeking converts to your religion.

This insecurity about being Jewish in a world that has given Jews ample reason for such insecurity is yet another reason why many Jews instinctively react negatively to Jewish proselytizing. Of course, a moment's thought would reveal to these Jews the benefits they would receive should many people become Jews. For one, having millions of non-Jewish families with a Jewish member in them would diminish antisemitism. Second, more Jews means a less inviting target for bullies. I discussed these and many other benefits to Jews in detail in Part I of this article.

A Lack of Appreciation of Judaism's Worth

It is easy to understand why Jews who are not particularly religious have little interest in seeking converts. Why would Jews who themselves do not care about Judaism want others to convert to Judaism? The real riddle concerns religious Jews: why don't they, who presumably love Judaism, want others to live Jewish lives?

Some answers have already been discussed—in particular, how centuries of persecution and isolation led many Jews to see themselves as inherently different from non-Jews. There is an additional one.

Over the course of centuries, a particularly unfortunate development took place within religious Jewish life. The notion took hold that reasons for the commandments were unknowable, that the commandments were to be obeyed not because of any inherent rational or moral excellence, but solely because God commanded them. Judaism therefore seemed to consist largely of nonrational practices. This in turn led to two inevitable consequences. One was that Jews began to lose sight of Judaism's meaning and purpose, and therefore lost any ability to rationally articulate its meaning to others. The second was that Judaism became an ethnic way of life rather than a world-embracing religion.

Thus, in addition to not wanting to offer Judaism to non-Jews, religious Jews became *unable* to offer Judaism to non-Jews. If you don't understand your laws, you cannot explain them to others, let alone make a convincing case that they live by them. And you will neither want nor be able to attract outsiders to a way of life that is ethnic ritual rather than universally relevant. People can convert to a religion and even to a people, but not to an ethnicity.

For this reason, most religious Jews became as incapable as nonreligious Jews of explaining Judaism to outsiders.

Of course, today, religious Jews would respond that they know very well the beauty and profundity of Jewish laws. But if that is so, on what grounds can they rationalize keeping something so beautiful to themselves? And on what grounds can they continue to ignore Judaism's explicit desire for converts? Either they are not convinced about their own and Judaism's ability to make the Jewish case in the marketplace of ideas, or they are a particularly selfish lot, desiring to keep as many people as possible away from such an enriching way of life.

HOW TO SEEK CONVERTS

Once Jews understand that they must seek converts for their own sakes and for the sake of the world, and that Judaism wants them to seek converts, the only remaining question is how to go about it.

The first thing Jews must do is to change their attitude toward seeking converts. This alone will lead to a profound shift in Jewish behavior. The moment Jews understand that they have a mission to the world, Judaism takes on a far deeper meaning, the outer world becomes far more real, and attitudes toward non-Jews undergo a very positive metamorphosis.

One example can illustrate all these points.

Few Jews invite non-Jews to their homes for a Shabbat meal. The reason is as plain as it is sad. Of the Jews who regularly invite non-Jews to their homes, few observe Shabbat, and of the Jews who observe Shabbat, few regularly have non-Jews to their homes. Yet, one way to get the word out that Jews welcome new Jews is for Jews who celebrate Shabbat to invite non-Jews to their homes.

This can be achieved in two ways: person-to-person and communally. In the first instance, Jews can invite non-Jewish colleagues and acquaintances to their homes. In the second, synagogues, federations, and other Jewish organizations can initiate programs, announced through notices in the general media, that anyone interested in learning about Judaism should contact them. In appropriate instances, people will be invited to spend a Shabbat or other Jewish holiday meal with Jewish families who volunteer for such activities. I offer an example of such a public notice.

(A sample advertisement)

You do not have to be Jewish to be saved—Judaism holds that God rewards all good people.

Therefore, if you are presently involved in a religion, this notice does not apply to you.

But if you are searching for religious meaning in this life, you may want to be Jewish. Contrary to what many people—including many Jews—believe, Judaism has always sought new adherents. That is why the Jewish tradition emphasizes that Abraham, the first Jew, was a convert.

If you are on a quest for truth, or for meaning, or for a moral way of life, or for sanctity in a secular world, or for religious meaning, or for all of these, we invite you to consider Judaism.

Contact any of the organizations listed here for further information on classes that culminate in a Sabbath experience with a Jewish family. And pick up any of the books listed below to better understand how Judaism can enrich your life.

Of course, experiencing Judaism in a Jewish home is hardly the only way to embark on Jewish outreach. I cite it only to make it clear that each individual Jew can play a major role in letting the world know that Jews welcome converts. But inviting non-Jews to Jewish homes achieves an additional goal that is as great as attracting people to Judaism: it engenders goodwill between Jews and non-Jews.

The most public and organized role must of course be played by Jewish organizations. Through newspaper ads, word of mouth, public forums, etc., Jewish organizations can make it known that the Jews are back in the business of taking the world seriously as Jews, that Judaism, too, has something distinctive to offer troubled humanity.

For God's sake, for the Jews' sake, and for the sake of a world that in this century produced the monstrous evils of Nazism, Communism, and other ideologies of mass cruelty, we must at least try.

I believe, almost "with perfect faith," that it would work.

NOTE

1. Reported by Professor Jakob Petuchowski, who heard Rabbi Baeck make this statement at a public lecture.

⤙ 7 ⤚

Egon Mayer

Why Not Judaism?

Dr, Egon Mayer, professor of sociology at Brooklyn College and the Center for Jewish Studies at the City University of New York, is perhaps the foremost expert on the statistics of intermarriage. He has been studying and writing about the subject for as long as it has been part of the Jewish communal agenda; indeed, his studies for the American Jewish Committee helped make the issue vital, as did his important book *Love and Tradition: Marriage Between Jews and Christians.*

Unsurprisingly, then, Dr. Mayer focuses on intermarriage in this article. He sees conversion to Judaism as one important potential answer to the perplexing questions aroused by intermarriage; it is one vital part of Jewish outreach. Dr. Mayer is director of the Jewish Outreach Institute, which is in the forefront of doing research in the area of outreach. Outreach itself is an evolving concept, and it should be understood that seeking converts is only part of its pluralistic goals.

———◆———

Evangelism, marketing and social work—in a delicate blend—comprise a newly emerging Jewish movement called outreach. Placing far greater emphasis on group survival and family harmony than on teaching salvation or any other doctrines of faith, outreach is the vehicle for a transformation of U.S. Jews. A demographic shift is occurring that will transform American Jews from "a people that dwell alone" into a unique American minority: one that takes advantage of cultural pluralism not only by *blending* into the majority but by *absorbing* large numbers of the majority as well.

If present trends continue—and they almost surely will—converts to Judaism—or Jews-by-choice, as many prefer to be called—will comprise a substantial and increasing proportion of the American Jewish population.

From about 1 percent in the first few decades of this century, they grew to about 3 percent in the 1970s and 1980s. It is entirely possible that Jews-by-choice will comprise between 7 and 10 percent of the American Jewish population by 2010.

According to the 1990 National Jewish Population Study (NJPS), about 120,000 American Jews have joined the fold by formal religious conversion. Another 65,000 identify themselves as Jewish even though they were not born Jewish and did not undergo formal conversion. These people are Jewish only by self-definition, without the benefit of clergy. Together, the two groups (generally referred to as Jews-by-choice) comprise 3.3 percent of the current American Jewish population of 5.5 million.

As small a minority as these two groups are at present, they nonetheless represent a novel development in the evolving relationship between Jews and gentiles in the modern world. They also suggest a source of demographic replenishment.

Probably fewer than a thousand gentiles per year became Jews-by-choice before 1965. The rate more than doubled between the mid-1960s and the early 1970s, to about 1,800 per year between 1965 and 1974 and 3,200 between 1975 and 1984. By the end of the 1980s and in the early 1990s, the number has risen to around 3,600 per year.

Aside from their demographic impact, these new Jews are having a wide-ranging impact on the institutional programs and policies of the organized Jewish community as well as on its ideological mindscape.

"Twenty-five or thirty years ago I would perform just a few conversions a year, privately in my study," say rabbis who have been in American synagogue pulpits for decades. Today there are formally organized "Introduction to Judaism" courses at such places as the 92nd Street YM-YWHA in New York, the University of Judaism in Los Angeles and at centers of the Union of American Hebrew Congregations throughout the country, with some enrolling as many as several hundred students a year.

The reason for the upsurge in conversions to Judaism is neither a new-found spirit of evangelism among Jews nor a sudden Mosaic epiphany among gentiles. The principal reason is interfaith marriage between Jews and gentiles.

According to the 1990 NJPS, more than half of all currently married Jews who married since 1985 have married someone who was not born or raised Jewish. This figure contrasts sharply with the approximately 11 percent of currently married Jews who chose non-Jewish partners prior to 1965. The first sign of change occurred between 1965 and 1974, when 31 percent of marrying Jews chose a spouse who was not born or raised Jewish. Among

Jews getting married between 1975 and 1984, about 51 percent chose a spouse who was not born or raised Jewish. Since the mid-1980s that figure has risen to about 53 percent.

Synagogues, Jewish community centers, Jewish family service agencies and even such national service organizations as Hadassah and B'nai B'rith Women are rushing to create outreach programs to cope with what appears to be a demographic revolution brewing in the melting pot—the large-scale entry of gentiles into the Jewish family. Though not all the programs have conversion as their main goal, all aim to help the interfaith married family, particularly the gentile spouse and children, feel more at home in the Jewish community.

Historians disagree about whether Judaism was ever a vigorously proselytizing faith. Dio Cassius, a Roman writer of the third century, asserts that when Jews flocked to Rome in the first and second century C.E., they converted many natives to their own ways. Seneca, the Roman philosopher and tragedian of the first century, moaned, "The customs of this most accursed race have prevailed to such an extent that they are everywhere received. The conquered have imposed their laws on the conquerors." References can also be found in the writings of ancient commentators like Juvenal and Tacitus about the apparently widespread acceptance of Judaism in the Graeco-Roman world. Philo, the first-century Alexandrian philosopher, wrote that "a great number of other nations imitate the Jewish way of living" and estimated that in his time as many as a million Jews lived in Egypt—a figure that would not have been possible without large scale conversion among the native Egyptian population.

The late Salo Baron of Columbia University, the most distinguished scholar of Jewish history in recent times, estimated that perhaps as much as 10 percent of the population of the ancient Roman empire was made up of Jews as a result of widespread conversions among the pagan populations who came under the influence of the exiles of ancient Judea.

Other scholars cite passages from the Talmud that suggest that the rabbis of ancient Israel accepted converts reluctantly as an accommodation to personal needs. "Converts are as troublesome to Israel as the plague of leprosy," says Rabbi Chelbo in the Talmud (*Yevamot* 47b). Other rabbis worry that proselytes "delay the coming of the messiah." It is not at all clear from the record of arcane ancient debates to what extent, if any, ordinary Jews extended themselves in their relations with the gentiles of the ancient world to try to bring them "under the canopy of the Torah."

One fact about the history of Jewish evangelism does stand out quite clearly. As Christianity became the dominant religion in the waning Roman

Empire, a succession of edicts made it increasingly risky for Jews to accept, much less to seek out, converts. In the year 339 C.E. Emperor Constantine ordered the confiscation of property of anyone who abetted the conversion of a Christian to Judaism. Subsequent imperial edicts decreed imprisonment, expulsion and even death for Jews who helped gentiles convert.

The rise of Islam in the seventh century added yet another impediment to any Jewish inclination for evangelizing. In 624 Mohammed began a war of annihilation against the Jews of Arabia. After his victories in 628, he promulgated a series of laws that forbade the remaining Jews from accepting any Moslem convert on the pain of death. A Moslem who converted on his own would face the loss of all his worldly possessions.

The historical record of the past 1,600 years gives ample evidence of the seriousness of these edicts in both the East and the West. As recently as 1849, Warder Cresson, a well-to-do Quaker from Philadelphia, found himself declared insane by his family because he converted to Judaism. Only after a protracted court battle was he able to establish his sanity. In 1749, Valentin Potocki, a Lithuanian nobleman, was burned at the stake in the middle of Vilnius because he chose to abandon his Christian faith and practice Judaism. Roughly at the same time in England, Lord George Gordon, a former president of the United Protestant League, was condemned to spend the rest of his life in prison on a concocted charge that thinly veiled his contemporaries' fury at the fact that Lord Gordon became Israel bar Abraham, a practicing Jew.

Because of the seriousness with which Christian and Moslem authorities clamped down on any incidence of Jewish conversion, rabbis from the early Middle Ages on took a highly restrictive attitude toward prospective proselytes. The *Code of Jewish Law (Shulchan Aruch)*, compiled in the late sixteenth century, pathetically informs the reader in its preface to the laws on conversion that its provisions apply "only where the civil authorities permit Jews to accept converts." It calls on Jews to discourage those seeking conversion. Only after the prospective convert refuses to be dissuaded are rabbis permitted to facilitate the Jewish education and conversion of the candidate.

In light of the long historical record of external constraints and internal restraints against seeking converts, Judaism has been regarded by both Jews and gentiles as a nonproselytizing religion.

Forced by ghetto walls into separatism, Judaism flowered in its intensity and intellectual fermentation even as Christianity and Islam spread in breadth. While the latter gained multitudes of adherents worldwide, the former sprouted a multitude of ideas about what Judaism means to its adherents who lived as minorities in tension with their dominant host cultures.

Yet, while world Jewry had long abandoned any programmatic effort to missionize to the gentiles, it never broke entirely with the creed of the prophet Isaiah, who believed that "Israel shall be a light unto the nations that My salvation may reach the end of the earth." David Belin, a prominent attorney from Des Moines, Iowa, who has played a major role in transforming American Jewish attitudes toward "outreach to the gentiles," founded the Jewish Outreach Institute in 1987, citing the Isaiah who looked to the day when the house of the one God would be called "a house of prayer for all people."

Not that Jews as a group ever believed that the faith of Israel is a prerequisite for spiritual salvation (as, for example, Christians believe in the necessity of accepting Jesus as savior). But most Jews have believed—and most probably continue to believe—in the world-perfecting efficacy of a life lived according to the social ethics of the Torah and the Talmud.

In radical departure from their long history, American Jews are increasingly becoming convinced that it would be better for themselves as individuals and for the Jewish people as a whole if hundreds of thousands of gentiles were to become Jews.

To be sure, no American Jew is likely anytime soon to knock on his Christian neighbors' door to try to bring them the "good news" of Moses or the Talmud. The new Jewish evangelism bears little resemblance to the more familiar Christian variants. Nor have American Jews experienced any theological change of heart. The Jewish belief system has always been pluralistic: "All God's children have a place in the world to come," regardless of whether they believe in the Buddha, Christ, Allah or Elohim. The emerging attitude is not about the salvation of the soul or even about the truth claims of a creed. Instead, it is about the survival of the Jewish family and, by extension, the Jewish community.

The mission and methods of the new Jewish outreach movement are not theological but sociological. They are driven by a growing fear that, due to the high and increasing incidence of marriage between Jews and gentiles, Jews are fast becoming a demographically endangered species. The potential for extinction this time, however, is not the result of hate and persecution but rather of love and absorption-by-matrimony into a benignly accepting majority.

The formal break with about 1,600 years of Jewish diffidence about welcoming converts actually occurred a little more than 10 years ago. Its consequences, however, are just beginning to crystallize in the lives of hundreds of thousands of families and in the multitude of Jewish institutions that comprise the organized Jewish community in modern America.

On December 2, 1978, Rabbi Alexander Schindler, president of the Union of American Hebrew Congregations (UAHC)—whose members comprise about one-third of American Jewry—proposed that Jews, or at least Reform Jews, begin to "reach out to" the religiously unaffiliated, particularly those who have married Jews.

"I believe," he said in his address to the Board of Trustees of the UAHC, "that it is time for our movement to launch a carefully conceived outreach program aimed at all Americans who are unchurched and who are seeking roots in religion. . . . My friends, we Jews possess the water that can slake the thirst, the bread that can sate the great hunger. Let us offer it freely, proudly—for *our* well-being and for the sake of those who earnestly seek what is ours to give."

Remarkable words for the religious leader of a portion of the community that has borne the reputation and practice, since the fall of the Roman Empire, of *not* seeking converts.

Schindler's words were not welcome in all Jewish quarters. Traditional Jews, particularly the Orthodox, were outraged at the chutzpah of a Reform rabbi proposing to "make Jews" by standards contrary to traditional Jewish law, known as *halachah*.

Apart from its general hesitancy in welcoming converts, *halachah* requires that converts "accept the yoke of the Torah," that is, obey the complex Jewish ritual system, undergo ritual immersion in a *mikveh* (ritual bath), a ceremony that is historically the forerunner of Christian baptism, and have themselves circumcised, in the case of males.

Even as it pioneered outreach, the Reform movement has not followed all of the traditional standards for conversion. For example, many Reform rabbis were quite ready to accept converts without requiring ritual immersion in the *mikveh* or requiring ritual circumcision for men. The Conservative and Reconstructionist movements (about 40 percent of American Jewry), which soon began to follow Reform's lead on outreach, also take a less stringent attitude toward the basis on which they'll accept converts to Judaism. While the rabbis of these two latter movements do require *mikveh* immersion and ritual circumcision for men, they are far more willing than their Orthodox counterparts to accept converts who wish to become Jews, even if the applicant is motivated by a prospective marriage to a Jew and is not committed to full practice of all the rituals required by the traditional religious system.

Indeed, the last 10 years of battle in the Israeli Knesset over the Law of Return—which revolves around the question of who is a Jew—has been largely stimulated by Schindler's 1978 manifesto and the programs of outreach that flowed from it.

One group of militant Orthodox rabbis, the Shofar Association, took out full-page advertisements in the *New York Times* and other newspapers warning readers: "Beware of Counterfeit Conversions" to Judaism. The Association of Sephardic Rabbis, also a highly traditional group, placed a complete ban on any and all conversions to Judaism.

Liberal and secular American Jews were frightened that Schindler's call for outreach would upset the détente in Jewish-Christian relations, in effect at least since Vatican II in 1965, which said Catholics would not actively seek to convert Jews. Some feared that a Jewish outreach program would rekindle theological antisemitism and possibly undermine American support for Israel.

More importantly, the masses of American Jews who were the target audience for Schindler's message do not possess the religious zeal it takes to fuel a missionary movement. Few could see themselves as "a light unto the nations" in any but the most secularized sense. More personally still, Jews who had married gentiles were most reluctant to upset the emotional balance that seems to regulate the handling of religious and cultural differences in interfaith families.

Tellingly, Jewish fears to the contrary notwithstanding, the reaction from Protestant and Catholic quarters has remained a resounding silence. As the renowned sociologist of religion, Peter Berger observed in a May 1979, article, "Converting the Gentiles?" in *Commentary* magazine,

> The mainline Christian churches are in a state of theological exhaustion and are most unlikely to be roused from it by a little Jewish proselytizing. . . . it seems unlikely that the conversion to Judaism of a few lapsed Presbyterians would provoke antisemitic reactions—except among those already so disposed. It is equally hard to imagine that irate Presbyterians [or anyone else] would launch a missionary counteroffensive.

But if the Christian denominations were not roused to "defend the faith" against the call for Jewish outreach, neither were the various branches of Judaism moved to *actively* seek out America's "unchurched" and bring them to temple. Although Schindler's Reform movement created a Commission on Outreach in 1983, its principal function was to create educational programs that would help interfaith married families and their children feel more comfortable in the Jewish community—to *facilitate* rather than to *instigate* conversion.

Though professing philosophical support for the idea of outreach, neither the Conservative nor the Reconstructionist branches of American Judaism made the least effort to seek out the religiously unaffiliated gentiles or even to aid those who are seeking entry into Judaism of their own volition.

All the while, the major secular Jewish organizations that each year collect hundreds of millions of dollars for Jewish philanthropies in Israel and in the United States and provide such services as local community centers for education, culture and recreation and social services for troubled families and the like have remained totally aloof from the issue. Even long-established community relations agencies, like the Anti-Defamation League of B'nai B'rith, the American Jewish Congress and the American Jewish Committee, which have many decades of experience in interfaith dialogue and cooperation, took a position of benign neglect when it came to promoting outreach.

They studied it, earnestly discussed it at conferences, maybe even hoped for it. But they did nothing to advance it.

How, then, did it happen that by the end of the 1980s there were nearly 200,000 new Jews—up from only about a third as many 25 years earlier?

A survey conducted in the summer of 1990 at the Center for Jewish Studies of the City University of New York Graduate School under the sponsorship of the Jewish Outreach Institute (JOI) has revealed a change of heart on the part of the American Jewish leadership on the issue of conversion. Tapping the attitudes of more than 2,000 rabbis, synagogue presidents, Jewish community service professionals and other lay leaders, the JOI survey found that 80 to 90 percent favored the conversion of the gentile partner to Judaism in interfaith marriage. That is a remarkably high rate of approval for a phenomenon that was virtually unheard of just three generations ago.

Moreover, those figures betoken a surprisingly high degree of consensus among people who are generally better known for fractiousness on issues of religious ideology.

The new welcoming attitude toward converts is not to be found in the policies of any of the denominations or organizations. Instead it is rooted in what might be called the conditional embrace of the Jewish family.

One facet of this conditional embrace, its matrimonial dimension, is captured in a vignette by the late Paul Cowan, coauthor of *Mixed Blessings: Marriage Between Jews and Christians* (Doubleday, 1987), reflecting on his wife's conversion to Judaism:

> For years I had thought I was completely indifferent to Rachel's religious decisions. She was the wife I loved, no matter what she chose to call herself. But now I knew I felt stronger because Rachel was one of us.

Paul's elation that "Rachel was one of us" is a feeling reported by almost all Jews whose gentile spouses convert to Judaism. With but rare exceptions, most Jews-by-choice will acknowledge that either in the courtship stage or after marriage they'd been made to feel, by spouse or in-laws, that they would be more enthusiastically loved and accepted by the Jewish family if they became Jewish themselves.

Perhaps psychological seduction is as bold as Jewish evangelism gets.

The conditional embrace that seems to be associated with Jewish conversion is not based on any theological ambitions for the salvation of the gentile spouse or in-laws. Instead it is based on a more mundane but very real existential concern about family continuity.

Jewish proselytizing is emerging as a desperate effort by American Jewish parents, whose adult children are increasingly choosing gentile marriage partners, to ensure that they will nevertheless have Jewish grandchildren. As Peter Berger put it in 1979, "It is reasonable to regard Rabbi Schindler's proposal as a sensible and low-risk measure of Jewish demographic self-defense."

The form taken by this measure of "demographic self-defense" is a new Jewish evangelism based not on zealous advocacy for a creed but anxiety about the survival of family identity. It is not a mission designed to replace a religious error with a religious truth. Instead it is a subtle effort, comprised largely of self-help workshops and educational programs, to assure Jewish family continuity by having gentile spouses and offspring converted and absorbed into a Jewish life-style.

Indeed, among the more surprising features of the new Jewish proselytizing effort is its total lack of religious zeal. In sharp contrast to religious missionary movements in general, the Jewish outreach is germinating among the least religious segments of the community. Among the most highly acculturated American Jews there is a growing fear that their very success in adapting to modern America may result in the rapid decline of the Jewish community within two or three generations.

Since the early 1970s, when marriage between Jews and gentiles began to skyrocket, the number of conversions has grown steadily. Nearly 90 percent of all conversions to Judaism take place within the context of interfaith marriage. While most conversions take place prior to marriage, about a third will occur sometime after the marriage. Gentile women are much more likely to convert to Judaism than are gentile men: About 80 percent of all converts to Judaism are women.

According to tradition, before a candidate can be considered for conversion, the supervising rabbis must be assured that the conversion is solely for the sake of religious conviction. *Halachah*, which still binds most Orthodox and some Conservative Jews, forbids the acceptance of converts if they are joining out of such ulterior motives as marriage to a Jewish spouse, desire to be better accepted by Jewish in-laws or desire to produce Jewish children.

But interfaith marriage is the single most powerful social force that is driving the high numbers of conversions to Judaism and the radical trans-formation of Jewish attitudes toward it. It is also, thereby, altering the age-old group relations between Jews and gentiles

The mass migration of Jews from Eastern Europe to America at the end of the nineteenth and early twentieth centuries and the subsequent killing in the Holocaust of those who remained behind produced a new climate in Jewish-gentile relations. From the perspective of immigrant Jews and their descendants, the remarkable hospitality of a pluralistic America evoked a sense of gratitude toward its culture. Jews embraced the civil religion of early twentieth century America, its emphasis on human equality, individualism, the right to be left alone, the abundant freedoms guaranteed by the Constitu-tion and the abundant economic opportunity.

Initially Jews happily ignored some of the more Christian elements of the American ethos—the quasi-official character of such Christian holidays as Christmas and Easter, certain forms of residential and occupational exclu-sion and the pervasive Christian influence on the arts, education and culture.

Perhaps as a result of their enthusiastic embrace of America, Jews, in turn, have also been enthusiastically embraced by the golden land. Public opinion polls since the mid-1950s have consistently registered the decline of prejudice against Jews. Conversely, tolerance among the American public for interfaith marriage between Jews and Christians has increased from about 59 percent in the late 1960s to nearly 80 percent in the late 1980s. The ques-tion usually asked to determine this is: "Would you accept a member of this group in marriage with your own children?" Respondents are offered a list of minorities such as Catholics, African-Americans, Jews and the like. In a matter of two or three generations American Jews became the paragon of the successful minority within the American mosaic.

One consequence of Jewish success as a favorite American minority is that as Jews secured the tolerance and amiability of their gentile neighbors they became less distinctive in their religious beliefs and life-style. Acceptance from the outside was increasingly reciprocated by blending from the inside.

Jewish entrée into the highest echelons of commerce, culture and politi-cal life has only increased pressure on American Jews to become just like their gentile peers—particularly since successful assimilation into modern secularized America has not required any Christian creedal affirmation. The increasing generational distance from immigrant ancestors has further attenuated the influence of tradition upon American Jewish lives. Thus, as the postwar baby-boom generation of America's Jews has come into middle age, they have increasingly come to take for granted the lack of Jewish distinctiveness in their everyday lives that their parents had cultivated only as a public strategy of adaptation to America. For their children it has come to prevail in private life as well, as the uniquely American form of Jewish identity.

In light of the Jewish emphasis on the family as the bearer and transmitter of tradition, the most alarming consequence of this transformation of Jewish identity has been its impact on Jewish mate selection. Quite simply, young American Jews since the end of the 1950s have found less reason to filter out their gentile friends as potential marriage mates. In short, interfaith marriage has been one of the inexorable results of the highly successful blending of Jews in America. From that perspective, one might have expected most Jews to rejoice about the marital trends of their children and grandchildren over the past three decades. But alarm, anxiety, even disapproval have been the far more common Jewish responses to interfaith marriage.

But, unlike their ancestors who, like the famed Tevye from *Fiddler on the Roof*, reacted with outrage when a child intermarried, modern American Jews have responded with a characteristically more pragmatic attitude.

As countless parents, facing the prospect of an interfaith marriage, have put it: "We don't want to lose our religion, but we don't want to lose our children and grandchildren either." This complex attitude, born from generalized American respect for one's ancestral roots, on the one hand, and the child-centered familism that uniquely animates American Jews, on the other, has had paradoxical consequences.

First, it has greatly diminished the age-old control Jewish parents had exercised over the mating choices of their children—thereby lessening the parental resistance to interfaith marriage.

Second, the child-centeredness of American Jewish family life has also spilled over into the expectation Jews have of their religious and communal institutions. Rather than wanting those institutions to be the steadfast bearers of an unchanging tradition, they look to those institutions to adapt to their own changing family needs.

In retrospect, Rabbi Schindler's call for Jewish outreach was more a signal for Jewish leaders to accommodate to the reality of interfaith marriage among their own children than a call to spiritual arms to save the souls of the unchurched. His call simply reflected the emerging reality of the 1980s: families are turning to their synagogues and communal institutions to help them deal with the fact of interfaith marriage rather than to help them fight it.

Where once they might have turned to those institutions for comfort in the face of a crisis like interfaith marriage—and perhaps to absolve them from a sense of personal failure because their children married gentiles—Jews now want solutions to the problem of stigma and exclusion by making their institutions more embracing. Where once they might have turned to a rabbi or other communal leader to help them prevent or emotionally cope with a family problem like interfaith marriage, Jews now want their leaders to mirror in communal policies the emotional acceptance that most express for their children's marriage choices.

Finally, the new welcoming attitude toward converts in the Jewish community reflects a new sense of realism about what it takes for a religious minority to survive, and maybe even thrive, in a free, open and pluralistic society. The realization that interfaith marriage cannot be stopped has led American Jews in most cases to a fundamental philosophical change, which might be summed up, albeit somewhat glibly in a twist on an old cliché: If we can't beat 'em, let 'em join us.

David Polish

Jewish Proselyting—Another Opinion

It should come as no surprise that these calls for seeking converts would meet resistance from within the Jewish community. David Polish, a Reform rabbi and former president of the Central Conference of Reform Rabbis, is one articulate dissenter. Rabbi Polish begins his analysis of Rabbi Schindler's call for an outreach program first by noting that Jewish tradition was one of welcoming converts. However, Rabbi Polish—in contrast to Ben Zion Wacholder's analysis of the Tosafists—believes that such efforts are not a *mitzvah* comparable to other *mitzvot*. Rabbi Polish also considers Rabbi Schindler's call to action as a counterpoint to the Christian world's retreat from a sense of reaching out to attract new members of the faith, at least in the ways Jews long associated with Christian missionary activities. After also considering the Jewish dissent aroused by different conversionary requirements, Rabbi Polish considers alternatives to Rabbi Schindler's proposal.

———•———

In 1962, Leon Fram made the following statement in a paper to the Central Conference of American Rabbis, entitled "What Is Judaism's Mission in the Contemporary World?": "In order to define our mission, we need not go far afield. We need not go exploring for some new cause to adopt. It is the same mission which the Prophets proclaimed and which the Pharisees sought to translate into the conduct of daily life. . . . In the Free World Order which is ahead of us, and which Judaism will be effective in bringing about, we can be free to resume the active missionary work we carried on in the days of the Pharisees. There are already some stirrings in this direction." While this was a personal statement on the part of Rabbi Fram, it was not at all uncharacteristic of a significant segment of the Reform rabbinate, as the discussion which followed his paper appeared to indicate.

Most recently, this was spelled out in greater detail by Alexander Schindler at the board meeting of the Union of American Hebrew Congregations in December 1978. Rabbi Schindler's presentation derives from his concern over the growing corrosive power of intermarriage and its consequent threat to American Judaism. The greater part of his address is devoted to this issue, on which he presents five points. First, "The conversion of the non-Jewish partner-to-be is clearly the first desideratum." Second, "Jews-by-choice have special needs and we need special guidance on how to meet them. . . . Newcomers to Judaism must embark, in effect, on a long-term naturalization process and they require knowledgeable and sympathetic guides to help them along the way." Third, "Our Reform congregations must do everything possible to draw into Jewish life the non-Jewish spouse of a mixed marriage." Fourth, "There is a possibility of the harmonization of tradition with modern need" in recognizing the Jewish legitimacy of a child born to an intermarried non-Jewish mother. Our movement has adhered to these principles, although we have not pursued items two and three as vigorously as we should. Rabbi Schindler's call in these areas should be given fullest support.

The fifth and the most controversial proposal is far more specific. "It is time for our movement to launch a carefully conceived outreach program aimed at all Americans who are unchurched and who are seeking roots in religion. . . . I call on our members to resume their time-honored vocation and to become champions for Judaism. . . . These words imply not just passive acceptance but affirmative action."

This was quickly ratified by the Union board, which resolved "to plan a special program to bring the message of Judaism to any and all who wish to examine or embrace it. [Note that the limitation to the unchurched is no longer in evidence, that instead "any and all" are invoked.] Judaism is not an exclusive club of born Jews [This is gratuitous. What responsible Jew ever said it was an exclusive club?]: It is a universal faith with an ancient tradition which has deep resonance for people alive today." (Note again that the unchurched have been replaced by "people alive today," and that universalism without any particulartistic mitigation is dominant.)

Rabbi Schindler's call emerges from the midst of our present condition, intermarriage, and it seeks validation in our "time-honored vocation." Leaving aside momentarily the merits of his program, his appeal to the past is authentic. The seminal scholarly works by our own colleagues, William Braude and Bernard Bamberger, give sound validation to the fact that in talmudic and early Christian times, converts were not only welcomed by our tradition but were sought and encouraged. "Both in Palestine and Babylonia—despite the fall of the state, despite persecution, despite the rise of Christianity, the Rabbis wanted converts and got them and held them. Their success in the face of such discouraging odds is the best proof of their missionary ardor" (Bamberger, *Proselytism in the Talmudic Period*, 291).

It is of considerable significance that in his *Hazal-Pirke Emunot V' Deot*, Ephraim Urbach cites Braude and Bamberger in a manner indicating that they have said all that can be said on the subject. I hypothesize that, much later, Judah Ha-Levi's *Kuzari* might have been more than an apologetic work and could have been a subtly disguised missionary document, intended not so much to defend Judaism as to persuade seekers. The narrative background in which Christian, Moslem, Philosopher and Jew compete for the Khazar's allegiance seems to support this. The passage in Part I (Hirschfeld edition, 79) describing the method of conversion in Judaism is suggestive. In such a context the historical record of the Khazars and their conversion gives implicit support to Ha-Levi's argument. Nor should we overlook the fact that Ha-Levi wrote his book in Arabic and in a milieu in which Jews partook "of the fullness of intellectual and economic opportunity" (Salo Baron). In such a milieu, Ha-Levi's discreet overtures could have been possible. I cite the documented rabbinic record and the tantalizing possibility concerning the *Kuzari* to stress that the appeal to the past is sound and convincing. But having said that, I must differ with Rabbi Schindler's fifth conclusion and the concurrent action by the UAHC board on the ground that for this time and for this issue, appeal to the past is irrelevant.

Before spelling out my argument, it should be pointed out that the tradition of Jewish proselyting is by no means to be equated with its critical importance in Christianity and also that it does not stand in the upper levels of the Jewish hierarchy of values. In New Testament and in apostolic Christianity, proselyting is *the* central *mitzvah*. Faith in Jesus is the central doctrine and, derivatively, the call to spread the gospel about him is *the* essential, indispensable act that must be performed. The New Testament abounds with calls to "come after me and I will make you become fishers of men" (Mark 1:17); "the gospel must first be published among all nations" (Mark 13:10); "by whom we have received grace and apostleship, for obedience to the faith among all nations, for his name" (Romans 1:5).

Most compelling of all is "Go ye into all the world and preach the gospel to every creature" (Mark 16:15). These are among the last words of Jesus to his disciples, to whom he appeared after his resurrection. This is his final and most urgent mandate, his last will and testament reinforced by the threat of damnation for those who do not believe, and here the dogma of "no salvation outside the church" originates. The Gospel according to Mark then concludes by telling that "they went forth and preached everywhere" (16:20).

This cardinal *mitzvah* was fulfilled with alacrity. Before the middle of the second century, Justin Martyr tells, "There exists not a people, whether Greek or Barbarian, or any other race . . . however ignorant of arts or agriculture, whether they dwell under tents or wander in covered wagons, among whom prayers are not offered in the name of a crucified Jesus to the Father of all things" (*Dialogue with Trypho*, 117).

Jewish proselyting, however, commands neither such urgency nor centrality. It is an important task, not a mandate. It was a high enterprise, not a compelling *mitzvah*. It was practiced zealously, but in a dimension other than those *mitzvot* for which Jews were required to make sacrifices, sometimes even unto death—*Shabbat, shofar, lulav,* teaching and learning Torah. There is no such principle as "no salvation outside the Synagogue." To the contrary, the doctrine that *"hasidei umot ha'olam* have a share in the world to come" presented an option to those outside the faith that was absent in Christianity. Isaiah 42:6 (*l'or goyim*), which is regarded as paradigmatic, at least in Reform, is not consensually treated as a call to proselyting. It has none of the compulsion of the resurrected Jesus' last words. Rashi interprets *l'or goyim,* "Every tribe (in Israel) is called *goy.*" Radak states that the passage has two connotations, the first being that the nations will enjoy peace because of Israel; the second, that the nations "will keep the seven laws [of Noah] and will go in a good way." *Metzudat David* states, "To light up the eyes of all the nations so that they will know that *Adonai* is God." This is hardly a fervent call to mission.

At issue in this discussion is not the prevalence or legitimacy of proselyting in Judaism during talmudic times but rather its position in the Jewish scale of values. We do not need to make gratuitous comparisons with such values as *Shabbat* and *milah,* which are not only paramount but occupy altogether different categories which we might call theocentric–covenantal. There is, however, an act of humanistic *hesed,* clearly defined as a *mitzvah,* which is analogous to proselyting inasmuch as it, too, is concerned with human redemption and restoration to the fold of Jewish life—*pidyon shvuyim.* This *mitzvah* has been both continuous and imperative in our history and clearly occupies a dominant place. In *Baba Batra* (8a–b), there is a discussion on whether even orphans are required to contribute to charity. R. Shmuel ben Yehudah determines that they are not required to do so, *even* for ransoming captives. The discussion continues: "Ifra Hormizd, the mother of King Shapur, sent a purse of dinars to R. Yoseph, with the request that it should be used for carrying out a great *mitzvah.* R. Yoseph considered what such a *mitzvah* could be, when Abaye said to him, 'Since R. Shmuel ben Yehudah has taught that money for charity is not to be raised from orphans even for the redemption of captives, we conclude that *pidyon shvuyim* is a very great *mitzvah*." The *Tosefta* adds that if a *Sefer Torah* may be sold so that one might teach Torah or marry a wife, it goes without saying that this also applies to *pidyon shvuyim*.

The urgency, imperativeness, and unabating continuity of this *mitzvah* that has truly commanded us down to this day is set forth with utmost clarity in these passages. Matthew could have said with even greater appropriateness, "Ye compass sea and land to rescue a single captive." The vocation of proselyting is thus not comparable with the intensity of the *mitzvah* of ransoming captives. It should finally be noted that, halachically, proselyting is not one of the *Taryag Mitzvot*, nor is it referred to as a *mitzvah* in talmudic literature, in the Rambam's *Mishneh Torah* or *Sefer Hamitzvot*.

We return to the issue of relevance. The impressive record of and commitment to Jewish proselyting had little bearing on the medieval Jewish strategy of desisting from the practice. No one in a Christian land would have insisted that, since this was our vocation, we should actively pursue it. Thousands were willing to die and be killed *al kiddush ha' shem*, but no one was willing to die in order to bring a Christian under the wings of the *Shechinah*. Hence, the suspension of Jewish proselyting was prompted not only for reasons of prudence and security, which Jews disregarded in other cases, but because it was not a supreme requirement.

I would now argue that for a different set of reasons, contemporary realities make the case for Jewish proselyting equally irrelevant. The first set of reasons pertains to our relationship with the non-Jewish world. (I will not consider the admonition that we proceed with sophistication and consideration for the sensitivity of Christians, and that we limit ourselves to the unchurched. These are matters of tactical policy which can easily be breached, as the Union board resolution, coming quick on the heels of Rabbi Schindler's address, would seem to indicate.) The Union board ratified a call to proselyting precisely at a time in religious affairs when a significant part of the Christian world has begun to withdraw if not retreat, and certainly to reassess its mission to the Jews. The magnitude of this event, for it is truly an historic event, can best be understood against the centrality of this commitment in New Testament Christianity. This could constitute virtually a revised exegesis of, if not an excision from, the very heart of Christian scripture. It would be somewhat similar to an expurgation from our *T'nach*, or at least an attenuation, of the concept of *Shivat Zion*. What a far cry from early Christianity, which was openly fighting Judaism for the souls of men. What a far cry from the first gathering of the World Council of Churches in Amsterdam only three years after World War II, when the declaration went forth to Christendom: "We cannot forget that we meet in a land from which 110,000 Jews were taken to be murdered. . . . All of our churches stand under the commission of our common Lord, 'Go ye into all the world and preach the Gospel to every creature.' The fulfillment of this commission requires that we include the Jewish people in our evangelistic task" (*Official Report*, The First Assembly of the World Council of Churches, 180).

The reassessment by various sectors in Christianity is not coming about primarily out of theological or intellectual considerations, but because of the Shoah. If the World Council of Churches was not abashed by its brazen and contemptible insensitivity, others may have been. In April 1958, Reinhold Niebuhr, writing in our own *Journal*, abjured the principle of carrying the gospel to the Jews. He wrote:

> The problem of the Christian majority, particularly in America, is therefore to come to terms with the stubborn will to live of the Jews as a peculiar people, both religiously and ethnically. The problem can be solved only if the Christian and Gentile majority accepts this fact and ceases to practice tolerance provisionally in the hope that it will encourage assimilation ethnically and conversion religiously. . . .
>
> The Christian majority can achieve a more genuine tolerance only if it assumes the continued refusal of the Jew to be assimilated, either ethnically or religiously. That recognition involves an appreciation of the resources of Jewish life, morally and religiously, which make Judaism something other than an inferior form of religion such as must ultimately recognize the superiority of the Christian faith and end its long resistance by capitulation and conversion.

The Vatican Council under Pope John XXIII withdrew by considerable lengths from its traditional *mitzvah*. It may not yet have forsworn its mandate, but it has gone far to inhibit it. "In company with the Prophets and the Apostle, the Church awaits that day, known to God alone, on which all peoples will address the Lord in a single voice and 'serve him shoulder to shoulder'" (Vatican II, *On the Jews*, October 1965). . . . "Relations between Christians and Jews have for the most part been no more than a monologue. A true dialogue must now be established. The dialogue, in effect, comprises a favored means for promoting better mutual understanding and a deepening of one's own tradition. The condition of dialogue is respect for the other as he is, for his faith and religious convictions. All intent of proselytizing and conversion is excluded" (Introduction to the discussions of the plenary session of bishop members of the Secretariat for Promoting Christian Unity, 1969).

The same applies to a segment of the evangelical world where there is, at least, a measure of inhibition about missionizing Jews. Even those evangelicals who anticipate that Jews will ultimately accept Jesus, though without Christian intervention, are thus revising their sacred writ. I believe that not modernity, but, to the contrary, the incursion of the Dark Ages as embodied in the Shoah, has brought this about. In a de facto sense, a theological "SALT" arrangement has been effected between Judaism and much of Christendom. Each will restrain its missals. A Jewish call to mission, however delicately couched, would represent a renunciation of the unwritten understanding. It could be considered a provocation by Jews for the resumption of Christian evangelism in our midst. There could be no more inopportune time than now to jeopardize a truce that could perhaps become a peace. Some would seize the pretext of lifting a reluctant suspension of their mission, perhaps blaming Jews for rejecting a profound Christian concession.

There are equally severe implications for intramural Jewish relations. Once more, the appeal to our traditional vocation holds little relevance. In very early Christian days, as well as later, Jewish proselyting was predicated on the principle of one *halachah*, binding on all Jews. Whatever differences may have existed within the halachic system, the indispensability of *milah* and *mikveh* for conversion was unassailable. Except, of course, for Paul. Whatever the theological and political reason for the rupture with Christianity, halachically it was *milah* that forced the break. This must say something very monitory to Reform. There no longer is a *halachah* acceptable to all Jews. Our position on nonhalachic conversion is well known, and it is a source of tension, especially with Israeli Orthodoxy, but it is a kind of controlled tension. As long as neither side presses the issue, we can manage to live under the formula of uneasy nonbelligerency. But whould we proclaim activism in the realm of proselyting, one of two results must ensue. Either we accept halachic conversion, which some Reform rabbis advocate, with the probability that Reform will become increasingly negligible as a concept, if not as an institution, or we will generate a struggle which could stir accusations of Paulinism against us. Reform has come too far to invite charges of schismatic heresy. Most Reform rabbis are not susceptible to submitting to the demands of halachic conversion and to do so would be to trade possible peace with Orthodoxy for certain conflict within Reform. While certainly prompted by the most earnest of motivations, a call for denominational proselyting, if implemented, could awaken vicious confrontations. A nonhalachic activist Reform mission, going beyond our more restrained present practice, would outrage others who would accuse us of blatant defiance of a sanctum. Were this outrage to take the form, however unlikely, of halachic countermission, there would be open conflict and scandal.

Are there authentic Jewish alternatives to active proselyting? I believe that there are and that, joined to Rabbi Schindler's first four points, they could meet our common concern over threats to Jewish survival and could bring greater numbers into Judaism than could outreach to the unchurched. It is commonplace to point to the obvious 50 percent in Jewish life who are unsynagogued, who belong to no Jewish organizations, who contribute nothing to Jewish causes, who give their children no, or virtually no, Jewish education. Yet should the prospect of attempting to win over even a portion of them be less challenging and less rewarding than seeking the unchurched? Are we ready to write them off? A program of renewal, perhaps shared by as many branches in Jewish life as care to participate, could arouse greater interest and contribute more to Jewish unity than approaches to non-Jews. We may now be giving the impression that our institutions are renouncing the estranged 50 percent of American Jewry. If one of our enemies is intermarriage, another more virulent is Zero Population Growth, which Jews have embraced with characteristically excessive zeal. Should we not engage in a united effort with other Jewish bodies, to restore the *mitzvah* of *p'ru u'r'vu*? To bring the obvious message that a mutilated and depleted people has the task, as well as the moral right, to replenish itself, just as dangerously teeming societies have the task to limit their populations? Let the adherents of situational ethics ponder that. It is not coincidental that Orthodoxy, which has so far been least affected by intermarriage, is also contributing most to the numerical restoration of our people. This proposal should not be evaluated in terms of its apparent difficulties. It is every bit as feasible as proselyting. It certainly commands priority and greater gravity in the scale of *mitzvot*.

A second objective should be the tragic plight of those unmarried Jewish women who encounter the severest difficulty in finding Jewish mates. Contemporary "pop" literature and conventional wisdom are full of stereotypes about the materialistic "Jewish princess" and the arrogant "Jewish prince" whom no sensitive person would have for a partner. This presents us with a dual challenge. In the first place, there may be enough validity to the perceptions to warrant an appraisal of how we are doing as a "kingdom of priests and a holy people." But this gargantuan task must be left for other instruments in Jewish life. The second challenge, however, is more manageable. Does the synagogue, does the Jewish community, have a responsibility, however costly, to take another look at the feasibility of sophisticated *shadchanut* under communal auspices? This would require the efforts of social scientists, psychologists, and rabbis who would attempt to reconcile young people's individualism and sense of independence with the need of many, clearly articulated, for finding mates. How earnestly are we pursuing alternatives to singles' bars?

A third objective should be an assessment of our educational systems. Are they working? Is Jewish commitment appreciably affected by Jewish education or noneducation? Do our communal leaders come out of Jewish school systems, or rather out of other environments more conducive to Jewish commitment? How effective are our outreach activities on campuses? Can we learn from the less conventional methods of other Jewish groups? What of the quality of Jewish life? Does it contribute to disaffection and alienation?

Finally, there are large numbers of Jews who for sociological as well as economic reasons will not join congregations or give their children Jewish educations. They are the poor and the socially insecure, the left-out. It is not that they lack the desire but rather that they are inhibited. Should we not be thinking how to offer their children free schooling without putting the parents through the humiliation of pleading poverty or social dislocation?

There should be no illusions about the magnitude of the task, but can any task be more life-giving and more in the spirit of our people's time-honored vocation?

⇥ 9 ⇤

Jonathan D. Sarna

Reform Jewish Leaders, Intermarriage, and Conversion

Jonathan Sarna, a professor of American Jewish history, sees intermarriage as the cost of living in a free society. He analyzes a study of Reform Jewish leaders and finds that intense Jewish identity and education reduce intermarriage, as would a concerted program to help single Jews meet each other. Dr. Sarna also notes the increase in the number of Jews-by-choice.

Dr. Sarna sees some problems for the integration of converts into the Jewish community, based on his analysis of the responses of Reform Jewish leaders who themselves were converts. For example, he thinks converts do not emphasize the ethnic dimensions of Judaism sufficiently, concentrating instead on the more purely religious factors. The most troubling finding in the study for him was that Reform converts were much more likely to accept intermarriage, say, for their children.

Dr. Sarna's fear is that converts will be one-generation Jews, that their children will either intermarry or themselves convert out of Judaism.

This analysis of Reform Jewish leaders focuses on the need to see conversion not simply as stopping after a conversion ceremony but as continuing after the ceremony to give new Jews a Jewish past, a sensibility, and a passionate attachment not just to a belief system but to a people and a culture, or, in Mordecai Kaplan's resonant summation, a civilization.

INTRODUCTION

Back in 1818, Attorney General William Wirt, one of the finest attorneys general in America's history, wondered in a private letter whether persecutions of the Jews, for all of their unhappy effects, perhaps held the key to Jewish unity. "I believe," he wrote to John Myers of Norfolk, Virginia, "that if those persecutions had never existed the Jews would have melted down into the general mass of the people of the world." He went on to suggest that if persecutions came to an end, the "children of Israel" might even then cease to exist as a separate nation. Within 150 years he was sure that they would be indistinguishable from the rest of mankind.[1]

Now, more than 150 years later, we know that Wirt was wrong: the Jewish people lives on. The relationship that Wirt posited between persecutions and Jewish identity may not be wrong, but to date, we have never had the opportunity to find out. Meanwhile, prophecies of doom have continued unabated. *Look* magazine some years ago featured a cover story on the "Vanishing American Jew." *Look* itself has since vanished, not just once but twice, and the Jewish people lives on. A volume entitled *The End of the Jewish People*, by the French sociologist George Friedman, has also come and gone. Again, the Jewish people lives on. Indeed, somebody once pointed out that prediction is very difficult, especially about the future. This may be particularly worth remembering today.[2]

In speaking about the future, most of us, when we are honest, speak about contemporary trends and extrapolate (usually quite wrongly) that they will continue ad infinitum. So it is that a task force examining the future of Reform Judaism sensibly began with a study of contemporary Reform Jewish leaders. We cannot begin to think about where we are going in the Reform movement until we know where we are now.

To my mind, this study, entitled *Leaders of Reform Judaism*,[3] offers us some very important information. It is an honest study, it is methodologically sophisticated, and it makes available a wealth of interesting data. Like all such studies, it must be used with discernment: the data base is necessarily small; women seem to be overrepresented (60 percent to 40 percent); East Coast Jews are underrepresented; and over 80 percent of the respondents are over the age of 40. Obviously, the leadership of the Reform movement is neither a microcosm of American Jewry nor a microcosm of the Reform movement as a whole. But this study can nevertheless teach us a great deal, especially about the complex question of intermarriage—the central focus, we are told, of the research task force's mandate.

JEWISH KNOWLEDGE

Before turning to this issue, however, I do want to lament that one subject was largely overlooked in this study, and that is the (to my mind) critical question of what Reform Jewish leaders know about Judaism in general and about Reform Judaism in particular. We are, to be sure, given the discouraging information that only about one in five Reform Jewish leaders knows modern Hebrew more than slightly, and that 44 percent have either little or no ability at all even to read prayer book Hebrew. But what about knowledge of Judaism? How many leaders could pass a minimal test in Jewish cultural literacy? Do they read Jewish books, study Jewish texts in translation, look back into Jewish history? I think that it would be important to know, and I furthermore think that if the answer is embarrassing we ought to do something about it. Leadership seminars, summer institutes, serious programs of continuing adult studies, scholarships for those who want to take Jewish studies courses at neighborhood universities—these and similar programs should, in my opinion, all be part of the agenda for the future of Reform Judaism. I believe that such programs would improve the caliber of Reform leaders and the quality of Reform Jewish life itself; and yes, in their own way, I think that such educational programs would also help to counteract intermarriage. I realize that educated Jews, too, meet and fall in love with non-Jews, but if they do, it is some comfort to know that they are at least able to explain why Judaism means so much to them, and why (we hope) they also want it to become the religion of their children.

INTERMARRIAGE

Intermarriage is, as I mentioned, the central focus of this overall study, and it deserves special comment. For just as Attorney General Wirt predicted, the decline of persecution and the rise of interfaith intimacy have made it harder and harder to maintain Jewish distinctiveness. Intermarriage, in other words, is the price we pay for living in a highly tolerant society where Jews and Christians interact freely. Most people today do not, as they once did, intermarry in order to escape Judaism; instead, they intermarry because they happen to meet and fall in love with a non-Jew.[4] Increasingly, for this reason, the intermarriage rates for men and women have converged. It is no longer the case that many more Jewish men intermarry than Jewish women. Bruce Phillips found that in Los Angeles, among under-thirty Jews, the opposite was true; more Jewish women intermarried than men. The conversion rate is similarly far more balanced today than in the past. Whereas among Reform leaders surveyed here 90 percent of the converts were women, today according to Phillips, men are converting at an even higher rate than women.[5] Clearly, then, neither intermarriage nor conversion should be seen as a sex-linked phenomenon. Relevant programs must be directed to men and women alike.

What can we do about intermarriage? The leadership study is pessimistic: "Given the cultural realities of contemporary North America," it concludes, "there is no necessary connection between the degree of one's Jewish religious background, activity and practice and the decision to marry a born non-Jew" (p. 90). Strictly speaking that is correct: there is no "necessary" connection; even ultra-Orthodox Jews occasionally marry born non-Jews. But there certainly is a *statistically significant* connection. This study, Steven M. Cohen's studies, and simple common sense all indicate that, generally speaking, the more intense one's Jewish commitment, the less likely one is to intermarry. Even if one does marry a born non-Jew, one is more likely, given a strong Jewish commitment, to insist that the non-Jewish partner convert.

There is no reason for us to hide or dispute these facts. Instead, I think that we should publicize them widely and use them to make the strongest possible case for encouraging worried Reform Jewish parents to begin nurturing Jewish consciousness early and to continue Jewish education and identity training long past Bar/Bat Mitzvah and Confirmation. This may not guarantee marriage to a nice Jewish boy or girl, but it does at least improve the odds.

Other ways of improving the odds need to be encouraged also. Clearly one of the most effective means of promoting in-group marriage is to place Jews in situations where they are most likely, just in the normal course of events, to meet other Jews. One of the reasons New York City has a lower intermarriage rate than most other Jewish communities in America is precisely this: in New York the odds of meeting a suitable mate who happens to be Jewish are relatively high. Some of our synagogues, temples, Jewish centers, and Hillel houses around the country achieve this same goal through extraordinarily successful Jewish singles activities. But a great many Jewish singles are not being reached by Jewish organizations. What we need for them, I believe, is a concerted nationwide outreach program (or to use Leonard Fein's term, and "in-reach program") designed to help single Jews meet other Jews wherever they are. Such a program, if sensibly and sensitively carried out and backed by sociological research and adequate funding, could go a long way in mitigating some of the problems of our singles and keeping them within our community.

I want to say a word at this point about the chapter in the leadership study dealing with rabbinic officiation at intermarriages. I for one found it illuminating to learn that lay leaders today are as divided on this subject as rabbis are. Perhaps understandably, those whose own children have intermarried often feel differently from those whose children have not. What we lack, however, is any adequate measure of the impact that rabbinic decisions (on whether or not to officiate) have actually made on the intermarrying couples themselves. I know from Mark Winer and Egon Mayer that such surveys are now underway, and I want to use this opportunity to sound a note of caution. The key question is not just mechanically quantitative, as these surveys would have us believe, but also elusively qualitative. In other words, before we can measure impact effectively we need to know not just whether a rabbi agreed to officiate but also how the rabbi explained his or her decision and then related to the couple beforehand and afterwards. There are rabbis who have a remarkable ability to say "no" graciously without losing their influence, and there are rabbis who, even if they do perform intermarriages, are more likely to drive people away from our faith than draw them near to it. I know of no current research that takes account of these qualitative aspects of rabbinic work, and I am, therefore, leery of drawing any meaningful conclusions at this time, much less of making policy recommendations for the future.

"JEWS BY CHOICE"

This brings me to what I consider to be the most innovative and compelling sections of this report, those that deal with converts to Judaism, or "Jews by Choice." Nobody knows how many converts have entered the Jewish fold, but estimating conservatively at 2 percent of America's 5.7 million Jews yields a population of over 115,000 men and women. If all of them lived in one community, it would be the ninth largest Jewish community in America, with more Jews than St. Louis, Minneapolis, and Cincinnati combined. This is an unprecedented situation not only in America but in all of modern Jewish history. It deserves a great deal more scholarly attention than it receives.

Only a small number of converts are actually included in this survey (41 converts, 51 born Jews married to converts). The conclusions drawn, however, correlate well with other surveys, notably those of Egon Mayer and Steven Huberman,[6] and are also supported by impressionistic evidence. Here I want to discuss three interrelated trends that to my mind hold especially important implications for the future.

First of all, all surveys agree that converts tend to emphasize religious and spiritual aspects of Judaism: they attend synagogue more often than born Jews do, they observe basic home rituals, and they look to the synagogue as their spiritual center. What Harold Kushner found in Conservative synagogues applies to Reform temples as well:

[Converts] define their Jewishness in terms familiar to them from their Christian upbringing: prayer and ritual observance. By their numbers and sincerity, they are reshaping American Judaism into a less ethnic, more spiritual community.[7]

The implications of these changes are not yet altogether clear; they may prove, despite my skepticism, to be wholly positive. Certainly, rabbis and congregational leaders need to be alert to what is going on, so that they may set appropriate priorities for the coming decades.

The second and more troubling trend that I see is the tendency of converts to subordinate the ethnic aspects of their Judaism. They score far below born Jews in the Jewish communalism index that Mark Winer describes. They are more diffident about *Kelal Yisrael* in general, particularly the idea that Jews should extend special help to fellow Jews in need. And their support of Israel is, statistically speaking, much lower than that of born Jews. These findings are not surprising; Egon Mayer found similar attitudes in his study. Nor are these findings hard to understand, since most Introduction to Judaism courses emphasize religion over ethnicity, and most converts come to Judaism from a religion that considers universalism more important than peoplehood. But if not surprising, these findings are deeply troubling, especially since even among born Reform Jews the values that have been traditionally associated with Jewish peoplehood seem to be eroding. *Kelal Yisrael* and *Ahavat Yisrael*—the fraternal feelings of love that bind Jews one to another even when they disagree—have weakened their hold on many of our leaders today. We are fast losing our ability to view the Jewish people in familial terms as one big *mishpoche*. Obviously, this problem is not unique to Reform Jews: the principles of *Kelal Yisrael* and *Ahavat Yisrael* are spurned by far too many Orthodox Jews as well, especially in Israel. But while this magnifies our challenge, it does not absolve us from the obligation to uphold these principles no matter who violates them. Bitter experience should have taught us that these principles are sacred; whenever Jews have not been responsible for one another, tragedy has resulted. So while others preach intra-Jewish hatred, we must learn to practice what Israel's great chief rabbi, Rav Kook, called *ahavat chinam*, boundless love. This means love for converts, love for Conservative and Orthodox Jews, yes, even love for Jews who don't love us. That is what the family of Israel is all about.

We are a long way from meeting this goal. Leaders of Reform Judaism score low on communalism, leaders who are converts score lower, and impressionistic evidence suggests that many ordinary Jews score lower still.

There is thus an urgent need for a vigorous new emphasis on Jewish communalism throughout the Reform movement (indeed, throughout all branches of Judaism), paying special attention to what *Kelal Yisrael* and *Ahavat Yisrael* mean and how both can be turned into working principles that govern our lives. No priority is more important in terms of safeguarding Jews everywhere and the future of the Jewish people as a whole.

CONVERTS' VIEWS OF INTERMARRIAGE

This brings me to the last trend pointed to in this survey that demands attention, and that is the views expressed by converts on the subject of intermarriage, particularly what they would do if their own children intermarried. Frighteningly, about 80 percent of converts or those married to converts scored high on the intermarriage acceptability index: they would not, by their own admission, feel too badly if their children married non-Jews. Egon Mayer's study showed that many converts would *not even discourage* their children from marrying someone who was not Jewish.[8] In the Reform leadership study, more than 50 percent of the converts responding—leaders, I remind you—would not even be bothered a great deal if their children *converted to Christianity*! (p. 109). There is here a world of difference between converts and born Jews, and one that augurs very badly indeed for our future. If today, when most Jewish parents still disapprove of intermarriage, we have such a significant intermarriage rate, tomorrow, when a substantial number will not disapprove, I fear that the figures will be very bleak indeed.

Now I obviously understand why many converts feel as they do, and in a sense I admire their consistency: they want their children to have the same freedom of choice that they had. The very term "Jew by Choice," so very popular today in Reform circles (some, indeed, argue that we are *all* "Jews by Choice") implies that members of the next generation are free to make a different choice, even if that means Christianity. But as people concerned about Judaism's future, it seems to me that we cannot look upon these statistics with equanimity and must wholeheartedly reject the proposition that conversion to Judaism is an ephemeral decision in no way binding on one's offspring. Instead we must help converts understand *why* we feel as strongly as we do about preventing intermarriage and apostasy and must emphasize that to our mind conversion implies not just a choice but a *permanent transformation*—a change in identity, traditionally even a change of name. Perhaps we should discard the very term "Jew by Choice" as misleading and replace it with a stronger term—a Jew by adoption, by conversion, by transformation. Certainly, it seems to me, as I have already argued, that we need to place new stress on the peoplehood aspects of Judaism, with appropriate educational and outreach programs.

Let us make no mistake; the data we now have at hand should serve as a dire warning: *Unless we act decisively, many of today's converts will be one-generation Jews—Jews with non-Jewish parents and non-Jewish children.* I say this with great personal sadness, since some of the finest, most courageous, and most dedicated Jews I know are proud "Jews by Choice," and the last thing I mean to do is to cast doubt on their sincerity. We are a better Jewish community thanks to those who have come to Judaism from the outside, and we should be grateful that our problems stem from those entering the Jewish fold rather than from those rushing headlong to abandon it. Still, the data here speak for themselves and are positively alarming. We will be accountable to posterity if, knowing what we now know, we close our eyes and do nothing.

CONCLUSION

Let me close with what I hope is a more comforting thought. Learned Jews and non-Jews have been making dire predictions about the future (or end) of the Jewish people for literally thousands of years—long before William Wirt and long after him—and, as we have seen, their predictions have proved consistently wrong. The reason, I think, has nothing to do with the quality of our prophets, but is rather to the credit of those who listened to them. Refusing to consider the future preordained, clearheaded Jews have always acted to avert the perils they were warned against, and in every case, to a greater or lesser extent, they were successful: the Jewish people lived on.

So it is today. We have prophets, we have wise leaders, and we have a future that is ours to shape. We can shape it well, or we can shape it poorly. May we find the wisdom to do a good job.

NOTES

Edited from a lecture delivered at the Workshop Seminar of the Research Task Force on the Future of Reform Judaism, held at HUC-JIR, New York, on October 9, 1988. I am grateful to Rabbi Sanford Seltzer for inviting me to prepare this lecture and for permitting me to publish it here.

1. William Wirt to John Myers, 12 June, 1818, Myers Family Papers, American Jewish Archives. For the background to this letter, see Jonathan D. Sarna, *Jacksonian Jew: The Two Worlds of Mordecai Noah* (New York: Holmes & Meier, 1981), p. 178.

2. See Stephen J. Whitfield's essay on "The End of Jewish History," in *Religion, Ideology and Nationalism in Europe and America: Essays Presented in Honor of Yehoshua Arieli* (Jerusalem: The Historical Society of Israel, 1986), pp. 385–407, and in a slightly different version in Whitfield's *American Space, Jewish Time* (Hamden, CT: Archon, 1988), pp. 171–191.

3. Mark L. Winer, Sanford Seltzer, and Steven J. Schwager, *Leaders of Reform Judaism: A Study of Jewish Identity, Religious Practices and Beliefs, and Marriage Patterns* (New York: Union of American Hebrew Congregations, 1987).

4. Jonathan D. Sarna, "Coping with Intermarriage," *Jewish Spectator* 47 (Summer 1982): 26–38.

5. Bruce Phillips, "Los Angeles Jewry: A Demographic Portrait," *American Jewish Year Book* 86 (1986): 145–147, 153, and 177–178.

6. Egon Mayer and Carl Sheingold, *Intermarriage and the Jewish Future* (New York: American Jewish Committee, 1979); Egon Mayer, *Children of Intermarriage* (New York: American Jewish Committee, 1983); Egon Mayer and Amy Avgar, *Conversion Among the Intermarried* (New York: American Jewish Committee, 1987); Steven Huberman, *New Jews: The Dynamics of Religious Conversion* (New York: Union of American Hebrew Congregations, 1979).

7. Harold Kushner, "The American Jewish Perspective: A Conservative Perspective," *Judaism* 123 (Summer 1982): 298.

8. Mayer, *Children of Intermarriage*, p. 34.

⊰ 10 ⊱

David Max Eichhorn
and Immanuel Jakobovits

Shall Jews Missionize?

After a concise introduction by Rabbi William Berkowitz, renowned Reform rabbi David Max Eichhorn and Orthodox rabbi Immanuel Jakobovits, former chief rabbi of the British Commonwealth, respond to questions about whether or not Jews should actively seek converts. Rabbi Eichhorn summarizes the pro-conversion stand very clearly. Interestingly, Rabbi Jakobovits appears to agree with a great deal, differing most importantly on the conditions under which proselytes are accepted. In this sense, he summarizes Orthodox concerns not about conversion in theory but about the requirements of a conversion, the acceptable motives for a conversion, and the qualifications of the rabbi performing the conversion.

The clash of views, so well presented under some very skillful questioning by Rabbi Berkowitz, remains prominent in Jewish life today.

———•———

W.B.: The theme we are to discuss is a current question in American Jewish life: Shall we have Jewish missionaries? Some people would give an unqualified yes to this question, but some feel otherwise and would say no. Perhaps, as we discuss this, we may find that there is no clear-cut yes or no answer. It is not a matter of black and white; perhaps it is gray. There are many sides to the subject, and we have chosen to explore two different points of view, with perhaps my own inserted from time to time as a third. To give you two disparate aspects of the subject of Jewish missionary activity, we have selected two rabbis who have had close relationships with the questions involved.

One of our authorities is Rabbi David Max Eichhorn. Dr. Eichhorn was the director of field operations of the Commission on Jewish Chaplaincy, National Jewish Welfare Board (J.W.B.). Before taking this post, he was a pulpit rabbi, and immediately before coming to the J.W.B. he served as a Jewish army chaplain in Europe during World War II. He is a theologian and philosopher who is deeply versed in the subject of proselytism; he is a noted lecturer and the author of several books.

The other authority has had a rich and colorful rabbinic career both here and abroad, having served as rabbi of the Great Synagogue of London and as the chief rabbi of Ireland. He is a prolific writer on Jewish law and has lectured extensively throughout the United States. He was the rabbi of the Fifth Avenue Synagogue in New York City and is now chief rabbi of the British Commonwealth—Rabbi Immanuel Jakobovits.

I would like to open our discussion with our usual procedure, giving an opportunity to each speaker to develop his particular point of view. The first problem is, I think, to establish a frame of reference, to set the background.

Rabbi Eichhorn, can you tell us the history of the development of missionary work in Judaism? Has Judaism traditionally been a proselytizing religion?

EICHHORN: The answer to that direct question, Rabbi Berkowitz, is an unqualified yes. The average Jewish person has a completely mixed-up picture of the attitude of Judaism toward proselytism, of the attitude of Judaism toward the convert, and of the historical picture in this whole field. Part of the difficulty is the fact that in Hebrew there is no word for *convert*. The word *convert* is a completely Christian term. It derives from the Latin *conversus*, which means *to change*. The Christian concept is that a person who becomes a Christian changes over from something else. He has a certain religious point of view one day. Then he has a great vision, or sees a great dream, or hears a great sermon, or he goes down on his knees and hits the sawdust trail. Yesterday, as the old story goes, he was a fish, and today he is a chicken; yesterday he was an unbeliever, and now he is a Christian. This miracle, this phenomenon that converts an individual from one religion to another, is completely absent in Judaism.

The Hebrew word that we use for convert—because we have to go along with the language of the country in which we reside—is *gair*. The Hebrew word *gair* comes from the root *goor*, which means "to live with," and when a non-Jew becomes a Jew he does not change over from one religious point of view to another. He approaches, he becomes part of, he comes to live with a group of people and becomes a member of a religious fellowship with whose point of view he has agreed for a long time, sometimes consciously, sometimes unconsciously. He has found a group of people whom he considers very worthwhile. Here is a theology and philosophy he wants to espouse, and so he comes into the group.

In the Bible this is very clear; the word for *sojourner*, the word for *stranger*, the word for *convert* are all in this word *gair*. In the Bible there are a number of types of *gairim* depicted. There is the type of *gair* who simply comes to live with the group, and there is another type of *gair* who comes not only to live with the group but also to become completely part of it. When, in the Book of Esther, the expression "to Judaize"—to become part of the Jewish people—is first used in the Bible, we have in this one verse in which this word is used something akin to the process of complete proselytism.

With the single exception of the Book of Ezra and Nehemiah (for these are really one book), the consistent attitude of the Bible is that we welcome those who wish to affiliate with us. Outside of this book, in which Jews who had married non-Jewish women were forced to divorce their wives and to put aside the children of these wives, the Bible maintains that we welcome others not only as fellow members of our group but as partners in a job that God has given to us. God has chosen us from among all peoples to teach His Law to the nations, to become, as the Bible says, very specifically, "a light unto the nations and unto all the peoples." So we are a people who wish to have additional adherents. We are a people that has a message to give to the world. This is stated hundreds of times in the Bible and in the Talmud.

W.B.: Dr. Eichhorn, I would like to interrupt. Now that we have established the premise, may I point out that this theme of missionary activity is appropriate to the *Sidra* that speaks of Abraham and Sarah, who went out to win new souls. My basic question to you is this: What has been our history from Abraham until, let us say, the present time? Has Judaism been a proselytizing religion?

EICHHORN: In the sense of sending out professional missionaries, in the sense of giving people food, clothing, medical help, and bribes in order to persuade them to adopt our religion, we have never been a missionary religion, and, please God, we never will be. We do not hold out any sort of inducement to anybody to enter our religious fold except that of finding a way of life that for him is better than the way of life that he has. I would categorically say that in Jewish history, professional people have never been employed for this purpose, but I would also say categorically that in Jewish history, from time immemorial, every Jew was destined and every Jew was bidden to be a missionary. The Bible tells us we are a kingdom of priests and a holy people.

What is the Bible trying to tell us but that as individuals and as a people we should be setting an example to the rest of the world, an example that we should be seeking to have the world follow.

What sort of people would we be and what sort of individuals would we be if we said to those who followed our example, "So far, no further. You can only come up to the door, but you cannot come in." This would be absolutely unthinkable. As I said before, there was no parallel in biblical times to what we today call a convert. The early Talmud period and the pre-Christian centuries contained synagogues that were filled with non-Jews who were interested in hearing sermons and attending services. There are numerous references in the Talmud to these people, especially women, because one of our problems was that we were very insistent on circumcision. This was a very dangerous and painful operation for a male to go through, especially in those early days of which we are speaking. So actual converts seemed to have been much more prevalent among females than among males.

The Christian Testament states that the Pharisees would cross land and sea to make one convert. This is somewhat of an exaggeration, of course, but among the Pharisees, among the Essenes, certainly among the Rabbis of the Talmud, we find again and again many evidences that there were people who did everything within their power to try to persuade non-Jews to become Jews. We have a famous story that has been authenticated by many historical proofs, that a whole kingdom, the Kingdom of Adiabene, lying between the Roman and Parthian empires, converted to Judaism. A Jewish traveling merchant from Palestine had come to the court of the king of Adiabene and, while selling silks to the king's daughter, interested her in Judaism so that she, her father, and her mother eventually converted. When the war broke out between the Romans and the Jews in the year 66, a whole regiment, a whole troop, from Adiabene fought alongside the Jews against the Romans. They perished to the last man, including two or three princes of the royal household. This country remained Jewish until it was overrun by the Parthians in about the year 100. This is just one among many instances.

W.B.: So we could say that, up to a point in Jewish history, the answer—for want of a better term—was that there was a more or less aggressive mission to non-Jews. Now, in which period of Jewish history did the attitude change to a "no" attitude?

EICHHORN: When the Christians entered the picture, the attitude became "no." When Constantine the Great made Christianity the official religion of the Holy Roman Empire, and when the Code of Justinian was instituted, one of the features of that code of law was that any Jew who tried to convert a Christian to Judaism would be put to death, and that any Christian who became converted to Judaism would likewise be put to death. This put a rather sharp and quick end to Jewish proselytizing efforts. Later on, when the Moslems came into that part of the world and instituted the Code of Omar, this code had exactly the same provision. By about the seventh century it was practically impossible for a Jew to try to convert either a Christian or a Moslem, and it was almost impossible for a Christian or a Moslem to become a Jew. As this situation continued on into the Middle Ages, the Jews began to adopt what we might call a sour-grapes attitude, or what is sometimes referred to as a religious inferiority complex. They thought, "If we cannot have them, then we do not want them." Later on, certain Jews became converts to Christianity and Islam in order to feather their own nests, and some of these not-so-nice people turned on their fellow Jews and became even more bitter oppressors than the Christians or Moslems. The Jewish attitude "If we cannot have them, then we do not want them" developed into suspicion and then into hatred. Because of the medieval experience with Jews who converted to other religions in order to benefit themselves, we turned that same suspicion, and sometimes even that same hatred, on those who tried to become Jews. A typical reaction of many Jews today toward people who want to adopt Judaism is, "What is in it for him; what does he expect to gain by it?" Or "She is looking for a rich husband," or "She knows that Jews make better husbands than non-Jews." This is the typical, unfair reaction.

W.B.: Would you say that this attitude is very prevalent today toward the non-Jew? Would you say it is characteristic? What is the Jewish attitude of the Jew toward the non-Jew?

EICHHORN: Well, I am not going to try to give a dissertation on the attitude of the Jew toward the non-Jew, but certainly with reference to some well-known non-Jews who converted to Judaism, there is a suspicion, on the part of many that one talks to, that these converts may be insincere. If you mention that a movie star is keeping a kosher home, someone points to last night's headline and says that she is getting a divorce. Well, a lot of Jewish-born women get divorces from Jewish husbands, too. The question that may be asked is, "How much of the conversion was dependent upon a real belief in the principles of Judaism and how much upon convenience?" We have an example in Norma Shearer, who converted to Judaism when she married the late Irving Thalberg. She became the president of the sisterhood of Rabbi Magnin's synagogue in Los Angeles. Then her next husband was a Catholic, and she converted to Roman Catholicism when she married him. So we certainly cannot claim Norma Shearer as a very sincere convert.

W.B.: Dr. Eichhorn, I note that the Reform rabbinate in 1950 organized a Committee for the Unaffiliated. I believe that this is vital to our issue under discussion. What does it mean? What does it do?

EICHHORN: That committee was formed after a very heated discussion at the 1950 convention of the Reform rabbinate, and the motion to form the committee squeaked through by a very narrow margin, just a little more than half. The committee was set up to explore ways and means of increasing the influence or acceptability of the Jewish religion.

It was a very innocuous kind of motion, but everybody knew what it meant. It meant the study of the possibility of going out into the non-Jewish world with some sort of a program of attracting unaffiliated non-Jews to Judaism. The idea of even studying this was so fearsome to even the most liberal Jewish groups of this country—at least those who consider themselves the most liberal—that this resolution had a hard time getting through. This committee, of which I had the honor to be chairman, met very regularly and studied the subject. In 1957, after many months of investigation, our committee came to the Reform rabbinate with the following recommendations: that to give as much information as possible on Judaism to the non-Jew is not only a right but an obligation and a responsibility; that we should make the non-Jew aware of the fact that we would welcome him warmly if he were to come to us voluntarily and state that he wishes to become a member of our religious group, agrees fully with our religious tenets, and wants to help promote them throughout the world.

W.B.: And after he is welcomed? Once he comes, what happens? Do you give him a course of study?

EICHHORN: Oh, yes. First, I would like to make one or two further points with regard to the program that this committee proposed. They proposed that texts be printed and distributed in hotels, in airports and railroad depots, and so on. There should be preaching missions at which non-Jews will be invited to listen to the teachings of Judaism, and there should be radio and television programs specifically devoted to the idea of disseminating knowledge of Judaism and letting non-Jews know that we would welcome them. This proposal, this proposed program on the part of the committee, was passed by something like three hundred members of the Central Conference of American Rabbis without a dissenting vote.

As far as the Reform rabbinate is concerned, I am glad to say there is a whole change of heart. I also have firsthand indications that some members of the Conservative and Orthodox rabbinates are rethinking this whole matter. We are going back to first principles. We are sweeping out some of the cobwebs that grew in the minds of some of us during our dark days in the ghettos during the Middle Ages.

W.B.: May I ask this question? When you mention putting signs in depots or inviting non-Jews to lectures and activities of this kind, would you not call this an aggressive mission to the Christian community? If not, how do you term this?

EICHHORN: No, I do not call this an aggressive mission to the Christian community. The texts, the missions, the radio and television programs will do one thing and one thing only: they will set forth positively and without apology exactly what Jews believe.

W.B.: What *is* an aggressive mission to the Christians?

EICHHORN: An aggressive mission to the Christians would be, as far as I am concerned, saying on that television program, "We've got the true religion. All other religions are false. Come to us and be saved." This is what the Christians say when they preach their religion, and we have no intention of doing this.

W.B.: What *will* you say when you get on television?

EICHHORN: We will say that for us Judaism is the religion that best meets our needs and best fits our desires. Those who share this feeling with us may, if they wish, come and join us. We will be very happy to have them. I hope that neither I nor anyone else will ever be guilty of saying that we have the only true religion, or that our religion is better than anybody else's religion. Nobody knows who has the true religion, and nobody knows who has the best religion.

W.B.: A few minutes ago, you mentioned "removing the cobwebs from our minds," of removing the ghetto thinking of the Dark Ages, and this point of view, you said, was shared by some Conservative and Orthodox Jews. I know of a questionnaire concerning this that you sent out in 1954. I think some of the statistics from that would be most interesting.

EICHHORN: First, approximately twenty-five hundred non-Jews are being converted to Judaism every year in the United States. Second, about five out of six of these are women. Let me put it this way: in the Conservative movement, five out of six are females, and in the Reform movement, four out of five are females. Why Reform does a little better with the males is traceable to the fact that Reform Judaism does not demand circumcision of the male convert, while Conservative Judaism does. Of the converts who are now coming in, fourteen out of fifteen are coming in because of an impending or an existing marriage. I wish we could develop the reasoning that I think is behind that. I hope that some day a student of this field will study this phenomenon. I think he will find that what attracts non-Jews to Jews is far more than just a physical attraction and far more than just the feeling that one partner—the non-Jew—is going to better himself. I have had a great deal of experience with mixed marriages and with conversion, and it is questionable in my mind who is the more fortunate member of the couple in many of these marriages. Sometimes the Jew is getting much the better of it, and I do not think we ought to pat ourselves on the back too hard.

Ninety-one percent of the Reform rabbis and 68 percent of the Conservative rabbis answered this questionnaire. Any of us who knows anything about questionnaires knows that this response is phenomenal. It means that rabbis are really deeply interested in this problem. These rabbis were asked to rate the converts who are members of their congregations as being low-average, average, or above-average Jews—comparing these with the born Jews in the congregation. A heavy majority of the Conservative and Reform rabbis stated that, on the average, the convert is a better member of the congregation than the born Jew. This also, I am sure, will come as a bit of a surprise to some who think that converts are not as good as other Jews.

W.B.: Now we turn to our second guest, Rabbi Jakobovits. Naturally, Rabbi Jakobovits's point of view might be different from Rabbi Eichhorn's. We will try to determine that difference. The first question, Rabbi Jakobovits, is, What is the attitude, not only of Jewish history but of Jewish law, toward proselytizing?

JAKOBOVITS: I agree in principle with a great deal of what has been said. I also say that we welcome proselytes with open arms, and that we make them feel not only at home but as equals in our midst. Where I differ is on the conditions under which we are to accept proselytes. While I will proceed to show that our conditions are extremely rigid and therefore will allow for the admission of only a tiny percentage of those who apply, the Reform attitude as presented here by Rabbi Eichhorn is that the net ought to be cast considerably wider. That is one difference. Second, I want to make it quite clear that I do not propose to give here what may appear to be my personal attitude on the matter. I will try as well as I can, and as objectively as I can, to give the attitude of Jewish law, as I find it, toward this question.

Now, concerning the specific question as to the Jewish attitude, I can put it quite simply: if the would-be convert is agreeable to the conditions that Jewish law lays down for his conversion, then we place no obstacle whatever in his way. In fact, we give every assistance to him and then, upon conversion, welcome him with open arms. I think that would sum up the answer.

W.B.: Now the question is the "if." What does "if they meet the requirements" mean? Can you define what the requirements are? And how would you determine sincerity?

JAKOBOVITS: Well, here we come to the heart of the problem. As far as Dr. Eichhorn's historic presentation is concerned, I must take issue with one item, and that is his allegation that the present-day lukewarm or rather hesitant attitude toward the acceptance of proselytes is the result of the sour-grapes attitude developed in the Middle Ages, when the hostile attitude of the Church toward allowing the Jew to convert others colored our own attitude. I think that this is an extremely arbitrary reading of history. All I know is that the Jewish law that governs today's attitude to conversion was laid down in the Talmud very expressly 2,000 years ago, long before there were any Middle Ages. This attitude has, by and large, remained constant in all authentic rabbinic writings on the subject. If at one time we did have larger proselytizing movements than at another, it was due simply to the exigencies of the times; at certain times people felt more attracted by the rigid conditions that Judaism placed before them, and at other times less so. So much about the historical element. As a matter of fact, you could cite the conversion to Judaism in the Middle Ages of the whole Khazar Kingdom in Russia as evidence of the fact that when the ground was fertile for such proselytizing, it could be done on a massive scale even in the Middle Ages.

Our attitude on this matter is governed by two principal considerations, which I want to spell out as well as I possibly can. First, we do not believe that God meant all humans to be Jewish and to perform the duties that Judaism imposes upon us in order to find favor in His eyes. In this respect, we differ radically from the Christians. We do not say that a non-Jew, in order to be perfect in God's eyes, in order to be saintly, or in order to fulfill his destiny as a human being, must eventually be a Jew and conform to Jewish law. We believe, on the contrary, that so long as the non-Jews observe the fundamental laws of Noah, as we call them, the certain basic cardinal laws of humanity, which include the basic moral law, then they are just as virtuous and just as meritorious in the eyes of God as the Jew who fulfills the entire rigid discipline of Jewish life.

Therefore, it was not anticipated by our prophets that the distinctions between religions will be obliterated even in the perfect days, when there will be universal peace, and when "the knowledge of God will cover the earth as the waters cover the sea." We do not believe that there will come a time when everyone will have to embrace the Jewish faith, as the Christians believe that in order to be saved one must be baptized and must embrace the Christian faith. This basic premise of Judaism, incidentally, means that Judaism is bound to be far more tolerant of other faiths than probably any other religion, certainly any other monotheistic religion.

Following from this premise comes my second one. Why then were we chosen to have our own religion—you might almost call it our own natural religion—identified with our people, and to retain this limitation? We believe that we were chosen to be pioneers in this world. We were chosen to accept a mission in this world that only the few can carry out. The demands, the sacrifices, the privations, the discipline that are required of the advance guard of an army are far greater than those of the ordinary soldier. We were placed into this world so that we might make the initial breaches in the walls of paganism or immorality, as they existed in the past. Once we have broken through, as a small advance guard, the area can then be broadened, and the masses—the infantry, as it were—can follow and mop up.

W.B.: Does that mean, if we follow this to its logical conclusion, that the Jewish people are therefore a superior people?

JAKOBOVITS: No, it does not mean anything of the sort. It depends upon how you measure inferiority and superiority. We believe that every nation is sent into this world to fulfill a specific role. We believe that the Romans were here to teach us, possibly, the arts of government and warfare. The Greeks were here for art, for science, and for philosophy. We believe the Jews are in this world to be the pioneers of monotheism, the pioneers of religion and social justice, the pioneers of a people that will live on a higher level, so that ultimately the time will come when God will be sovereign of the whole world, yet without Judaism ruling the whole world.

The Bible itself is very specific on this matter. The Bible tells us, the Torah tells us, that we Jews are chosen people because we were the smallest of all peoples. With a small group you can achieve more, you can demand more, than with a big mass. Had we, in the days of the rise of Christianity, competed with the Church at that time, the chances are that today we would be a mass religion, counting hundreds of millions of people all over the world. We did not go in for this. We did not compete with the missionaries of the Church at that time, because we felt that we would then lose the ability to remain what we were and do what we were meant to do—that is, to live on a supreme level of self-discipline and self-sacrifice, which cannot be asked of the masses. Since it is in the smallness of our numbers that our strength lies, the overall attitude has been one of the greatest caution in admitting those who we were not convinced would carry the historic responsibility that we believe destiny and Providence have placed upon us.

These are the two basic considerations that, to my mind, govern the Jewish religious attitude toward conversion. Now, to complete the answer to the question that has been posed, What does Jewish law demand? Under what conditions do we accept converts? Let me give you some statistics. In this country we have no overall statistics of applicants and admissions. In England, where virtually all would-be converts apply to the London Beit Din, the central religious agency to which the majority of English Jewry owes allegiance, there are something like four hundred to five hundred applicants for conversion each year. Out of these, hardly more than 1 percent are admitted. One percent of all the applicants! And we ask, Why is this? I think Dr. Eichhorn has given the answer. He said that [in the U.S.] fourteen out of fifteen people are admitted *not* because they fall in love with Judaism but because they fall in love with a Jewish person. And this is precisely where I take issue. We say that if the motive for joining Judaism is not an appreciation of what Judaism as such stands for, if a person is unwilling to impose upon himself or herself all the rigors of Jewish law without exception, if the motive is the convenience of a marriage that might otherwise not be successful, or the bringing up of children who might otherwise have to grow up in a spiritual or religious no-man's land rejected by Jews and by Christians alike, if a party has fallen in love with a Jew instead of with Judaism—if all this is so—then we believe that such a person will not be able to join our ranks to the extent required by our law.

W.B.: There is a talmudic statement, which I have quoted frequently but which comes to mind again: *M'toch shelo l'shmuh buh l'shmuh*, that is, When someone does not *come* for its own sake, he nevertheless will end up doing it *l'shmuh, for* its own sake. Statistics tell of women who convert because of marriage and who then go on to lead full and fruitful Jewish lives. In the face of these statements, and in terms of experience, why would your position still be as it is?

JAKOBOVITS: The whole question here is what in fact constitutes *l'shmuh,* "for its own sake"? On this, of course, we may differ. Let us say that a person tells us that he or she will adopt the entire range of Jewish law, will keep a kosher home, will observe the moral and ethical requirements of Judaism, the business relations, the Sabbath, but that he or she cannot subscribe to, takes exception to, and cannot fulfill one law. We will reject this applicant. You may say very logically that such a person will be a far better Jew than most of those who were born Jewish; therefore, why should we turn down a person who, out of all the 613 laws, rejects one? Let me give you the answer. If you have a child of your own, then good, bad, or indifferent, he remains your child and you cannot disown him. If that child turns out to be bad, he is still your own child, because you have given birth to that child, and you share, as it were, in the fortunes and misfortunes of this child. But if you adopt a child, take a child in and make it your own by adoption, the matter is different. There you can choose. You can say, "The child who is going to prove an asset, I am going to adopt. One who I know has had a bad history, or comes from a family with a proclivity to crime or ill health," you will say, "I do not want to adopt." After all, you are making an open, free choice. That is our attitude here. If Jews are born as Jews and they ignore Jewish law, reject Jewish law, may not even remember that they are Jews, we still recognize them as Jews. We say, *"Yisrael af al pi shechata Yisrael hu."* A Jew, even though he sins, even though he is a renegade, even though he may be baptized, is still looked upon as a Jew. He is our child. He is born into our people. You cannot escape from Judaism. If, however, we are to adopt a Jew, if we are to invite one who is not born Jewish to assume these responsibilities and make him into one of ourselves, we can ask to be assured that he will be an asset to us. If he will be a liability, if he becomes a lawbreaker, why should we impose the burden on him?

If I apply for American citizenship, I will appear before a judge and be asked to take an oath of loyalty to this country, and I will be told that I will have to swear that I will abide by the Constitution of this country and by all its laws and regulations. Now, imagine that I tell this judge that I am quite ready to fulfill all the clauses of your Constitution except one, which I do not like. I am not going to abide by one clause in your Constitution or one law that your congress has passed because I have a conscientious objection against it. He will say, Go home and retain the passport that you had before. I will then ask the judge, Why are you stricter with me than with your own Americans? You have many Americans who are traitors and who are lawbreakers and who are in prisons, and they are still Americans. You have not taken away their nationality. I come to you, I want to fulfill 99.9 percent of all your laws, I make a little exception, and you reject me. He will answer, quite rightly, that I am being naturalized. I am being accepted as an American citizen and he will not allow me to make exceptions, though he may have to allow people who were born Americans to be exceptions. If we naturalize a non-Jew to become a Jew, we adopt precisely the same perfectly logical attitude. I would not argue with that judge, any more than I would like a would-be convert to argue with me, were I to give him the same answer.

There is another aspect of this problem on which I want to lay great emphasis. It is often suggested, and this is part of my answer to your question, that Orthodox rabbis who see these would-be converts and who reject them or who at least do not make it very easy for them are callous and perhaps ignore the human duties that they owe their fellow human beings when they come for help. It is this aspect that I would like to put in its proper perspective. If I had a part as a rabbi in converting a non-Jewish woman to Judaism, then, first of all, I must realize that I do not convert only her; I automatically convert her children and her children's children for all future generations. My act is converting them as well. Therefore, the decision I have to make is a crushing responsibility, purely from this point of view. Next, if this woman, before she was converted, worked on the Sabbath, she did nothing wrong in the eyes of God. She was perfectly honest, law-abiding, religious, and devout, in the eyes of God. The Sabbath was not given to her in our sense. If *after* I convert her she works on the Sabbath, thereby desecrating it, I am aiding and abetting her in the desecration of Jewish law.

W.B.: I would like to bring some of these things into perspective. You state that if you were to convert this woman, you realize that this is a crushing responsibility because you also convert her children and children's children. On the other hand, if you do not convert this woman, and she marries a Jew and has a home that is non-Jewish, what about *that* crushing responsibility?

JAKOBOVITS: It is the same crushing responsibility. If I reject the woman who potentially could have fulfilled the conditions of Jewish law and become converted, then I face at least the same responsibility by this withholding of what we call the Wings of the Divine Presence from the person who should rightfully enjoy that protection of Jewish law. Therefore, the responsibility works both ways. The crushing responsibility to say yes as well as no. But I want to explain that it is not callous of a rabbi if he conscientiously feels, after having explored the case, that he must come to a negative decision in the matter.

Let me just develop this idea of responsibility. I was saying that I will have a share in every religious offense that she commits, because through my conversion of her she becomes a lawbreaker. Through my converting, through my act, laws may be broken that will be on my shoulders to an extent that I could have foreseen. We are all only human. We are only expected to be human. But we should be at least human, and we should genuinely explore and examine the case, possibly through years of trial, in the same way that America keeps me waiting for five years until I can apply for naturalization.

We believe that a change of religion is rather a more serious matter than a change of national allegiance. It is not just a change of passport, it is a change of heart. I always tell people who apply to me that I do not convert them; they convert themselves. If the change has occurred in their hearts, they will feel as a Jew feels: when Jews are suffering anywhere in the world their hearts will bleed as Jewish hearts; if they see Jewish triumphs, their hearts will rejoice as Jews; if they see Jewish law being broken, they will grieve, and in them there will be a pain at the violation of Jewish law. If it came to the point that the supreme sacrifice were demanded of them, a supreme act of heroism, martyrdom, these people would say, "I will lay down my life for my faith." If this is their attitude, then we will adopt them.

Ruth, the most famous convert of all times, said to her mother-in-law, "*El asher telchi elech*," "Where you go, I will go." But she went on, "*uva'asher tolini olin*," "and where you spend the night, I will spend the night": even in the darkness when there is persecution, I will share that darkness with you. I will feel as a Jew in whatever circumstances may come to me.

I cannot help fearing what is happening today, when large-scale conversions are being performed. We have had the figure of 2,500 in this country alone. Each year 2,500 are converted. Do not forget these conversions are not all recognized by many Conservative rabbis, and none by the Orthodox rabbis. This is creating a situation in which we are raising generations of people whom one Jew will call a Jew and another Jew will call a non-Jew. You can imagine the havoc that this has wrought in Jewish ranks. I know of it. I have been chief rabbi in a country [Ireland] where every such case had to come to me, and have seen the agony, the misery, the suffering that has been inflicted as a result of the make-believe that has taken place, where one has stamped someone into a Jew, and somebody else, following his law, cannot recognize this conversion. It has led to untold misery and suffering and often to the infliction of the sins of the parents on innocent children.

A sense of responsibility is necessary here to a degree that is required in perhaps no other rabbinic decision. We decide on an issue that affects the very deepest and innermost feelings of a person's heart. And we do not have spiritual X-ray eyes that can look into the heart. But at least one thing we can do is to try, and—by living with that person, sharing experiences with that person, and by showing that person what a Jewish life is—to be able to judge after two or three years whether his heart is in fact now a Jewish heart, 100 percent and not 99 percent.

W.B.: Would you, for example, accept someone as a candidate, work with him for two or three years, and then at the end of that period determine whether you would convert him, or would you immediately reject a candidate when he or she comes to your study? Are you not then setting yourself up in authority as a judge to determine who is really sincere and who is not sincere in terms of your particular point of view?

JAKOBOVITS: The point I am making is this: when you apply for citizenship the judge is not going to question you in detail. He will ask whether you accept the Constitution. You will say yes or you will say no.

You raised the point that if the convert violates one of the 613 laws, we reject him; it then becomes not only a quantitative but also a qualitative matter. If you say, after having worked with the person for two or three years, that you feel the person is not ready, fine. But can you say at the very outset that you do not believe him to be a fit candidate?

I can give you a very categorical answer to this. I have myself participated in a number of conversions, and I can assure you that those people I have converted have remained true Jews. I can assure you that to this day, they and their children are, so far as I know of them and have remained in contact with them, an asset rather than a liability.

Now you ask, how can we set ourselves up as judges? I am afraid that a rabbi, in making 101 decisions every day, has to be a judge. If he has to advise people, he has to be a judge, to show them what is the right course. I do not believe that when I reject a candidate for conversion I do that person any harm. I think, on the contrary, that in rejecting a person who is not in fact converted at heart, I do that person a favor. And I believe that ultimately that person will come back to me and thank me for it.

W.B.: Providing that you are right. You are operating on the premise that you are right. When someone comes to my study to discuss something with me, I then try to guide him. I never tell him to do this or not to do that. I speak for Rabbi Eichhorn and I speak for myself when I say we have not been reckless in our conversions, and I can cite examples of people who have been equally devoted and equally sincere. Who am I to sit in judgment and say to Miss X, who comes for conversion because of marriage, that it will never work out? Who are you, with all due deference and respect, to say that if Miss X comes for conversion because of marriage, or Miss Y comes for some other reason, it will work out or it will not? This categorical yes or no makes for a problem.

JAKOBOVITS: I do not think the problem actually exists. This is quite simple. You say I am operating on the assumption that I am right. I presume that you do the same. If you thought you were wrong you would act differently. Again, I did not suggest that if someone comes who is married to a Jewish party and therefore wants to be converted, that I necessarily reject him. But I have to find out the primary motive, the innermost motive. Does this person want to live a Jewish life? Is that person fascinated and enamored with Judaism, or is it merely a matter of using Judaism as a cloak for an easier marriage relationship? This I must explore, and I explore it as honestly as I can. I spend hours with every applicant. And even if I form my own impression the first moment that the young people walk in, I still spend a few hours with them, if only to explain what our attitude is. I do not want them to walk out of my office without feeling that whatever judgment I have given them is a justified judgment, a rational, logical judgment. I can say that, as a rule, if they cannot share my views they at least respect them. They feel that there is here an attitude of law that is perfectly consistent.

Dr. Eichhorn mentioned the celebrity conversions that have taken place. One is getting married, another is getting a divorce, and the third is very sick. I can only say that this is precisely why we want to be strict. We do not want Judaism to be used for the glamour of Hollywood. We do not want our religion to be dragged down to a point at which a woman is going to have as many religions in her life as she is going to have husbands. To me, this is sickening. I believe in drawing the line somewhere by laying down the basic conditions that we want these people to accept, not this, that, and the other law in detail but the totality of Jewish law, just as I am expected to accept the totality of the Constitution of the United States. If I say that I will not accept that totality, that I will make an exception, I will be rejected as an American citizen. If anyone comes to me and says that he cannot accept the totality of the Jewish law — the Jewish constitution of life — then I must say, for precisely the same reason, that I cannot assume the responsibility for converting him.

W.B.: It cannot be stated more clearly than it has been stated here. We have heard two differing attitudes toward the acceptance of converts to Judaism, yet a central ideal, it seems to me, is common to the presentations made by both of the speakers: Judaism welcomes sincere converts to our faith. Such differences as have been expressed seem to lie mainly in the definition of sincerity and devotion to our Law, and this definition is colored by the backgrounds of the speakers.

I conclude with this point. I believe that it cannot be denied that there is a burning need for Jewish missionaries today. However, I also believe that our generation requires Jewish missionaries to the Jews, for there are too many Jews who are ours in name only. And likewise, many thoughtful Christians recognize the need for Christian missionaries to the Christians. The task of such consecrated spirits must be to win those who are Jews or Christians merely by accident of birth to a fervent and enlightened loyalty toward their ancestral religions. A religion that demands nothing is worth nothing. Like everything else that is worthwhile, true religion must begin at home.

III

CONVERSION
AND THE INTERMARRIED

⊰ 11 ⊱

Dru Greenwood

Reform Jewish Outreach

Because so much of the contemporary debate about conversion takes place in the context of a discussion of intermarriage, it is vital to see how American Judaism deals with the combination of these questions. Both Reform and Conservative Jews, the two largest groupings within American Judaism, have developed ideas and programs to deal with the question of intermarriage,

No one is better able to trace the development of outreach in the Reform movement than Dru Greenwood, director of the Commission of Reform Jewish Outreach. She notes that, for the Reform movement, outreach to interfaith couples is seen as a seamless addition to encouraging conversion.

———•———

Judaism offers life, not death. It teaches free will, not the surrender of body and soul to another human being. The Jew prays directly to God, not through an intermediary who stands between him and his God. Judaism is a religion of hope, not despair. Judaism insists that man and society are perfectible. Judaism has an enormous wealth of wisdom and experience to offer this troubled world, and we Jews ought to be proud to speak about it, frankly and freely, with enthusiasm and with dignity.

Rabbi Alexander Schindler, president
Union of American Hebrew Congregations

With these words Rabbi Schindler concluded his remarks to the UAHC executive committee in Houston, Texas, in December 1978, in a historic speech that marks the beginning of the Reform movement's formal efforts of outreach to new Jews-by-choice, to interfaith couples and their families, and to all who seek what Judaism has to offer. Through these words as well the tone was set for an outreach that not only responds to demographic trends in the Jewish community that include a high intermarriage rate, but, even more, finds its compelling motivation within Judaism itself. Through Outreach, Jews open the door and offer a way in to those who would join our people and our faith.

TRANSFORMATION OF APPROACH

In the years since 1978, Reform Jewish Outreach has transformed the way Jews in modern times view conversion to Judaism. Creating a warm welcome in synagogues, teaching newcomers about Judaism and Jewish life, and developing programs and resources to help bridge the transition from non-Jew to Jew—these became first the mandate, then the standard of the Reform movement.

From where we sit now, evidenced in part by the publication of this very book, it is hard to remember how much change has occurred over the past fifteen years. Here are a few examples. The term "Jew-by-choice," in place of "convert" with its Christian overtones, was coined and generally adopted to indicate the positive decision being made by those entering Judaism. For the first time, with the publication of Lydia Kukoff's *Choosing Judaism*, conversion as a *process* of growing into Judaism—including personal, intrafamilial, and community adjustments along the way—was opened up for discussion and normalized. Individuals in the process of conversion no longer felt alone. "Conversion" classes became "Introduction to Judaism" classes, removing impediments for those who were just beginning to explore the possibility of Judaism for themselves but were not yet ready to make a commitment. These classes also shifted their focus and integrated the strictly academic approach that had prevailed with one that included hands-on practice in Jewish living as well. *Na'aseh v'nishma*—"All that the Lord has spoken we shall *do* and we shall hear" became the subscript of the new *Introduction to Judaism* curriculum (1983). (I have fond memories of the times I brought the dough and braided and baked challah with forty to forty-five Intro students. Community and a sense of proud ownership came along with the good smells and tastes.) Public conversion ceremonies began to take place in synagogues, allowing the new Jew to be fully welcomed into his or her community and, equally important, giving Jews in the congregation the opportunity to learn about conversion and celebrate it as part of the life cycle of many Jews. Following the establishment of the national Commission on Reform Jewish Outreach of the Union of American Hebrew Congregations and the Central Conference of American Rabbis, outreach committees were established in Reform synagogues to plan programs and provide an institutional address for concerns about conversion. Each one of these changes was revolutionary. Together they prepared the ground for further changes.

INVITING JEWISH CHOICES

In much of the discussion of outreach in the Jewish community, there tends to be a distinction made between encouraging or inviting conversion (on which there is general agreement) and reaching out to interfaith couples and their children (about which there is less consensus). Reform Jewish Outreach does not make this distinction but rather opens the door to Judaism for all, whether they currently intend to become Jews or not. Inviting Jewish choices is the overall rubric of Outreach. The consequence of this open approach is that programs designed specifically to invite the tentative Jewish explorations of interfaith couples (the second phase of Outreach) in fact enable many people to find a home in Judaism who otherwise would not. Anecdotal evidence suggests that we are seeing in the Reform movement a greater percentage of conversions taking place at a later point in the life cycle, after an individual has spent many years establishing a Jewish home and living a Jewish life. There are no guarantees; conversion to Judaism is not for everyone. However, providing a positive experience of Judaism in a caring and respectful way and an opportunity to work through religious issues between partners in a nonjudgmental and supportive setting does open Jewish possibilities to many. Interfaith couples discussion groups, holiday workshops, learners' minyanim, and other related programs all accomplish this goal. Although Jewish tradition warns against recalling the non-Jewish past of a convert, it is nevertheless important to remember as we plan programs that everyone who converts to Judaism was once not Jewish.

As Outreach has matured over the past fifteen years, other related program areas and resources have developed as well to support the mission of inviting Jewish choices. Support for Jewish parents whose children intermarry, programs for adolescents who are considering the meaning of their own Jewish identity and their decisions about interdating and intermarriage, "Stepping Stones: To a Jewish Me" for children of intermarried couples who have not yet made a decision about the religious upbringing of their children, films and programs to enable the Jewish community to understand the issues facing interfaith couples and new Jews-by-choice and thereby to provide a welcome to Judaism—all are designed to strengthen Jewish identity and offer a way in. More than half of Reform congregations now have Outreach committees that plan ongoing programs, and professional Outreach

staff in UAHC regions throughout North America support congregational
Outreach efforts, counsel interfaith couples and those in the process of conversion, and plan regional events. Program guides are available in all of these
areas from the William and Lottie Daniel Department of Outreach at the
UAHC, 838 Fifth Avenue, New York, NY 10021, or call (212) 249-0100.

LOOKING AHEAD

Based on the institutional structure and program resources that have been
developed thus far, the Reform movement continues to advocate a Judaism
that is open to all. At the 1993 Biennial Convention of the UAHC in San
Francisco, Rabbi Schindler reiterated his initial call for outreach "to all who
are seeking religious meaning in their lives," urging the Reform movement
more assertively to seek out and invite in proselytes, to reclaim our historic
role as "champions of Judaism." Steps in this direction are being taken with
the publication of such pamphlets as "What Judaism Offers for You: A Reform
Perspective" and "Inviting Someone You Love to Become a Jew." Introduction to Judaism classes, advertised in the secular press as "open to the public," are bringing many who previously felt themselves unwelcome to discover a rich and meaningful way of life and an open door to Judaism.

For thousands of people whose lives have been transformed by their
coming to Judaism, Reform Jewish Outreach has provided and will continue
to provide a pathway.

⊰ 12 ⊱

Avis D. Miller

Outreach to Intermarried: Parameters and Outlines

In this essay, Rabbi Miller lays out a carefully calibrated stragegy for the Conservative movement to deal with intermarriage. She focuses a lot on prevention and outreach (sometimes called *keruv*, or drawing toward, in the Conservative movement) as well as the place of conversion in such efforts.

Rabbi Avis Miller is senior rabbi at Adas Israel Congregation in Washington, D.C. She chairs the Rabbinical Assembly's Committee on Outreach.

———•———

In the wake of the National Jewish Population Study commissioned by the Council of Jewish Federations, our American Jewish community has been grappling with new urgency over questions of Jewish continuity. The survey confirmed the trend toward intermarriage that Jewish leaders had been observing in their own communities. Intermarriage is occurring among all segments of our community, and it is on the increase. The rate is higher among unaffiliated Jews than among those from ongoing religious communities, and it is highest of all among the children of those who have intermarried. In these times when we have exhausted our ethnic capital, affiliation with an ongoing religious community seems to be essential for Jewish continuity, and the institution that offers the setting for ongoing religious commitment is the synagogue.

Only a few short years ago, the case was being made that intermarriage could actually benefit our community. If two Jews married non-Jews rather than each other, went the argument, then we would have two potentially Jewish families instead of one. No one can pretend any more that intermarriage is "good for the Jews."

We now confront without hopeful illusions this question: Given the rate of intermarriage, and our recognition of its personal pain and communal destructiveness, what do we do? If a solution can be found, then the synagogue will have the major role to play.

The Conservative movement has developed a three-tier strategy to confront the challenge. Our first line of defense, *l'hatchilah* (a priori), is to emphasize the mitzvah of endogamy. We must continue to articulate that it is important for Jews to marry other Jews. This means that we must be willing to discuss the issue forthrightly from our pulpits, in our schools, and in our youth groups. We must be willing to do so with firmness but without rancor, sensitive to the pain borne by growing numbers of congregants who have intermarriages in their families. Our young people and their families must comprehend the direct relationship between interdating and intermarriage. If the message of the necessity for endogamy is not heard from the rabbi and the synagogue, then it will not be taken seriously anywhere.

The United Synagogue of Conservative Judaism is to be applauded for its timely development of teaching materials and programs devoted to promoting endogamy. Included in their publications on the subject are: *Intermarriage—Our Grounds for Concern: 14 Questions, 14 Answers*; *Interdating—Intermarriage: Intervention*; *Intermarriage: What Can We Do? What Should We Do?*; *A Return to the Mitzvah of Endogamy*; *Principles and Compassion: Guidelines and Casebook for Teaching Children of Intermarried Parents in Our Synagogue Schools*; and *Future Thinking: The Effects of Intermarriage*. The National Federation of Jewish Men's Clubs has also produced a booklet on the impossibility of raising children in a home in which both Judaism and Christianity are practiced.

If despite efforts at prevention an intermarriage seems likely to occur, we must encourage those involved to consider the option of conversion to Judaism. Sincere Jews-by-choice add enthusiasm and strength to our community. They enrich us by their adult understanding of Jewish values, by their open quest for spiritual sustenance, and by their commitment to living a Jewish life. Unfortunately, many people, Jews as well as non-Jews, are unaware of what it takes to become a Jew-by-choice. To this end, the Rabbinical Assembly has begun producing materials, including a fine booklet entitled: *Are You Considering Conversion to Judaism?* Available in quantity, these booklets are for distribution to those already engaged or married to Jews.

Finally, *b'diavad* (ex post facto), if an intermarriage does occur, our third line of defense is outreach to the intermarried, in the hope that a Jewish family will result.

It would be easy for us to open our doors wide and welcome intermarrieds without qualification. The American climate of political correctness rejects the notion of boundaries that separate people into groups and endorses policies of inclusivity. If we were to open our doors without limits, the numbers affiliated with our institutions would surely balloon with those seeking Jewish legitimation in the face of intermarriage, and in the short term we would likely be very successful. But in the process, we would lose our integrity and dilute our community with one-generation Jews. For those who are not willing to understand our standards would be like cut flowers, who may bloom brightly for a while, but who do not have enough Jewish nourishment to last beyond their own lifetime, to pass on to the next generation.

We have a considerable challenge educating offspring of endogamous marriages to choose a Jewish lifestyle over the competing lures of secular life. *Kal vahomer*, how much more of an uphill battle will we have with the products of intermarriage, who we know intermarry at a rate approaching the random selection of a mate, without reference to religious background. Opening the doors of our synagogues will result in short-term communal gains more than offset by long-term losses.

In the interests of long-term continuity, we cannot afford to offer outreach that sacrifices our standards. In this regard, Rabbi Alan Silverstein has suggested that we reconsider our terminology to reflect what we are really trying to bring about: "In contrast to the notion of 'outreach' in which we change our self-definition in order to count the mixed-married among our numbers, *keruv* connotes the attempt to bring Jews and their non-Jewish spouses closer to us and to our established communal standards."

We cannot offer membership in a Jewish institution to non-Jews who are unable to subscribe wholeheartedly to the purpose of that institution. Offering membership to non-Jewish spouses would not avoid the problem in any case, since the line would have to be drawn elsewhere, causing congregational conflict by disallowing them a voice on the ritual committee, for example, or a committee chairmanship, or membership in the board of trustees. Our American ideal of democracy tells us that we cannot grant someone institutional membership, on the one hand, and deny them the rights and privileges of membership on the other hand.

Likewise in the realm of the ritual life of the congregation, there are Jewish rituals and mitzvot that are inappropriate for non-Jews to perform, just as it would be inappropriate for a non-Catholic, for example, to take part in certain sacraments of the Catholic Church. An aliyah to the Torah or the wearing of a tallit makes no religious sense for a non-Jew who is not bound by the covenant to observe Jewish practices. It is also not reasonable to expect a Conservative synagogue, as a Jewish institution that recognizes the communal dangers of intermarriage, to acknowledge formally and congratulate families when such marriages take place. We must distinguish between personal wishes for a couple's happiness, which individuals may choose to extend, and public expressions, which indicate communal endorsement.

With these standards in mind, we ask ourselves: In what context shall we pursue a policy of *keruv*? Our first answer is that whenever possible, within our standards, our synagogues should reflect our concern that we not reject any Jew or any family sincerely trying to be part of our community. Without violating any halachic principles, we may certainly address mail to an entire family, even if that family includes non-Jews. In life-cycle events, some may include a non-Jewish parent or spouse in some meaningful but nonritual way. We may offer non-Jews in our midst free High Holy Day tickets. We should make special efforts to invite non-Jewish spouses to participate in adult-education offerings such as Hebrew Literacy or Learners' Minyan, in the hopes that exposure to the Jewish way of life and friendship with Jewish families will bolster them in their attempts to create a Jewish home and raise a Jewish family, and may even result in conversion.

Many Conservative congregations around the country are offering entry-level courses in Jewish living, explicitly inviting intermarried couples trying to raise a Jewish child, along with others who may be interested in increasing their Jewish literacy. Targeted along with intermarrieds are Jews who never went to Hebrew school and those who have forgotten everything they ever learned there; those with Jewish ancestry, usually young adults with a Jewish father and a non-Jewish mother, who want to explore their Jewish heritage; and those considering conversion who want to know a little more before committing themselves to the conversion process.

Wherever these courses in Jewish literacy are offered, they have a number of features in common. First, the course is announced in the secular media. Second, and very important, the outreach to intermarrieds is explicit but not exclusive. Intermarried couples are welcome along with others who are within the orbit of the Jewish community. Usually these courses attract substantial numbers of our members who want to learn more, as well as unaffiliated and marginal Jews looking to enter the institutional Jewish community. Third, the courses provide not just information but affect social contact with Jews as well. Teachers are encouraged to share their own personal enthusiasm with Judaism. Other committed members of the community join the classes to socialize with those hesitating on the fringes of Jewish life. Fourth, documentation is kept concerning who joins these classes and why, and what kinds of Jewish opportunities they are seeking. Finally, follow-up courses are offered in areas of interest to the participants. The idea is to encourage not just entrance but long-term participation in an ongoing Jewish community, which appears to be the sine qua non of Jewish continuity.

We have discovered that contrary to popular wisdom, many intermarried and unaffiliated Jews are willing to come into a religious institution, if the right program is offered and the right atmosphere prevails. We have learned lessons in *keruv* from experiences such as Project Link, in Northern New Jersey: that Jewish study can lead to conversion; that *keruv* programs can result in separable goals that are important to us, including not only conversion but also raising Jewish children and integrating mixed families into synagogue life, as we try to draw them closer to us. Our communal resources are finite, and those already committed to raising Jewish children, particularly those who are willing to come directly into the synagogue, are the most accessible targets for successful *keruv*.

We have also discovered that groups exclusively for intermarried couples may develop in directions not compatible with the synagogue's interest in integrating such families into congregational life. The limited resources in a synagogue should be devoted to the encouragement and enrichment of Jewish life rather than to other social and psychological purposes. Some couples, for instance, may wish to focus on how to accommodate two religious traditions in the home, an issue in which the synagogue has no vested interest.

The dynamics of congregational life suggest that groups set up to deal with issues of intermarriage and outreach be composed not just of those with an immediate, familial connection with the problem but also of those from the mainstream of congregational life, who may represent a broader perspective of community norms and goals.

We have seen the success of sensitive synagogue *keruv* within fixed parameters. Such efforts *can* succeed, and they *must* succeed if Jewish continuity is to be assured. The day is short, and the work is great.

IV

CONVERSION TO JUDAISM
IN ISRAEL

⊰ 13 ⊱

Moshe Samet

Who Is a Jew (1958–1988)

This essay, abridged and updated by Myla Sherman, traces the legal question of who is a Jew in the Israeli court system. Much of the question of Jewish identity focuses on questions of conversion. It is no surprise that one significant area of potential contention between American and Israeli Jewry rests in who is legally Jewish, who is allowed to conduct conversions, and related questions. The attempt to amend the Law of Return, guaranteeing citizenship for almost all Jews to immigrate to Israel, was based on the question of conversion. The religious authorities in Israel wish to amend the Law of Return to note that a person is Jewish if born of a Jewish mother or if converted "according to *halachah.*" This phrase, interpreted in Israel and the United States as meaning converted by an Orthodox religious court, and not, for instance, by rabbis affiliated with the Reform or Conservative movement, would functionally delegitimize non-Orthodox rabbis and, to some interpreters, non-Orthodox Judaism. Attempts to amend the law have met strong opposition from American Jewish groups.

Because this matter can change through upcoming court cases, I thought it most useful to provide a background for those following the current debate.

INTRODUCTION

It was in 1958 that the question of "who is a Jew" under Israeli law first arose in all its fury. Thirty years later, this issue continues to be the cause for great controversy in Israel, appearing regularly on the government and Knesset agenda. Moreover, it has created dissension between Israel and major sections of Diaspora Jewry, and in the Diaspora itself.

Originally, the question seemed to be purely technical: Was the Interior Ministry authorized to inquire into the accuracy of declarations by new immigrants concerning their Jewish origins? Yet this seemingly marginal matter generated a fierce and bitter debate about the state's fidelity to Jewish law and about the content of Jewish identity in our time. The question was a harsh one: Is it possible to be a Jew by nationality alone, without any religious affiliation, or are the two inextricably linked?

In Israel there is a whole set of laws relating to Jewish citizens exclusively. Of these the most important are the Rabbinical Courts Law, 1953, which gives religion a monopoly over marriage and divorce; the Law of Return, 1950, which grants every Jew the automatic right to immigrate to Israel; and the Citizenship Law, 1952, which automatically grants Israeli citizenship to all Jewish immigrants under the Law of Return.

In the first ten years of statehood, the rabbinical courts in Israel had maintained a lenient approach to conversion. In contrast, the Orthodox rabbinical courts abroad, and particularly in the West, tended to be very severe, whether in defiance of Reform Jewry or in order to combat growing assimilation via mixed marriages. Candidates for conversion who were turned down by rabbinical courts in their own countries often came to Israel to obtain the desired certificate in that period. Policy in Israel eventually hardened due to protests by rabbis abroad and pressure from the increasingly fundamentalist Orthodox establishment in Israel. Moreover, the wave of emigration from Eastern Europe in 1956, with its large number of mixed couples, led the rabbinate to adopt a more stringent attitude toward the conversion process.

In 1957, the director of the registration department in the Interior Ministry, a member of the National Religious Party (NRP), ordered that the "religion" clause in new immigrants' papers be subjected to meticulous examination; a mere declaration by the immigrant would no longer be enough. In response, Attorney General Haim Cohen and Interior Minister Israel Bar-Yehuda issued new guidelines in March 1958 stating that a declaration made in good faith by new immigrants concerning their Jewishness was to be regarded as sufficient. Infuriated by the new guidelines, the NRP leadership demanded their cancellation because they constituted a violation of the status quo, according to which "questionable" converts underwent reconversion upon their arrival in Israel. Unmoved by various changes in the proposed formulation, or by attempts at conciliation and compromise, the NRP withdrew from the government in June 1958.

To cope with the ferment, Ben-Gurion at the end of 1958 consulted a group of 50 rabbis and intellectuals he called the "Sages of Israel." Some 82 percent advocated the NRP's stand, and Ben-Gurion therefore announced in July 1959 that the guidelines were being revoked. Many of these "sages" had made previous statements to the effect that they supported the traditionalist position; Ben-Gurion was apparently looking for an honorable way out and for constraints that would justify the surrender to "religious coercion." When NRP leader Moshe Haim Shapira became the interior minister in 1959, he hastened to issue new guidelines. These directives defined a Jew— for the purposes of the population registry—as a person whose mother was Jewish or who had been converted according to the halakha (Orthodox Jewish law), which requires circumcision, ritual immersion, and acceptance of all the traditional Jewish commandments and practices.

In the coalition agreement of the Fifth Knesset, the NRP was assured that legislation would be enacted to make the Interior Ministry's guidelines the law of the land, but public pressure prevented this.

Although key laws in Israel relate to Jews only, in none of them was a Jew defined for the purpose of applying those laws. This was not an oversight of the legislature but a deliberate omission, since consensus on the matter could not be reached. NRP leaders justifiably found it illogical that although a person's Jewishness was defined by the Rabbinical Court Jurisdiction Law in terms of the halakha, a different definition applied for the Law of Return. "Secularists," on the other hand, claimed that the halakhic test for determining a person's Jewishness would deter mixed couples from settling in Israel—against the interest of the state, which sought to increase its population—and would adversely affect its image as a progressive country.

THE SHALIT CASE

The Shalit case, resolved in 1970, was a watershed in the "who is a Jew" controversy and a key factor in its Israeli solution. Binyamin Shalit, an Israeli naval officer, wanted to register his children as Jews even though his gentile wife refused to convert, but was refused by the registry official in accordance with the current directives. He then petitioned the High Court of Justice, arguing that it was not up to the registry official to decide whether or not his children were Jews. The question was passed back and forth between the court and the government until the court ruled by a vote of 5–4 in favor of Shalit. The NRP ministers threatened to leave the coalition unless the government overturned the court's ruling by means of legal validation, but a compromise was found that proved acceptable to both sides. The NRP's stand was adopted with respect to registration, meaning that a child of a non-Jewish mother would not be registered as a Jew unless the mother converted to Judaism, while gentiles in the family of a Jewish immigrant would benefit from the Law of Return even without conversion.

The final bill gave the rabbinate a monopoly over conversion in Israel, effectively ending the "who is a Jew" stage in the conversion debate. The amendment asserted explicitly that a person's Jewishness is determined according to criteria of Jewish religious law, that is, one must have been born to a Jewish mother or have undergone conversion. The second stage of the debate focuses on the question of who is authorized to perform conversions abroad, since with respect to Israel it was definitively decided that conversion is the exclusive domain of the rabbinate. In other words, those who wish to further amend the Law of Return are actually seeking the intervention of the state in the relations between religious streams outside Israel and wish to bring about the delegitimization of non-Orthodox institutions, rabbis and sages abroad.

RECONVERSION OF NON-ORTHODOX CONVERTS THE NORM

In terms of the existing procedures favored by the Israel Chief Rabbinate (in practice, not according to the law and in violation of its spirit) converts who immigrate to Israel and whose conversion was performed by a non-Orthodox rabbinical court have been forced to undergo reconversion. Therefore, advocates of the additional amendment intend to give legal status to a procedure that exists in practice. It would not be out of place to cite the conclusions of a halakhic-religious study conducted by the author on the subject of conversion, which shows that the entire matter is a marginal one in the halakha. Not one mishnah was devoted to the subject, and the Talmud itself still contains deliberations that lead to extremely lenient conclusions on the matter. The source of the current procedure by which a convert must accept the commandments in a valid rabbinical court lies in the *Shulhan Aruch*, yet there, too, it appears in retrospect that conversions were performed as the religious judges saw fit.

A detached analysis shows that the compromise was a fair one and that each side obtained the maximum possible, and in fact, the "secular" side considered the matter closed. Although the religious Zionist leadership still wanted the Law of Return to qualify converts by the powerful words "according to the halakha," they realized that the addition would effectively sever hundreds of thousands of members of Conservative and Reform congregations from the Jewish community. In May 1970, however, the NRP executive decided that it could not be responsible for registration that recognized as Jews persons whom the halakha did not so recognize. It therefore called for an explicit amendment to the law, stating clearly that every conversion had to be approved "by the authorized religious body—the Chief Rabbinate of Israel."

A few days later the Chief Rabbinate Council convened to discuss the question. It published three resolutions: first, that conversion not performed according to the halakha was invalid, "whether in Israel or abroad"; the second barred the Population Registry Office "from registering a non-Jew as long as he has not undergone conversion according to halakha"; and the third strongly urged the government to amend the Law of Return by adding "according to the halakha" at the appropriate place.

The major development in 1971 concerned Jews from the USSR at a transit camp in Vienna, where the Jewish Agency had arranged for the conversion of Israel-bound immigrants by one of the most distinguished rabbis in Europe. In order to placate the Habad movement, which maintained that the conversion process was too hasty, the Chief Rabbinate of Israel decided that some of the converts would undergo reconversion upon their arrival in Israel.

THE NRP VS. AGUDAT YISRAEL AND HABAD

In August 1972 the ultra-Orthodox Agudat Yisrael Knesset faction submitted a motion of no confidence in the government because of its refusal to add the words "according to the halakha" to the Law of Return and to the Population Registry Law. Heavy pressure was exerted on the NRP to join Agudat Yisrael in voting no confidence, with the primary movers being Habad. Among those who tended to vote against the government were MK's Rabbi Neriya, Yitzhak Rafael and Deputy Education Minister Avner Sciaky. Prime Minister Golda Meir offered the NRP a package deal whereby her party would not support a bill authorizing civil marriages for those the rabbinate had ruled unfit to marry—in return for which the NRP would abstain when the Agudat's no-confidence vote was called. The proposal was accepted and the NRP abided by its part of the bargain. Sciaky, however, who voted with Agudat Yisrael, was forced to resign from the government at Mrs. Meir's insistence. He later wrote a two-part comprehensive essay entitled, "Who Is a Jew Under the Laws of the State of Israel" (1977–1978).

Attacked for trading in religious principles in return for political gains, the NRP was forced to justify itself and make all manner of pledges to its Orthodox following. The party argued that passage of a law allowing civil marriages could have been far more detrimental to religion and to the state's

Jewish character than the current situation with respect to the Law of Return. At the fourth NRP convention, in March 1973, the conversion issue proved to be the stormiest subject on the agenda. Both Yitzhak Rafael's faction and the Young Guard called for the adoption of a resolution whereby the NRP would not join the next government unless the Law of Return were amended. A compromise was finally worked out: in the final resolution, the words "to amend the law" were replaced by the less binding phrase, "to amend the situation."

THE 1973 ELECTIONS

In the elections that were held in late 1973 the parties of the left lost ground to the right, enhancing the bargaining power of the NRP. Since Golda Meir was adamant in her refusal to co-opt Shulamit Aloni's faction to the government, she found herself unable to form a majority government without the NRP. As a result that party was able to negotiate an unprecedentedly generous agreement on practical matters, including an acknowledgment that conversion was a halakhic concept. It was also agreed that the cabinet would urgently establish a committee, composed of the prime minister and the ministers of religious affairs, justice and the interior, with the aim of working out legislation within one year.

This formula did not satisfy the NRP's Young Guard, however, which insisted on an amendment to the Law of Return and the Population Registry Law in full and without any compromises. Finally, the party requested that the Chief Rabbinate resolve the dispute—an unprecedented step for religious Zionism, which did not make a habit of involving professional spiritual leaders in political questions. The Chief Rabbinical Council supported the Young Guard, and under public pressure the NRP was forced to retract its agreement to join the government. Coalition negotiations were later reopened due to developments related to the pre-Yom Kippur War security situation, and the NRP gained even more—the prime minister gave her written consent to a declaration confirming the Interior Ministry's practice of blocking the registration as a Jew of any non-Jew who had not been converted according to Jewish law.

HABAD MOVEMENT BLOCKS ATTEMPT TO REACH
A CONSENSUS AMONG THE STREAMS

Yitzhak Rafael, the new religious affairs minister, set out immediately to prove that the "who is a Jew" problem could be resolved while the NRP was in the government. As chairman of the ministerial committee on conversion that was formed under the coalition agreement, Rafael first approached leaders of the Conservative movement and obtained their consent that conversion in Israel be performed according to the halakha. He also obtained the agreement of Rabbi Herbert Wiener, one of the leaders of the Reform movement in America. Rafael was also successful in his approach to the Chief Rabbis. They ruled that conversion was not to be invalidated on the basis of the convert's membership in one religious branch or another, but that each case was to be judged on its own merits. In the United States, however, Rafael quickly found that his optimism had been unwarranted. It was out of the question to impose "the halakha" on the Reform rabbis en masse — neither for conversion nor for other matters, although there remained the possibility of cooperation between the Orthodox and the Conservatives. The latter were known for their positive attitude in principle toward the halakha as a whole, including conversion, although they rejected the contention that only the Orthodox were authorized to interpret the halakha. The difference actually lay in the approach to interpretation and in procedures for rendering judgments.

The Conservatives agreed to accept two proposals: the creation of a special local court for conversion, with the participation of non-Orthodox rabbis who were deemed worthy; and the formation of a Conservative rabbinical court for conversions that would be recognized by the Chief Rabbinate of Israel. "Modern Orthodox" leader Rabbi J. B. Soloveitchik, however, rejected the establishment of a joint rabbinical court and recommended a "sit and wait" policy on the idea of a Conservative rabbinical court for conversions. He was apprehensive that the extremist ultra-Orthodox haredis would take such a step to mean Israeli recognition of the Conservative movement and would therefore renew their incitement against the State of Israel.

Dr. Rafael's visit to the United States provoked vicious slanders and denunciations by the Habad movement, which had long been furious at the NRP's failure to have the words "according to the halakha" added to the Law of Return and the Population Registry Law. This failure of Dr. Rafael's led the NRP to drop any further attempts to champion the "who is a convert" issue. Stung by his failure and by the insulting treatment he had received at the hands of Orthodox circles in America, Dr. Rafael subsequently expressed a favorable attitude toward the Conservative movement, maintaining that it was moving closer to the halakha.

THE LIKUD YEARS

The 1977 Knesset elections produced a political turnabout: the right took over the reins of government from Labor. Herut, the dominant element of the Likud, was quite sympathetic to Jewish tradition even before the elections, resolving to support a Knesset bill calling for "conversion according to the halakha." Its leader, Menachem Begin, had pledged to adopt the Lubavitcher Rebbe's position and ensure that it was affirmed by the Herut convention. Thus it was not by chance that the non-Zionist Agudat Yisrael was invited to join his coalition and that it accepted in return for commitments on religious matters. The coalition agreement clauses relating to the "who is a convert" issue contained a pledge by the prime minister that he would make a personal effort to drum up support for the passage of a private members' bill to have the law amended.

In a visit to the U.S. shortly after the establishment of the new government, Prime Minister Begin met in New York with leaders of Judaism's three branches. He was received warmly by Orthodox leaders, but at a joint session with Conservative and Reform movement heads, Begin was criticized for his government's intention of changing the policy on converts. The rabbis spoke of the injustice that would be done to their communities if the status quo were changed, while the fund-raisers stressed the damage that Israel would sustain because most major donors were members of non-Orthodox congregations. Mr. Begin surprised these people by revealing that he personally supported the idea of conversion according to the halakha out of principle and not because he was yielding to the demands of his coalition partners. He had believed in this all his life, he said, and now that he had the power he intended to put his belief into practice. Although Begin would not consent to any postponement of the matter, he did agree to discuss the particulars of the amendment and its ramifications with Interior Minister Burg in Jerusalem.

CONSERVATIVE AND REFORM RABBIS
JOIN TO FIGHT LEGISLATION

On August 15, 1977, a joint delegation of Conservative and Reform rabbis arrived in Israel—a historic event in terms of the religious life of American Jewry. The delegation remained in Israel for about a week. It was joined by Rabbi Tuvia Friedman, former president of the Rabbinical Assembly and a member of the Jewish Agency executive on behalf of the Conservative movement, along with Rabbi Richard Hirsch, the leader of the Movement for Progressive Judaism in Israel, which was affiliated with Reform Jewry.

Two meetings were held with Prime Minister Begin in his office; also present were Interior Minister Burg and Religious Affairs Minister Aharon Abuhatzeira. Prior to the meetings the delegation members drew up a joint working paper, in Hebrew and English, which was addressed to the prime minister and served as the basis for the talks. This memorandum warned of the possible implications of passing the amendment to the Law of Return: "the State of Israel, which is the principal force uniting the Jewish people, would become the agent of its division."

It also levelled sharp criticism at the Orthodox movement:

> The issue in dispute is not the halakha but who is to determine what constitutes the halakha, and who controls and uses the religious institutions. All the Conservative rabbis and a number of Progressive rabbis perform conversions while adhering to the three halakhic requirements: circumcision, ritual immersion, and acceptance of the burden of the commandments. In the many discussions which have been held from time to time between representatives of Orthodoxy and non-Orthodoxy, it has been suggested that conversions performed by non-Orthodox rabbis according to the halakha be granted recognition. The Orthodox rabbinate has persisted in its refusal to recognize these conversions, maintaining that the converting rabbi was not authorized to perform the conversion; in other words, it is not the ceremony which is at issue but the presiding rabbi, who bears no authority in the eyes of Orthodoxy. Hence the conclusion must be that the intention of the Orthodox rabbinate is not to preserve the halakha itself but to preserve their control over the halakha.

It should be emphasized that the document attests to a change in the position of the Reform movement, which now agreed in principle to a halakhic solution—and also a change in the opposite direction on the part of the Conservatives, who now sought to have the Reform representatives included in the joint arrangements that would be made to resolve the conversion problem.

During the first meeting in the prime minister's office, Mr. Begin tried to interest the guests in a compromise proposed by emissaries of the Lubavitcher Rebbe, according to which the Rebbe would agree to conversions being performed with the participation of non-Orthodox rabbis, provided the president of the rabbinical court was always Orthodox. This insulting suggestion was quickly rejected. The prime minister then raised the idea of a joint rabbinical court and pledged to look into the matter personally.

BEGIN PROPOSES JOINT RABBINICAL COURT ON CONVERSIONS

At the second meeting the change in Mr. Begin's position was marked: he agreed to postpone the submission of the bill for several months until the question of a joint rabbinical court could be examined. Begin's previous eagerness to support the Orthodox stand was noticeably dampened at this point, possibly in reaction to the Orthodox opposition to this idea. In any case, when the idea of establishing a joint rabbinical court abroad became known in Israel, Agudat Yisrael announced that such a development would force them to withdraw from the coalition. Begin then asked for a year to consider the matter, and his request was granted by all the coalition members, including Agudat Yisrael.

The NRP, having withdrawn from the debate over the conversion issue at the end of 1974, did not actually take up the matter again during the remainder of the Tenth Knesset. On the other hand, it seemed initially that this would be the great hour of Agudat Yisrael, which in the Ninth and Tenth Knessets had been the self-appointed leader and sponsor of "Orthodox-initiated religious legislation." Yet despite its major legislative successes in other areas and its spectacular achievements in financing its various institutions, the party was unable, in this period, to resolve the conversion issue according to its own conception.

Superficially, it appears that the Agudah's repeated attempts over six years to have the words "according to the halakha" introduced into the Law of Return and the Population Registry Law were overruled by the objections of the Likud's Liberal Party wing. A closer look, however, reveals a more complex picture: Agudat Yisrael did not give the matter top priority because of an essential lack of unity regarding the importance of the conversion issue and solutions to it.

HABAD MOVEMENT LEADS FIGHT
TO CHANGE LAW ON "WHO IS A JEW"

The one group for which the conversion issue did in fact become the major issue was the Habad movement, which, following the political turnabout, returned to center stage. As early as 1972 they had set up a special lobby whose aim was to badger the religious factions in the Knesset, the Prime Ministry, the Chief Rabbinate and the entire religious establishment, the Interior Ministry, the daily papers in Israel, the Orthodox leadership and the Jewish press abroad. In the summer of 1978, over a year after the signing of the coalition agreement, they began publishing a slick publication called *Shlemut* (*Integrity*), which was a continuation of the internal circulars they had begun issuing three years earlier under the name of "The Committee for the Integrity of the Jewish People."

While this kind of activity was typical of public life in America, it was an innovation on the Israeli scene. In fact the lobby gave the issue a wholly disproportionate significance, to the point where it might have seemed that the survival of the Jewish people hinged on the addition of one phrase to two administrative laws.

DIVISION WITHIN AGUDAT YISRAEL
THWARTS ATTEMPTS TO PASS AMENDMENT

As we have seen, in the Ninth Knesset Agudat Yisrael gave Mr. Begin a year's grace regarding halakhic conversion. This only heightened suspicion among fervent supporters of the amendment, and attacks on the Agudah's failure intensified. Habad's suspicions were confirmed by a letter leaked to the press in November 1977: in this letter, Agudah MK's Lorincz and Porush requested that other religious legislation be expedited in order to enable Agudat Yisrael to withstand the pressure caused by the Law of Return issue. Habad followers in the U.S. subsequently launched a new attack on Agudat Yisrael, accusing it of not taking the issue seriously. The debate raged in the newspapers of the rival ultra-Orthodox factions, which treat internal disputes even more harshly than their attacks on the "secularists," "Zionists," etc.

July 25, 1978, was a turning point. In a surprise move, MK Kalman Kahane, a Poalei Agudat Yisrael representative who had not joined the coalition, got the bill to amend the Law of Return through the Knesset on preliminary reading; the bill was now referred to the Constitution, Law and Justice Committee, headed by NRP MK David Glass. Once in the hands of this committee, however, the bill was left untouched for over a year. Only the Poalei Agudat Yisrael representative demanded that it be put to a vote, while the other committee members insisted that other issues were more urgent. The committee did not conclude its discussion of the bill until November 28, 1979, and after another 15 months of foot-dragging it was voted down (March 24, 1981).

As the "months of grace" granted to the government drew to a close, new matters of considerable importance to haredi circles cropped up. These were the termination of El Al flights on the Sabbath and the City of David archaeological excavations, and the bill to prevent fraud in kashrut. Also, Prime Minister Begin was too preoccupied at this time with the evacuation of Yamit to deal effectively with the conversion issue, and the Agudah did not insist that he adhere to his timetable. Toward the end of the Knesset's 1981 winter session, Agudat Yisrael MK Avraham Shapira tried to submit the amendment with the help of Alignment representatives. The opposition, which anticipated the government's fall over the conversion issue, informed him that coalition discipline would be enforced, and Shapira was forced to drop his plan.

The 1982 summer session saw a repetition of the well-known scenes in which Habad and its supporters demanded that the issue be raised as an ultimatum, while Porush and Lorincz shrugged off its importance. When the Lebanon War broke out at the beginning of June, the "who is a Jew," or more accurately "who is a convert" issue seemed likely to fade away for the time being. By the time of the new winter session Shapira's resolve had also been weakened, and he acceded to Begin's request to defer the matter because of the latter's U.S. visit. Shapira's fourth retreat was not long in coming. On November 28, 1982, the representative of the Rabbi of Vishnitz, MK Alpert, submitted a bill by which the words "according to the halakha" would be appended to the laws of immigration and registration. Alpert's move was a kind of "parliamentary ambush," since a group of the bill's opponents were in Brazil at the time and a majority in favor was feasible. However, once again Shapira was convinced by Begin to withdraw the bill, this time because of the Zionist Congress session in Israel. As compensation, a committee composed of Begin, Shapira and MK Rabbi Druckman was set up to ensure the subject's advancement.

VIOLENT DISSENT AMONG THE RELIGIOUS FACTIONS

A split in Agudat Yisrael became imminent in the winter of 1982, when the quarrels between Hasidim and Mitnagdim over the distribution of financial aid to the yeshivas reached its peak. Rabbi A. Schlesinger, son-in-law of MK Shlomo Lorincz and a fierce polemicist who represented the stand of the Mitnagdim on the "who is a Jew" issue, was the target of attack by several Gur Hasidim. The walls of his house as well as the walls of quite a few synagogues were defaced, apparently by his ultra-Orthodox opponents, with drawings of swastikas and death threats to him and his family.

The Habad-sponsored Committee for the Integrity of the Jewish People now also took a new step by taking the issue outside the parliamentary framework. To that end a kind of sub-lobby was founded, entitled "The Committee for the Prevention of Assimilation of the Jewish People," with the task of organizing "a series of meetings and mass assemblies." The new lobby was affiliated with the Gur Hasidim and the Habad movement. The latter two bodies deliberately maintained a low profile, however, as a defense against the contention that Habad was exploiting the conversion issue in order to drive a deeper wedge between Hasidim and Mitnagdim in Agudat Yisrael and trying to break up the party.

A mass gathering of haredi groups was held at the Jerusalem Convention Hall on January 9, 1983, but it turned out to be a failure. No agreement could be reached on the "who is a Jew" question, and the Mitnagdim boycotted the assembly altogether. Even Habad was disappointed by the decisions reached at the assembly, because their ultimatum was not included. Moreover, in the final formulation the term "in accordance with the Shulhan Aruch" was appended to the phrase "according to the halakha"; Habad did not accept this addition, maintaining that according to the Shulhan Aruch it would not be possible to reject all non-Orthodox conversions.

THE RABBINICAL COURTS LAW

As early as the coalition negotiations in the summer of 1981, a proposal had been raised that instead of adding "according to the halakha" to the Law of Return, an amendment that encountered fierce resistance because it was blatantly aimed at the non-Orthodox streams and was, according to legal experts, of no value in any case, the proper way to proceed was to append the conversion issue to a bill for the amendment of the Rabbinical Courts Law. This was a subject that had already appeared in the coalition agreement for the Ninth Knesset and was mentioned again in the agreement for the Tenth Knesset, where it was explicitly stated that the bill in question would be submitted to the government within six months. The first paragraph of the Rabbinical Courts Law, 1953, states: "Matters of marriage and divorce of Jews et al. shall be under the exclusive jurisdiction of rabbinical courts." Now being proposed was the following formulation: "Matters of marriage and divorce of Jews and the determination of Jewishness" etc. In other words, a certificate of conversion from abroad, like a certificate of marriage or divorce, would not be valid in Israel until it received rabbinical approval.

It now emerged that this alternative to the solution of the conversion question via the amendment of the Law of Return was supported chiefly by the NRP, which had borne responsibility for the rabbinate since the establishment of the state. However, according to the press, it appeared that Agudat Yisrael had also considered this possibility during the coalition negotiations in 1981. The idea itself was scornfully rejected by the Lubavitcher Rebbe, who called it a "combination" and a "compromise." Actually, it is difficult to know whether the Agudah MK's who opted for a solution of the conversion problem within the framework of an amendment of the Rabbinical Courts Law rather than via an amendment of the Law of Return were serious or whether this was no more than delaying tactics, as the Lubavitcher followers maintained. The bill, which set out to rectify the undermining of the rabbinical courts' authority, contained 38 clauses; deliberations were liable to be protracted.

The Habad Hasidim were amazed at the ardor with which the Mitnagdim in the Agudah were seeking to reinforce the standing of the rabbinical courts and thereby glorify, if only indirectly, the State of Israel. There is no doubt that from the outset Agudat Yisrael's attitude toward this bill was ambivalent because that party had absolutely no interest in aggrandizing the institutions of the Zionist rabbinate. On the other hand, it was not totally opposed to the state's rabbinical institutions. Agudat Yisrael rejected the Chief Rabbinate, the kashrut department, and so forth, but the majority of them made use of the marriage and divorce services of the rabbinical courts, and indeed, they manned most of the religious judges' posts. In this way it was possible to understand the support for solving the conversion issue within the framework of the Rabbinical Courts Law. As long as Rabbis Goren and Yosef—who were known for their leniency in matters of conversion—served as Chief Rabbis, it was difficult to reject Habad's arguments against the alternative, but with the advent of the new and more conservative Chief Rabbis (March 1982), the path was open to placing the conversion question in the hands of the rabbinical courts.

LUBAVITCHERS' MAIN GOAL: DELEGITIMIZING THE NON-ORTHODOX RABBIS

Three alternatives thus emerged: (1) amendment of the Law of Return by adding the phrase "according to halakha" as Habad demanded; (2) the above with an addition to read "according to halakha in accordance with the Shulhan Aruch," as called for in the draft resolution adopted at the Jerusalem Convention Hall assembly presided over by the Rabbi of Gur; (3) addition of "determination of Jewishness" to the first paragraph of the Rabbinical Courts Law.

This new situation only aggravated the debate within the haredi community, the more so because of Habad's insistence on advocating the least likely of the three alternatives. It emerged that the Lubavitchers were more interested in the symbolic universal aspect, namely, in delegitimizing conversions performed by non-Orthodox rabbis abroad, and not necessarily in solving the problem of the Jewishness of immigrants to Israel. The debate over the three alternatives both weakened and isolated Habad, which led to an acceleration of their messianic activity. We should recall that in March 1980 Rabbi Schneerson launched an active messianic process, in which the "who is a Jew" question was integrated. Toward the end of the term of the Ninth Knesset the Rebbe's followers often maintained that the conversion problem was delaying the advent of the Redemption.

A series of events within the haredi community during 1982 and 1983 eventually led to the decline of the conversion issue and its supporters alike. It is against this backdrop that MK Shapira raised the matter in the Knesset on March 21, 1983, even though he was not assured of a majority in favor; as anticipated, the motion was defeated by a majority of eight votes. According to Ma'ariv of the following day, Shapira had stated in advance that the defeat of the motion would not generate a governmental crisis. About a month later, advocates of the amendment were shocked when they read two interviews given by MK Lorincz to the New York Hebrew paper *Yisrael Shelanu*. In the first (April 29, 1983) Lorincz said the amendment was of importance only in principle and not in practice, while in the second (May 6, 1983) he stated that Habad was out to intensify the dispute within the party and intimated that their intentions were not entirely pure. These declarations triggered a furious reaction in both Habad and Gur and thereby overshadowed a more serious development.

Immediately after the defeat in the Knesset vote, the Rabbi of Gur demanded that the Agudah faction representatives refrain from voting for a sixth Liberal Party minister to replace the late Simcha Ehrlich. This was a reaction to the Liberals' behavior in abstaining and voting against the "who is a Jew" amendment. Yet at the cabinet meeting of May 1, 1983, the appointment (of Sarah Doron) was approved with Agudat Yisrael's assent. And, despite the Rabbi of Gur's explicit order not to do so, Agudah members voted for confirmation of the appointment on July 5, 1983. In compensation, they received from Prime Minister Begin a new letter in which "will try to make every effort" was replaced by "is obligated to make every effort." The intention was that six months after the latest vote the prime minister would bear personal responsibility for ensuring the success of the vote in the Knesset.

SHAMIR BECOMES PRIME MINISTER: HABAD CONTINUES TO PRESS FOR CHANGE IN "WHO IS A JEW"

We cannot know whether Mr. Begin would have done his part in the matter, because as the date neared on which he was to fulfill his commitment, the prime minister resigned. His successor, Yitzhak Shamir, whose government received Knesset confirmation on October 10, 1983, was not bound by Begin's personal undertaking. Nevertheless, the supporters of the "integrity of the people" lobby did not overlook the fact that Shamir was in desperate need of Agudat Yisrael's votes in the Knesset; thus a new opportunity presented itself for pressure on the conversion issue. The lobby demanded absolutely that Agudat Yisrael take advantage of it, but their demand was disregarded, forcing the Lubavitchers to the conclusion that even the hasidic wing of the faction had cooled to the issue and was no longer reliable.

The bill did not come up again in the final year of the Tenth Knesset's term, even though according to the regulations it could have been raised several more times. With Agudat Yisrael having washed its hands of the matter, the NRP could now take the issue under its wing once more. At the end of December the public learned that preparation of the bill to amend the Rabbinical Courts Law had been completed. The 38-clause bill would give the rabbis exclusive jurisdiction in matters of conversion and determining Jewishness. This development blocked, for the time being, the possibility of adopting the Lubavitchers' demand regarding the amendment of the Law of Return, a matter that had in fact become superfluous from the Israeli perspective.

HEMDAT: A COALITION FOR PLURALISM FORMED

Early in 1984 a coalition working for pluralism and against changing the definition of who is a Jew was formed. The new movement, called HEMDAT (Council for Freedom of Science, Religion and Culture in Israel), was composed of the non-Orthodox religious movements in Israel (The Movement of Masorti Judaism in Israel [Conservative], The Israel Movement for Progressive Judaism [Reform], and the independent Mevakshai Derekh Congregation) together with secular groups such as the Movement for Humanistic Secular Judaism, Na'amat and the World Labor Zionist Movement. The leading figures behind the new movement included the late Professor Yigal Yadin, former Supreme Court Justice Haim Cohen, as well as the leaders of Na'amat and the Reform, Conservative and Secular Humanist movements. The formation of a unified lobby against changing the Law of Return based on established groups in Israel was a turning point in the "who is a Jew" struggle, since for the first time the Conservative and Reform movements joined together with like-minded secular supporters of the concept of pluralism in a coalition for active lobbying and education—not just on the "who is a Jew" issue but for the broader goal of freedom of science, religion, and culture.

HABAD INTENSIFIES CAMPAIGN
WITH HUGE EXPENDITURES

Several manifestations relating to the heart of the debate and to its fringes bear recording. At the beginning of 1984 Habad launched new initiatives. On January 21, 1984, they began holding protest watches outside the homes of Agudat Yisrael faction members. About two weeks later they expanded this campaign to include members of the NRP Knesset faction in order to demonstrate that the issue had nothing to do with the dispute between them and Agudat Yisrael. In mid-February, a campaign was concluded in which they claimed that "one million" Israelis signed a petition calling on Prime Minister Shamir to amend the Law of Return.

More significant was Habad's filing of two petitions in the High Court of Justice requesting the court to order the Treasury not to transfer the special allocations that Agudah representatives personally distributed to their favored institutions. Habad, through its various front organizations, spent huge sums of money on these campaigns. Apparently most of the money was raised in the United States, including major contributions from unwitting members of the Reform and Conservative movements.

With the Tenth Knesset drawing to an early close, and with the defeat of the bill to amend the Law of Return, the campaign over the issue appeared to be at an end. Habad, whose funds were drained by the prolonged debate, immersed itself in its own financial problems and lost the bill's last enthusiastic supporter, MK Avraham Shapira. However, the rather surprising results of the elections for the Eleventh Knesset generated new hopes among the amendment's backers. The stalemate between the two major parties meant added leverage for the religious parties.

Although the rifts among the ultra-Orthodox representatives ran deep, they did have 12 MKs in the new Knesset: four from the NRP, two each from Agudat Yisrael and Morasha, and four more from the new Sephardi Torah Guardians list (Shas). Also elected were one representative each from Tami and Rabbi Kahane's party—both from the Orthodox camp—and two religious members of Tehiya. Thus there were from the outset 16 MKs who were known to be advocates of the amendment. Furthermore, the platforms of both the Likud and Tehiya referred positively to the need to solve the conversion problem, and the religious parties had given a written commitment to the Committee for the Integrity of the Jewish People to work for the speedy passage of the amendment as formulated by the Lubavitcher Rebbe.

A rift developed within the religious representation during the coalition talks, however, resulting in an effective loss of bargaining power when the national unity government was formed. Therefore the coalition agreement contained no explicit undertaking to amend the "who is a Jew" law. Compounding the weakness of the religious bloc in the Eleventh Knesset was pressure exerted by Jewish religious and political organizations in the United States against changing the status quo. The Lebanon War had intensified a creeping process of a cooling in the attitude of American Jewry toward Israel, and any surrender by the new government to the Orthodox wing's demand to undercut the non-Orthodox branches of Judaism would have lent added impetus to this process.

In any case, the bill to amend the Law of Return was submitted at a preliminary session of the new Knesset so that it could be debated immediately upon the opening of the winter session of the House. When the winter session opened, however, it became evident that neither the coalition executive nor the Knesset presidium were anxious to push the issue forward. The religious parties' prospects for making headway with other legislation became doubtful; they therefore decided to establish a lobby that would also include religious MKs from Tami, Tehiya, the Alignment, and the Likud. The immediate test case was the "who is a Jew" issue. This now had the enthusiastic backing of Morasha and Shas, Agudat Yisrael's Avraham Shapira, and the NRP's Sciaky; others in the NRP, led by Dr. Burg, followed suit, although with some reservations. More than a goal in itself, the issue now seemed to serve as a means to cement the religious lobby and to test its strength.

RELIGIOUS LOBBY REFUSES TO COMPROMISE

The efforts to push forward the bill to amend the Law of Return included the submission, on December 27, 1984, of a Private Member's bill by MK Aharon Abuhatzeira. The bill was basically identical to Section 12 of the bill to amend the Rabbinical Courts Law in a manner designed to place the entire matter in the hands of the rabbinate, which had gained NRP support in the previous Knesset. To avoid the inevitable delays of passing the bill with all its 38 sections, Abuhatzeira proposed extracting one section only, which would be assured of swift passage. The idea was that all conversion certificates from abroad would require ratification by the rabbinical courts in Israel. Because even Orthodox certificates would be subject to this stricture, the other religious streams could not possibly object. However, this scheme, which stood a chance of obtaining a Knesset majority, was rejected by the religious lobby. It united around the Lubavitch position: that the phrase "according to the halakha" must be added to the Law of Return and the Population Registry Law. The Lubavitchers argued that although Abuhatzeira's proposal would solve the problem of converts immigrating to Israel, it would not succeed in achieving their primary objective of depriving non-Orthodox rabbis throughout the world of their legitimacy and thus would not check assimilation.

The vote on the bill submitted by the religious lobby at Habad's behest took place on January 16, 1985; it was defeated 62–51. Harsh threats voiced by Jews overseas and the active lobbying by the HEMDAT coalition in Israel led Prime Minister Peres to impose party discipline in the vote and to recruit the three members of Yahad and five Arab representatives. On the other side, only 32 of the Likud's promised 38 MKs voted for the bill. MK Benny Shalita, one of those who had submitted the bill, joined some members of the Liberal Party, led by MK Sarah Doron, in voting against it, while others abstained. The five Tehiya members voted for the bill.

HABAD AND THE CONVERSION ISSUE

It goes without saying that the Habad movement was severely jolted, sustaining yet another defeat in a struggle with which it persisted for fifteen years, in the hope that it would impose the Rebbe's will on the majority of the nation. It should be asked why this movement—which inscribed on its banner the slogan of love of the Jewish people and among whose supporters are many nonobservant Jews and prominent activists in the non-Orthodox sects abroad—saw fit to throw its entire weight behind a matter of no practical importance. Yet a deeper perspective reveals an internal connection between this subject and the essence of the Lubavitch movement in its American incarnation. It is particularly connected to Lubavitch's attitude toward the question of Zionism and the state. In its origin Habad was the most scholarly and intellectual of the hasidic sects. After it was uprooted from Europe and transplanted in America, an Americanizing component was injected into the movement, and today it is fundamentally an "American Jewish organization." Habad's American character has led it to place the emphasis on attaining overt, spectacular achievements, even if they are no more than public relations events. Habad's primary objective, however, is to achieve through the political leverage of coalition agreements in Israel a Knesset decision that will, in effect, delegitimize the Reform and Conservative movements and their rabbis in America and throughout the world.

THE SHOSHANA MILLER AFFAIR

Since 1985 the "who is a Jew" controversy has taken on new impetus, under a new and more activist policy on the Reform movement in Israel, with Reform converts resolving their status in Israel by appealing to the courts.

There have also been numerous unsuccessful attempts to push amendments on the conversion issue through the Knesset, and the issue continues to be high on the Knesset's agenda.

The Shoshana Miller affair, which began in 1985 and was disputed for three years, may be seen as a turning point in Israel's dealings with immigrants converted abroad by non-Orthodox rabbis. Miller, a Reform convert from the U.S., immigrated to Israel under the Law of Return, but the Interior Ministry was not willing to issue her an identity card identifying her as a Jew. With the active assistance of new, young, Israel-born leadership of the Reform movement, she appealed to the High Court, and in response Interior Minister Yitzhak Peretz announced a new policy whereby all converts, Orthodox as well as Reform, were to be identified as "Jew (convert)" on their identity cards. This infuriated much of the Orthodox rabbinate, both because it equated Orthodox and non-Orthodox conversions and because it contradicted the religious precept that one should not "humiliate" converts by reminding them of their non-Jewish origins. HEMDAT organized an effective mass demonstration against the public branding of converts, and this policy was not implemented. The court eventually instructed the Interior Ministry to register Miller as a Jew, causing Interior Minister Yitzhak Peretz to resign in protest.

In addition to supporting efforts to amend the Law of Return, Shas made several unsuccessful attempts in this period to circumvent the issue by ensuring in other ways that conversion is controlled by the Orthodox establishment. In July 1985 they proposed an amendment to section five of the Rabbinical Courts Law on marriage and divorce, adding three conditions: first, that the rabbinical court will have exclusive jurisdiction over matters of conversion and authorization of Judaism; second, that conversions will not be performed in Israel except by the rabbinical court; and third, that conversions performed out of Israel will require the rabbinical court's approval. In February 1987 the Knesset voted down a proposal by the Likud and Shas that would have obligated every convert who wishes to be registered as a Jew to present a document bearing the name of the rabbi who converted him abroad.

AMERICAN REFORM AND CONSERVATIVE JEWS TURN THE TIDE

The depth of the WZO's concern about the "who is a Jew" issue in the American Jewish community was clearly demonstrated in the 1987 election of delegates to the Thirty-first Zionist Congress. The Zionist organizations formed by the Conservative movement (Mercaz) and the Reform movement

(American Reform Zionist Association—ARZA), made spectacular gains over the Zionist Organization of America, identified with the Likud and Hadassah, whose stands on this issue were less outspoken. The Likud candidate for chairman of the WZO, Minister Gideon Patt, tried to overcome the handicap of years of Likud cooperation with the religious parties. As part of this effort, Prime Minister Yitzhak Shamir in a speech before the Greater New York Board of Rabbis on November 22, 1987, declared that he believed the "who is a Jew" issue did not belong in politics and should be decided by consensus reached through dialogue between representatives of the religious streams in Judaism.

These belated pleas were of little avail, and a coalition formed by Labor, Conservatives, Reform and the Zionist Confederation (which included Hadassah) won the chairmanship of the WZO for their candidate, MK Simha Dinitz, on a platform of pluralism and opposition to any change on "who is a Jew." This was the first time since the establishment of Israel in 1948 that the voice of Diaspora Jewry had such a decisive impact on a matter of policy that, theoretically at least, was exclusively an issue to be decided by the Knesset.

Late in 1985, Shas MK Shimon Ben-Shlomo had proposed an amendment to a pre-state law (1927) that required persons wishing to convert to another faith to get the approval of the "head of that faith." The amendment would have officially designated the Chief Rabbinate in Israel as head of the Jewish faith, requiring that "no legal registration be performed of the faith of anyone in Israel if it is different from the religion of his birth or if he was not born into any faith"—except with the approval of the head of the faith, which of course would be the Chief Rabbinate. This amendment, which was again voted down in 1988, was an unusual attempt to circumvent the entire conversion issue by twisting a law from the Mandate days, when an entirely different situation prevailed.

MILLER VICTORY DOES NOT CHANGE
INTERIOR MINISTRY POLICY

Throughout this period, the Interior Ministry adamantly refused to register Reform converts as Jews. Shoshana Miller formally won her case in February of 1988, when the High Court of Justice ruled that the Interior Ministry's population administration must register her as a Jew. Upon the request of Miller's attorney, the Supreme Court ordered the population administration to report within one week whether she had been registered as a Jew. This led to furious reactions among the religious parties in the Knesset and a surprising response by Head Ashkenazi Rabbi Avraham Shapira, who called for having separate family lineage records for religious and secular Jews. Such a system had been proposed years before but had never been supported by a Zionist-religious rabbinate. In any case, the Interior Ministry agreed to register Miller but claimed that the ruling referred only to her and did not constitute a precedent. Court orders were therefore required to compel the Interior Ministry to register several other Reform converts as Jews, and the High Court continues to intervene in individual cases in which converts are refused registration. Meanwhile, the Interior Ministry avoids registering Reform converts as Jews until the High Court rules on the Shas appeal against this policy.

The dispute over "who is a Jew" or "who is a convert" continues to appear regularly on the Knesset agenda. The most recent attempt to amend the Law of Return (June 14, 1988) was rejected by the Knesset by a vote of 60 to 53, along with another attempt by Shas to designate the Chief Rabbinate as head of the Jewish faith, thereby putting conversion under its control. This vote was distinguished by vigorous lobbying for the amendment by Habad and other Orthodox groups and effective counterlobbying led by HEMDAT, Reform and Conservative leaders, the Movement for Secular Humanistic Judaism and various American Jewish organizations. This campaign included, for the first time, large ads in the Israeli press by the previously "nonpolitical" American and Canadian leadership of the United Jewish Appeal (UJA) and the Council of Jewish Federations (CJF). This latest defeat can partially be attributed to bad timing. Still the champion of the "who is a Jew" issue, MK Avner Sciaky insisted that the preliminary reading of the law be held on the same day as the vote on the very controversial electoral reform proposal, which was fully attended by the Alignment and Left factions. These parties swung the vote in favor of electoral reform and against the religious legislation, causing tension between the Likud and the religious parties. In a statement to the press, Shas leader Yitzhak Peretz accused the Likud of committing "the greatest betrayal ever against observant Jewry in Israel," and warned of future repercussions.

The extent of the brutal pressure applied by the Habad and the religious parties on their main political ally—the Likud—is typified by the fact that MK Ehud Olmert and Eliyahu Ben Elissar, who had always abstained or voted against the "who is a Jew" amendment, succumbed this time to party pressure and voted for the amendment. Of the Liberal Party Faction in the Likud, this time only MK Sarah Doron had the courage to vote against the amendment, although this faction was allowed freedom of conscience concerning all votes on religious issues.

Prime Minister Shamir, despite his pledge to the Greater New York Board of Rabbis on November 23, 1987, which he reconfirmed in a statement before the Association of Presidents of Jewish Organizations in June 1988, voted together with the Likud and religious parties to support the change in "who is a Jew" legislation in the Knesset vote of June 14, 1988. Apparently, coalition agreements are more binding than commitments made to Jewish leaders abroad.

CONSENSUS AMONG THE STREAMS OF JUDAISM OR DECISION BY KNESSET VOTE

As polarization of world Jewry increases over the "who is a Jew" issue, voices calling for moderation and dialogue have been growing in the Orthodox camp. The Rabbinical Council of America (RCA), which represents some 80 percent of American Orthodox rabbis, has come out against the constant raising of the "who is a Jew" issue in Knesset. Some of their leaders have pleaded with their colleagues in Israel to remove this religious issue from the secular political arena, since they feel that it is causing needless tension among Jews in the Diaspora. Rabbi Lookstein, one of the leading American Orthodox thinkers, has called for a dialogue between the religious streams in Judaism in order to reach an agreed-upon formula for conversions to Judaism in the U.S.

A HEMDAT delegation, including representatives of the Reform and Masorti (Conservative) movements in Israel, appeared before the Ministerial Committee on Conversions and recommended the establishment of a committee of rabbis and scholars with equal representation for each stream and a chairman acceptable to all. This committee would be granted the mandate to reach an acceptable solution to the conversion issue, which would be binding on all movements.

While the more moderate and pluralistic-minded American Orthodox RCA might have found such a solution acceptable, it was rejected by the Israel ultra-Orthodox parties, Shas and Agudat Yisrael, as well as the Habad movement. They were not prepared to accept any solution if it meant including Reform and Conservative rabbis and scholars in the same committee with Orthodox rabbis. Their main motive still remains delegitimizing the Reform and Conservative movements, while being less interested in finding an acceptable solution to conversions and maintaining the unity of the Jewish People.

If the moderate Orthodox forces in America manage to free themselves from the veto of the ultra-Orthodox groups in Israel and the U.S. and on their own initiate a dialogue with the Reform and Conservative movements, there is a real possibility of a feasible solution being achieved. If not, this issue will be raised continuously in the political arena in Israel, where, based on the leverage of coalition agreements and political horse trading, attempts will be made by the religious parties to decide by a vote in the secular Knesset the sensitive religious issue, which could permanently divide the Jewish People and seriously affect the relations of the majority of Diaspora Jews to the State of Israel.

❧ 14 ❧

Edward Alexander

Converts in Zion: Judaism vs. Ethnicity

Edward Alexander, a professor of English at Tel Aviv University and the University of Washington, offers a stirring defense of Judaism as a religion, not an ethnicity. His argument takes shape in viewing the harsh treatment given to converts to Judaism in Israel, despite the fact that these converts underwent a halachic conversion Professor Alexander's perceptive comments show that even in the Jewish homeland, among the Orthodox and among the secular, there is a strong resistance to accepting converts. Professor Alexander suggests that this resistance is due to seeing Judaism more as an ethnicity than a religion, for in a religion all adherents to the religion, independent of other factors, would be seen as equals.

Despite, then, the long history of conversion in Jewish thought and history, despite the voices calling for the actual seeking of converts, despite the potential for conversion to serve as one counterstrategy to intermarriage, conversion remains in Israel, and in the United States, still not a fully accepted part of Jewish life.

That task, to which Professor Alexander contributed this analysis in 1986, remains to be accomplished.

———•———

On June 19, 1984, the Israeli courts lifted their ban against publication of the names of the 28 men accused of participation in acts of terror organized by the "Jewish underground." Photographs and short biographies of all of them immediately appeared in the press and on television. The biographies usually mentioned army experience, if any, of the accused, the particular deeds or plots in which he was implicated, the yeshivot in which he had studied or taught. Since all of the accused were religious, individual religious histories went unmentioned—in every instance but one. This was Dan Be'eri, identified by the television reporters and by *Ha'aretz* as a *ger tzedek* (sincere proselyte, or proselyte by conviction) and by the English-language *Jerusalem Post* as "originally a French Catholic [who] immigrated to Israel some 15 years ago and became a deeply religious convert to Judaism."

In a country where it is considered normal and indeed necessary to identify and label converts at every opportunity, very few people are likely to have been surprised at an anomaly that elsewhere, certainly in the United States, would have caused a scandal. Even a weak imagination can vividly conceive the storm that would ensue if an American television reporter felt called upon to reveal that of 28 members of a recently captured gang of Christian fundamentalist terrorists one was a convert from Judaism and now, odd though it might seem, a "deeply religious" Christian. But in Israel it is routinely accepted that a convert never sheds the taint of his Gentile origins.

Questions regarding the halachic definition of Jewish identity receive much attention in Israel because the religious political parties periodically attempt to bully their coalition partners into bringing to the floor of the Knesset the "Who Is a Jew" bill (one version of which was defeated in January 1985). The intent of such bills is to amend Israel's Law of Return so that it would apply only to those Jews born of a Jewish mother or converted in strict accordance with Halacha, Jewish religious law. The question receives even more attention among Diaspora Jewry because of the contention between Orthodox Jews and those Jews who resent their desire to "monopolize" conversion. The irony in all this fire and fury is that it is much ado about nothing. The attention that the "Who Is a Jew" question receives is grotesquely out of proportion to its human relevance. The number of Diaspora converts to Judaism whose nonhalachic conversion might, under a new Law of Return, cause them difficulties when they came to settle in Israel is infinitesimal. There are few prospective immigrants trying to make their way to Zion these days, and still fewer who need to break open the gates of Halacha in order to do so.

The real question about converts in Israel has virtually nothing to do with Halacha but everything to do with the degradation of Jewish religion into ethnicity. It is this that causes Israeli society such trouble in accepting Jews who have been converted in complete accordance with Halacha. In Israel as in America, these Jews are to be found in all walks of life, among the secular and the religious, the uninstructed and the educated; but in Israel, far more than in America, their status as strangers is likely to be a permanent one.

A few personal reminiscences, selected from too vast a storehouse, will serve to illustrate my point. When I began to teach at Tel Aviv University, no fewer than three of my colleagues took it upon themselves to inform me that a student in my graduate seminar was a convert to Judaism from Roman Catholicism. It was not clear why I needed this information. Was it to explain in advance any peculiarities in his manners, or perhaps the fact that, unlike many other students, he might *have* manners? Was it to excuse him for some deficiency in Jewish learning, or to justify some unseemly endowment of Christian knowledge? Since no explanation was forthcoming I could only guess.

A convert's history almost invariably becomes a subject for research and an occasion for uneasiness when marriage is in question. An observant (not to say ultraobservant) friend of mine came to me in distress over the doubts that had been raised about his daughter's "Jewishness" by her fiancé's family. Upon emerging from the Bais Ya'akov school system she had become engaged, after the accustomed fashion of Orthodox matchmaking, to a yeshiva *bocher*. But her pedigree was called into question because her mother is a convert to Judaism. There was not the slightest doubt about the halachic validity of that long-ago conversion or about the rigid Orthodoxy of the mother's life as a Jew. Nevertheless, her daughter clearly lacked *yichus* and was looked down upon as an unworthy match for the scion of a rabbinical family.

Despite the fact that Israel's population is one of the most ethnically diverse in the world, and physical appearance varies from the "blackness" of Ethiopian Jews to the preternatural "whiteness" of many of the inhabitants of Mea Shearim, converts who do not "look Jewish" to the ignorant are in for a hard time, especially (a further irony) with the most secular and "assimilated" Israelis. Members of families that include converts to Judaism tell me that they can count on an average of five incidents a month in which they are "shamed in public" because of what strikes Israeli connoisseurs of physical appearance as "non-Jewish" looks. One of them told me how one of his colleagues—a university professor, no less—made a point of phoning him to report her amazed impression that "your son looks like a real *goy!*"

Since Jews are a "people" and a "nation" as well as adherents of a religion, it was perhaps to be expected that halachic standards of admission to Jewish identity would prove inadequate in the actual world. But if Jewish religion is something less than Jewish peoplehood and nationality, surely Jewish peoplehood and nationality are more than mannerisms and appearances and transient political prejudices. Some Israelis think that Jewishness consists of universalist ethics and leftist politics; others have a vague notion that you demonstrate your Jewish identity when, in arguing a point, you strike two fingers of one hand in the palm of the other. The difficulty that many

Israelis have in accepting converts is in exact proportion to their attachment to these grotesque travesties of Jewish identity. Indeed, the converts themselves afford a kind of litmus test for distinguishing between what is genuinely Jewish and what is meretricious, transient, and merely "ethnic" in Israeli Jews.

The degradation of Judaism into ethnicity did not, of course, begin in the state of Israel. Every illustration of it just given will be only too familiar to Jews of the Diaspora. Indeed, if we can trust the historical imagination of Isaac Bashevis Singer, it had already begun as far back as the seventeenth century in Poland. In his novel *The Slave*, the hero Jacob converts Wanda, the Polish widow of a drunken peasant, to Judaism. When she comes to live with him in a Jewish community, she is re-created as "Dumb Sarah." She feigns muteness because her imperfect Yiddish would very likely reveal her Gentile origins, and Polish law punished by death the "crime" of converting a Christian to Judaism. But she also feels keenly the need to conceal her Gentile origins from her Jewish neighbors. "True, Dumb Sarah behaved as a Jewess should, went to the ritual bath, soaked the meat and salted it, on Friday prepared the Sabbath pudding . . . blessed the candles; on the Sabbath, she stood in the women's section of the synagogue and moved her lips as though praying." This is all very well, but it cannot eradicate the taint of her "non-Jewish" manners and looks. She sometimes walks barefooted, has "unblemished peasant-like teeth," works like a country woman ("and for nothing"), and swims naked in the river. For these unspeakable offenses Sarah is slandered and rejected by the Jewish community, none of whose members appears to recall that Moses himself had taken an Ethiopian as his wife. An emissary from Palestine whom Jacob meets after Sarah's death tells him that "before the Messiah will come, all the pious Gentiles will have been convened." He does not add, since the entire book makes this irresistibly clear, that these righteous converts will find it easier to be Jews in the next world than in this one.

But it is not in the land of fiction that the tendency of Jews to slide from religion into ethnic clannishness has been expressed in its most extreme form. In the "Antisemitism" section of her *Origins of Totalitarianism* (1951), Hannah Arendt called attention to the fact that in nineteenth-century Western Europe "assimilation as a program led much more frequently to conversion than to mixed marriage." She refers to the widespread tendency among baptized Jews to marry only other Jews, whether baptized or not. Jewish religion had come to mean far less to such people than "Jewish" family, familiarity, and manners. It goes without saying that these apostates felt more at home with other Jews who had become Christians than with Christians who had become Jews.

It would be a poor conclusion to one crucial aspect of the Zionist enterprise if, in its desire to create a new, "normal" Jew, it only led us back to these desperate perversions of Judaism. For it was precisely these perversions, as much as external persecution, that justified the longing for an independent Jewish state in the first place. Ethnic homogeneity is neither possible nor desirable in a country whose inhabitants have been ingathered from every corner of the exile, bringing with them a rich variety of physiognomy, of culture, of manners. That Israeli identity is not based on religion according to Halacha is self-evident. But it is based on religion, for—as even very "secular" Israelis understand only too well—merely to live in this country, a country hedged round by enemies bent on its destruction, a country whose war for independence has already lasted nearly forty years—is to belong to what Hillel Halkin calls "a community of faith."

"Many a man," wrote John Henry Newman, "will live and die upon a dogma; nobody will be a martyr for a conclusion." The Israeli version of this dogma is that there is a transcendent meaning in Jewish collective existence that justifies the hardship and suffering that life in this country entails. Few people are better situated to recognize this truth with perfect clarity than those converts who, by choosing to live in Israel, have taken upon themselves not only the God but the fate of the Jews; for they know that to the idea of transcendent meaning ethnicity contributes exactly nothing.

Credits

Index

ABOUT THE EDITOR

Lawrence J. Epstein is a professor of English at Suffolk Community College in Selden, New York. The author of *Samuel Goldwyn* (1981), *Zion's Call* (1984), *A Treasury of Jewish Anecdotes* (1989), *The Theory and Practice of Welcoming Converts to Judaism* (1992), *A Treasury of Jewish Inspirational Stories* (1993), and *Conversion to Judaism: A Guidebook* (1994), he has also written more than 100 articles, stories, and reviews on Jewish life that have appeared in major Jewish periodicals. Dr. Epstein served as Middle East adviser to a United States member of Congress from 1981 to 1986 and currently lives in New York State with his wife, Sharon, and their four children.